OTHER BOOKS BY HARVEY COX

God's Revolution and Man's Responsibility
The Secular City.
On Not Leaving It to the Snake
*The Feast of Fools: A Theological Essay on
Festivity and Fantasy*
The Seduction of the Spirit
Turning East

RELIGION IN THE SECULAR CITY

Toward a Postmodern Theology

by Harvey Cox
author of *The Secular City*

A TOUCHSTONE BOOK
Published by Simon & Schuster, Inc.
NEW YORK

First Touchstone Edition, 1984
Published by Simon & Schuster, Inc.
Simon & Schuster Building
Rockefeller Center
1230 Avenue of the Americas
New York, New York 10020

TOUCHSTONE and colophon are registered trademarks
of Simon & Schuster, Inc.

Designed by Eve Kirch

Manufactured in the United States of America

1 3 5 7 9 10 8 6 4 2
1 3 5 7 9 10 8 6 4 2 Pbk.

Library of Congress Cataloging in Publication Data

Cox, Harvey Gallagher.
Religion in the secular city.
Bibliography: p.
Includes index.
1. Theology—20th century. I. Title.
BT75.2.C69 1984   230   83-19619

ISBN 0-671-45344-0
ISBN 0-671-52805-X Pbk.

ACKNOWLEDGMENTS

I was able to complete the research and a large part of the writing of this book because of a Fellowship in the Humanities granted to me in 1981–82 by the Rockefeller Foundation, for which I am deeply grateful. I would also like to express my appreciation to the members of my Advanced Seminar on "Religion in the Postmodern World," which met at Harvard Divinity School during the fall term of 1982; they helped me work through the original draft, chapter by chapter, in a truly collegial manner. My faculty colleagues at the Divinity School also subjected the opening chapters to a friendly critical analysis, as did the students in the M. Div. Senior Seminar in the spring term of 1983. By now the list of typists and retypists has grown too long to record, but I wish to thank all who helped in the preparation of the manuscript. Most of all I would like to say *muchas gracias* to the courageous people of the tiny Christian base community in the Latin American village I have called "La Chispa," and to the many thousands of similar communities all over that continent who have shared their faith, hope and love with me in a measure that exceeds any possibility of repayment.

Cambridge, Massachusetts
July 19, 1983

ACKNOWLEDGMENTS

This book is dedicated to
My Friends in Commonplace
in gratitude for ten years together.

CONTENTS

Introduction   Religion Returns to the Secular City   *11*

Part One.   Praying for the Children at the Gate:
The Conservative Critique of Modern Theology

1. "To Bring the Nation Back . . ."   29
   The Revival of Redneck Religion

2. Fundamentalism and the Tradition of Religious   38
   Antimodernism

3. True Reason, True Science, and True Faith: 49
   The Burden of Fundamentalist Theology

4. Populist Piety: Fundamentalism as Ideology   60

5. Fundamentalism and Postmodern Theology   72

Part Two.   "How Shall They Possess the Earth?"
The Radical Critique of Modern Theology

6. Foreigners in Consumer City: 85
   The Rise of Revolutionary Christianity

7. Questionable Concordat: 91
   The Radical *Ruptura* from Modern Theology

8. La Chispa and St. Francis Xavier   98

9. A Church of the Poor?   107
    The Birth of the Basic Christian Communities

10. Upending the Pyramid: Christian Base Communities in   118
    Europe and the United States

11. The New Nuclei   126

12. Liberation Theology: The Voices of the Uninvited   135

13. But Is It Really Theology?   150

14. Christian Radicals and the Failure of Modern Theology   159

**Part Three.   From the Bottom and from the Edges:
Sources of a Postmodern Theology**

15. The Great Inversion   175

16. "The Devil Is a Modernist"   181

17. The Gelding of God and the Birth of Modern Religion   191

18. The Resurrection of Life   205

19. Toward a Postmodern Theology   216

20. The Ancient Runes Speak—Postmodern Theology and   222
    the World Faiths

21. Carnival Faith—People's Religion and   240
    Postmodern Theology

22. A New Reformation?   262

    Notes   269

    Bibliography   282

    Index   294

INTRODUCTION

Religion Returns to the
Secular City

Not many years ago the world was full of dire prophecies about the future of religion. The great "sea of faith" which Matthew Arnold had once watched receding with a roar at Dover Beach seemed to have reached such a low ebb that it would never return again. We were entering, it was said, into a post-Christian era. The influence of religious institutions and traditional forms of piety were in irreversible decline. The distinguished Italian sociologist Sabino Acquaviva wrote in his book *The Decline of the Sacred in Industrial Society*, "From the religious point of view, humanity has entered a long night that will become darker and darker with the passing of the generations, and of which no end can yet be seen."[1]

Not everyone viewed the prospect of a religionless future with the same feelings. Preachers bewailed it, especially the erosion of spiritual influence on public morals. The latter-day children of the Enlightenment on the other hand greeted it as a liberation from ignorance and credulity. Theologians began to ponder the meaning of the "death of God."

Even the United States, which because of the strong religious influences on its early history had stood out as an exception to the global sweep of secularization, no longer appeared to be exempt. Religion was persisting here, the scholars declared, but only because it had settled for a much reduced place in the sun.

Students of religion were of the nearly unanimous opinion that whatever religion remained would have no connection with the public political realm. It would be restricted completely to the sphere of personal and family values. In a widely heralded article published in 1972, the American sociologist Richard Fenn said that here, as in all modern industrial societies, ". . . a normative order based on religious beliefs and values is no longer possible." The fact that political systems in such societies as ours had achieved "considerable independence from political control," he added, might well "reduce to near zero the level of interdependence between social factors and religious change." Consumption and political participation were what people wanted now, Fenn said; therefore, "Cultural integration on the level of religious beliefs and values is . . . under these conditions no longer possible or even necessary for the maintenance of motivation and order." [2]

What Fenn and his colleagues were arguing was that secularization does not actually drive religion from modern society completely. Rather, it fosters a type of private religion that has no real function for the society as a whole. In other words, despite the upsurge of gurus and charismatic revivals, the link between religion and the public domain—politics—was gone forever.

When theologians heard these forecasts about the decline of religion they naturally began to speculate about the theological and ethical implications. It did not seem premature or irreverent to think about how God and faith and morality could be envisioned in a world in which at least traditional forms of religion were disappearing. The once puzzling ideas of the German theologian Dietrich Bonhoeffer about a "world come of age" and a "nonreligious interpretation of the Gospel" now appeared more plausible. [3] By the late 1970s and early 1980s, however, the ebb tide appeared to be turning. Religion seemed to be staging a comeback.

One particularly powerful symbol of the sea change occurred on January 26, 1979. On that day a green-and-white Alitalia DC-10 landed in Mexico City and the newly elected Pope John Paul II climbed down the stairs and knelt to kiss the runway. I was teaching in Mexico City at the time, and I watched the pontiff's arrival on a tiny color TV screen with some friends in the San Angel section of the city. None of them found it all that significant. But I saw something click into place, the kind of sharp image that suddenly appears when a kaleidoscope is turned one more notch. Why I thought I discerned an epiphany when my companions saw only a middle-aged prelate kissing some asphalt will take a little explaining.

Mexico City—at least legally and constitutionally—is one of the most secular cities in the world. It is the capital of Mexico, and since the constitution of 1861 Mexico has been an officially secular state. Its laws controlling religion are severe. Parochial schools are technically illegal. It is against the law to wear a Roman collar or any other clerical costume on the streets. All religious properties, including church buildings, are the legal property of the state. Holding religious ceremonies including masses, in public, is prohibited. Diego Rivera's vivid murals depicting bloated priests and armored conquistadores maiming Indians and plundering their gold embellish the walls of official government buildings. On the surface, Mexico City is the embodiment of a sprawling, modern secular megalopolis, one of the largest in the world.

But underneath it all does Mexico City, like New York or maybe even Moscow or Beijing, conceal some artesian religious quality, barely covered by its veneer of official secularity? Does some subcutaneous spirituality still animate not only its people but millions of others all over the modern world despite the enormous impact made by public education, scientific technology, urbanization, and other allegedly secularizing forces? Furthermore, is there something in the air that has brought this dormant piety to the surface? Has the sleeping giant of traditional religion awakened? For me, the coming of Pope John Paul II, the head of the oldest and largest Christian church in the world, to what may be the world's largest "secular city" posed all these questions in a single flash.

In their own way, Mexican politicians were impressed by the Pope's arrival, too. Whatever its religious significance, for them the papal journey was also a *political* event. It made them jittery. Admittedly there seemed to be some reason for the apprehensiveness. Just a few weeks earlier another religious leader, the Ayatollah Khomeini, had returned to an allegedly secular country and displaced the whole government. No one thought John Paul II had that in mind, but officials knew that the Catholic bishops in Brazil had become the main opposition to the military regime there. They were aware that nuns and priests were cooperating with insurgent movements in Central America, just across the border. The new Bishop of Rome was an unknown quantity. The night before his arrival a queasy minor official told me he had dreamed that the Pope stood up in his open limousine, pointed to the president's palace, and said, "Seize it!" and the crowd had drawn machetes and obeyed.

The Pope of course gave no such command. But from any politician's perspective, his visit was an enviable success. Millions of people lined the Avenida de la Reforma, named, ironically, for the secular Reform of 1861 which had resulted in the expropriation of the church's property, to cheer and wave. With blithe disregard for the anticlerical laws, John Paul II appeared everywhere in resplendent white papal garb, and celebrated mass in public. Watching the huge crowds, members of the ruling party could not help but reflect on the efforts needed to cajole even small and unenthusiastic groups into attending their appearances. As the departing Pope's plane circled the city on its way back to Rome and thousands of Mexicans flashed *adiós* with tiny hand mirrors (the ideal of an enterprising local glassware dealer), one could almost hear the collective sigh of relief that went up from the Palacio Nacional.

The surprising weight attached by the local politicians to the visit of a priest from Cracow who commands no divisions highlighted another issue. Not only are we witnessing a resurgence of traditional religion in the world, this resurgence has an undeniable—if still indeterminate—*political* significance.

The ambiguous character of this political dimension of the new revival of religion was underlined for me by two visits I made in the summer of 1982. While making a return trip to Mexico in July, I stopped in Lynchburg, Virginia, to acquaint myself with the work of the Reverend Mr. Jerry Falwell, minister of the Thomas Road Baptist Church there and the founder and president of Moral Majority, Inc. During my brief stay I attended the Bible Study Hour and the regular Sunday morning service at Thomas Road Baptist Church. I visited Liberty Baptist College and Seminary, also founded and headed by Mr. Falwell. I inspected the imposing headquarters of the Old Time Gospel Hour, Mr. Falwell's widely viewed national network TV program. I talked at some length to the staff members of Moral Majority, Inc., about their efforts to enlist hundreds of thousands of Americans into bringing a conservative influence to bear on public policy in

America. Mr. Falwell himself served as my affable host for a luncheon at the local Hilton Hotel restaurant. I left Lynchburg with the impression that I had met a man who personifies the most conservative side of the return of religion—both religiously and politically—one was likely to find anywhere in the world today.

A few weeks after my visit to Lynchburg I attended Sunday mass at the venerable old cathedral in the city of Cuernavaca, Mexico. The Bishop of Cuernavaca, then in his final weeks of service before his retirement, was Don Sergio Mendez Arceo, one of the most prominent voices of the "Catholic left" in Latin America. The guest preacher for the day was Father Ernesto Cardenal, the controversial priest, poet, and symbol of Christian participation in revolution. A few months later Pope John Paul II, during a visit to Nicaragua, would publicly scold Cardenal for remaining at his post as his country's Minister of Cultural Affairs. Standing next to the high altar that day in August, however, Cardenal did not appear to be a man who would be much affected by scolding. He spoke with great feeling about how Christians were becoming active in the struggle for justice all over the continent, especially in El Salvador and Guatemala. Within the span of a couple weeks I had touched down on the two most antipodal outposts of Christianity to be found today: Jerry Falwell and Ernesto Cardenal represent the polar antitheses of the Christian world.

Falwell and Cardenal are not merely mirror images of each other. They are enormously different men temperamentally, and they occupy different places in the two wings of the religious movements they represent. Nonetheless, there are some intriguing similarities. Both underwent life-changing religious conversions as young men. Both moved from a deep suspicion of the world of politics toward finding themselves immersed in it. Both are charismatic figures whose persuasiveness springs more from personal conviction than from polished eloquence. Both take positions that sometimes embarrass their more cautious colleagues. Still, Falwell and Cardenal embody both the return of religion and its powerful but contradictory political significance as well as anyone could. Taken together, the question they pose is this: What is the meaning of the present dramatic reappearance of religion as a potent political force all over the world just when the experts had thought it was all over?

Subsequent events in the world have made this question increasingly more pressing. Shortly after the Pope's visit to Mexico a band of Shiite Moslems seized the American Embassy in Tehran and held a number of its staff as hostages. Back home the average American was not only angry but confused. Having heard for years that our nation's enemies were godless atheists, they found it hard to understand bearded mullahs who called the United States "Satan" and were depicted in the news as religious fanatics. Then, in December 1980, four American Roman Catholic women missionaries were shot to death in El Salvador, not, it appeared, either by godless Communists or by fanatic Moslems but by soldiers carrying rifles supplied to them through the ruling junta by the United States government. Religion and politics were not only being mixed but in highly unfamiliar ways.

Every week new evidence suggested something was astir. The Roman Catholic bishops of Canada issued a sharp criticism of their government's economic policies, claiming discrimination against the poor. The *New York Times Magazine* carried a cover article about the Protestant and Catholic churches of South Korea and their strong public opposition to the regime there.[4] The Catholic Bishop of Manila called on the businessmen of his nation to join him in opposing the Marcos government. Even in Communist countries religion appeared to be assuming a more prominent public role. In Poland, members of the Solidarity trade union movement, which was repressed by a martial law decree in December 1981, sang hymns at their rallies and carried pictures of the Blessed Virgin on marches. The leaders, including Lech Walesa, appeared to be motivated by Roman Catholic values. Visitors to the USSR reported a growing interest in traditional Russian Orthodoxy among young people and intellectuals. And in February 1982 nearly four thousand youthful East Germans gathered in a Protestant Church in Dresden to listen to talks by two Lutheran pastors in support of European nuclear disarmament. They met under a banner stretched across the baroque organ pipes that bore the motto "Frieden schaffen ohne Waffen" (build peace without weapons), a phrase which directly contradicts the official East German government's position expressed by the slogan "Peace Must Be Armed."[5]

In Western Europe also, once thought of as the epicenter of secularism, churches reappeared in the public realm. A popular movement against nuclear weapons suddenly came into world visibility in 1981, and the churches—of Holland and West Germany especially —were at its core. Laurens J. Hogebrink, a Protestant pastor, often spoke for the Dutch Interchurch Peace Council. The British campaign for nuclear disarmament was led by a Roman Catholic priest, Monsignor Bruce Kent. Even in Sicily, Protestants and Catholics were working together to oppose the stationing of nuclear missiles in the small city of Comiso.

In the United States the new vitality of religion in the public sphere assumed a more ambiguous form. Falwell had organized Moral Majority, Inc., in 1979, and in the fall of 1980 he and other TV evangelists—strongly hinting that they had helped elect Ronald Reagan President—began to push vigorously for government action on restoring prayer to the schools, banning pornography, outlawing abortion, and controlling what they considered immoral themes in the mass media. By the fall of 1982, however, none of these goals had been attained, and nearly all candidates running on these issues lost their electoral contests. The question of how much influence political fundamentalism would have on American society remained unanswered.

Church members also began to notice a renewed series of attacks on the National Council of Churches and the World Council of Churches. They were often orchestrated by a politically conservative group called the Institute for Religion and Democracy, and their polemics focused on certain activities of these ecumenical bodies that their critics asserted did not reflect the ideas of the average person in the pew.[6] But there no longer seemed to be a one-to-one correlation between conservative theology and conservative politics. In 1978 an organization appeared called Evangelicals for Social Action, which presented itself as offering "education, support, and analysis toward biblical social change." Its statement of purpose declares:

> We are unique in that our agenda for social change is not derived from liberal or conservative social agendas, but from the Scriptures.[7]

Today ESA describes itself as adhering to a "pro-life" stance on "such issues as peace and nuclear disarmament; the rights of the unborn;

wealth and poverty; the sacredness of the family; the elimination of racial and sex discrimination; human rights at home and abroad; and the protection of the environment." The Sojourners Fellowship in Washington, D.C., an influential group of theologically conservative but politically radical Christians, resembles ESA but puts more emphasis on direct action, pacifism, and the development of new forms of spiritual community.[8]

Evangelicals in fact were emerging as a "third force" between the vociferous fundamentalist and the establishment-liberal wings of American Protestantism. As they did, they were leaving behind the posture which at least since the 1930s had made theological and political conservatism synonymous. Dr. Billy Graham, once viewed by most Americans as a streamlined version of sawdust-trail revivalism and a stalwart defender of conservative causes, had assumed a new role in his mature years. He was becoming a kind of church statesman, mediating between the various theological currents, and a vigorous critic of nuclear armament. Against the advice of the State Department he made a highly publicized visit to Moscow in June 1982, both to preach and to attend a peace conference. He had become "ecumenical," with only the far-fundamentalist right and the ultraliberal left continuing to regard him with suspicion.[9]

In 1982 the role of the American Roman Catholic bishops in the formation of public policy also took a dramatic turn. Issuing a draft of a pastoral letter on war and peace that was highly critical of American nuclear weapons policy, the bishops served notice that Catholics were not interested merely in abortion or the institutional problems of parochial schools. Monsignor Vincent Yzermans, who once served as information director for the U.S. Catholic hierarchy, wrote in November 1981:

> Something is stirring in the Roman Catholic Church in the United States that portends an explosion between church and state that will make the abortion issue, the school-aid controversy and the tax-exempt status of churches look like a child's sparkler on the Fourth of July. Stated simply, the church in the United States is becoming a "peace" church. . . . This revolution is being waged painfully in the hearts and minds of Catholic thinkers and leaders. . . . The American bishops are shouldering their responsibility of

leading this revolution, at times to the chagrin and vocal opposition of their flocks.[10]

Monsignor Yzermans emphasizes the Catholic bishops' collective support for nuclear disarmament. Some individual bishops have gone further. Archbishop Raymond Hunthausen of Seattle announced that he would withhold the portion of his income tax going for military purposes, and Bishop Leroy Matthiesen of Amarillo, Texas, has asked Catholics who work in any phase of nuclear weapons development to consider seeking employment elsewhere. In addition the bishops have sharply criticized the U.S. policy of supplying arms to repressive Central American regimes. Although the "explosion" Yzermans predicts has not occurred, both the Vice President and the Secretary of State have publicly questioned the bishops' policies.

By the early 1980s it had begun to look as though a revival of religion, one with important implications for political life, was underway everywhere. The old secular city just wasn't what it used to be. The evidence pointed to a resurrection of religion, and of traditional and theologically orthodox religion at that, worldwide. It appeared to be a revival, furthermore, which was not restricting itself to the sanctuary but was reaching into the barricades and the corridors of power. But there are still gnawing questions. Is it simply that the dirge was played prematurely? Is the death of God, or at least of religion, simply taking longer than expected? Are we witnessing a genuine revival of traditional religion, or is the new religious wave a creature of the mass media, or the fevered bloom on the cheek of a dying consumptive? Is it no more than a cynical misuse of religion for extraneous purposes? If there is a genuine spiritual upsurge, why has it assumed such a political stance, and why are the political postures so disparate—revolutionary in Latin America; democratic in Poland; mixed in the United States?

In 1965, much under the influence of Bonhoeffer's theology and greatly concerned about what the expected decline of traditional religion might do to the relevance of Christianity, I wrote a book called *The Secular City*.[11] In it I drew upon the anticultic preaching of the Hebrew prophets and Jesus' opposition to the priestly establishment of his own day to argue that religion is not always and everywhere a good thing, and that secularization might not be the unmitigated scourge it was often seen to be. I suggested that instead of bemoaning the waning of ecclesial power or the disappearance of the sacral, Christians should concentrate instead on the positive role they could play in the modern secular world. I still believe in that thesis. The problem is that the world of declining religion to which my earlier book was addressed has begun to change in ways that few people anticipated. A new age that some call the "postmodern" has begun to appear. No one is quite sure just what the postmodern era will be like, but one thing seems clear. Rather than an age of rampant secularization and religious decline, it appears to be more of an era of religious revival and the return of the sacral. No one talks much today about the long night of religion or the zero level of its influence on politics.

The current reappearance of religion does not, however, make the message of *The Secular City* obsolete. It remains true that biblical faith is often critical of human religiousness. The Hebrew prophets inveighed against solemn assemblies. The religious authorities of his day saw Jesus as a dangerous threat. If secularization was not always bad, religion is not always good. If the challenge modern theology took on was to define and defend the faith in an era of religious decline, the task of a postmodern theology is to interpret the Christian message at a time when the rebirth of religion, rather than its disappearance, poses the most serious questions.

This is a book about the unexpected return of religion as a potent social force in a world many thought was leaving it behind. It is about the place religion has come to occupy in the modern age and about the role it should play in the postmodern world presently coming to birth. I write as a theologian. In doing so I accept that theology is an old-fashioned discipline that deals not just with what is but with what ought to be. Clearly, theologians possess no monopoly on the study of religion. Historians, sociologists, psychologists, psychiatrists roam freely through its sacred precincts as well. Still, there is a difference. When anthropologists and sociologists move as they often do from description to prescription, from telling us what religion is to advising us what it ought to be, then we must ask: What normative vision of religion and what plumbline of its proper relation to the secular world inform their prescription? Where do they get their oughts and shoulds? As soon as they begin to answer such questions we will have left social science and crossed over into theology.

Theology is unapologetically *prescriptive*. It does not claim to be value-free or neutral. Theologians draw upon the beliefs of a particular tradition to suggest a course of action, an appropriate response, a way of life commensurate with what the faith teaches. Theology can be wrong; it cannot be noncommittal.

In this sense, then, this book is not just *about* religion in the postmodern world. It makes a theological case which is in three parts.

The *first* is that with the passing of the modern age, the epoch of "modern theology" which tried to interpret Christianity in the face of secularization is also over. A fundamentally new theological approach is needed.

The *second* is that the essential rudiments of that new theology need not be invented out of whole cloth but are already appearing, borne by vigorous antimodernist religious movements. They need only to be discerned, clarified, and articulated.

The *third*, however, is that these indispensable components of the coming theology can be assembled only if we appreciate and use the accomplishments of modern theology, including "liberal" theology, rather than rescind them. I am writing not to bury modern theology but—at least in some measure—to praise it, or at least to learn from the courageous way it tackled the modern world how we might now begin to tackle its postmodern successor.

Where will the resources for a postmodern theology come from? My thesis in this book is that they will come not from the center but from the bottom and from the edge. They will come from those sectors of the modern social edifice that for various reasons—usually to do with class or color or gender—have been consigned to its lower stories and excluded from the chance to help formulate its religious vision. They will come from those parts of the world geopoliticians classify as the "periphery," regions also largely left out of participation in the centers of modern theological discourse which are located in the Western political and cultural milieu.

Before the bottom and the edge can be heard from, the present weakened "center" will have to be dismantled. Not destroyed, for there are parts of it which will be not only useful but essential to theology's next phase. Pope John Paul's arrival symbolized the return

Parallel in Technology *pest of past + present or Appropriate feeh.*

of religion to the secular city and the mixed political consequences of that return. It also brought together the two main agents of modern theology's end: the traditional and the radical. If the new theology will come from the edge and the bottom, I believe traditional religion will provide its content in some still unforeseen combination with radical Christianity. Here in the Pope's arrival were signaled all the elements—bottom and edge, tradition and radicality. Here the most archaic and the most avant-garde wings of Christianity seemed, for a moment at least, to squeeze out the middle completely. Here Poland was meeting Latin America, and Rome was kissing the Third World.

The Polish Pope is an exemplary conservative religious leader. His opposition to birth control and his insistence on clerical celibacy and an exclusively male priesthood make this painfully clear to American and European liberal Catholics. He is also a traditionalist who has made highly publicized pilgrimages to the Black Madonna of Czestochwa in Poland, Fatima in Portugal, and the basilica of Our Lady of Guadalupe in Mexico. He is a staunchly *Roman* Catholic who will not permit his interest in Christian unity to erode what he believes are the unshakable pillars of the True Faith. But in climbing out of his jet onto Latin American soil, John Paul II—the custodian of traditional religion—arrived in the habitat of Christianity's most revolutionary wing. He was stepping onto the continent where young Catholics sing a song called "The Cross of Light," honoring the memory of the Colombian guerrilla-priest Camilo Torres, and others light candles before photographs of the martyred Salvadoran Archbishop Oscar Romero; where Brazilian Bishop Paulo Everisto Ahrns opened the churches of his diocese in São Paulo to illegally striking workers whom the military government had forbidden to meet; where the highly controversial "basic Christian communities," lay-led grassroots congregations involved in Bible study and political action, are blossoming by the thousands, and the much disputed "theology of liberation" originated.

The Pope's visit to Mexico brought the juxtaposition between traditional and radical Christianity into sharp profile. But it also revealed some elements of convergence between the two, not the least of which is their common aversion to "modern theology," the attempt to adapt Christianity to the modern world. The Pope's social pronouncements do not please conservative American advocates of supply-side and *laissez faire* economics. For their part, the revolutionary Christians of Latin America are quite traditional in some ways. They puzzle moral majoritarians who prefer to believe that all revolutionaries are devoted to the destruction of monogamy and the abolition of religion. An acquaintance of mine, a priest who identifies himself with the Catholic left in Brazil, once told me that the problem with North American theologians is that they will "never understand that we Latin Americans *like* tradition and ritual and hierarchy." Liberation theologians are cautious about the way liberal theologians apply modern historical methods to the study of the Bible, not because they oppose such methods but because they tend to confuse and mystify the ordinary people for whom the message is intended. As for public morals, when Ernesto Cardenal became Minister of Cultural Affairs in Nicaragua after the victory of the Sandinist revolution, he immediately banned the importation of pornographic films. The meeting of the two wings of antimodernist Christianity involves consensus as well as collision.

These then are the two columns now engaged in ambushing the remnants of secular society and modern theology. But both wings are themselves improbable conglomerates. The conservative battalion, symbolized by the Pope, encompasses both arcadian poets who loathe television and Protestant preachers who own whole networks. It includes fashionable "neoconservatives," many of them Jewish, who write for *Commentary* magazine and whose grandmothers would light an extra Sabbath candle if they knew their progeny were keeping company with Texan revivalists and Polish prelates. Still, their shock could not exceed that of the shirt-sleeved fundamentalist predecessors of Mr. Falwell if they had seen the picture of a Romish Pope that was in a spring 1982 issue of *Moral Majority Report.* Whatever happened to "Rum, Romanism and Rebellion"?

Politics always makes strange bedfellows, especially when mixed with religion. If the conservative wing of the uprising against modern theology is a potpourri, the radical party is also a choir of mixed voices. It brings together not only Latin American Catholics but an increasing number of Asian and African Christians; a growing group of feminist religious thinkers; black American theologians; a scattering of white American inner-city Catholics and Appalachian Protestants, and—more recently—voices from the Asian American and Mexican American subcultures. Like the pope's division, this list includes people who until recently might have crossed the street to avoid meeting each other.

At first the convergence of the traditionalists and radicals seems odd. The conservatives dismiss the radicals and their liberation theology either as a collapsing of the faith into a political ideology or as just the latest sellout to modernity. The Latin Americans and their allies in the radical camp lump the sophisticated conservatives along with the fundamentalists as variations of the same religiously tinctured bourgeois ideology. But when it comes to evaluating modern theology, the two warring schools agree: they both find it a failure. Can a postmodern theology arise out of such cacophony?

I think it will, but one should not try to answer this question at the theological level alone. Theologies, unlike philosophical schools or scientific paradigms, do not make much headway in the world unless they are borne along by vigorous religious movements. They need a social base. The emergence of a postmodern theology from the bottom and the edges of the modern world will happen only as religious movements incorporating powerful critiques of modern theology and the religious sensibility on which it is based come more and more into prominence. Consequently, the first sections of this book examine the "religious" attacks on modern society and its theology; then we will turn to the dawning attempts to replace modern theology with something very different.

I have chosen to examine two representative antimodernist religious movements, one traditional and one radical, in considerable detail:

1. The dramatic reappearance of *political fundamentalism* and its recent marriage to the *electronic media* in the United States and, even more recently, in other countries as well; and,

2. The equally dramatic appearance of the *Christian base communities* and of *liberation theology*, which has occurred in many places, but chiefly in Latin America.

Both movements are growing rapidly. Both are profoundly antagonistic to modern theology, especially what they call "liberal" or "progressive" theology, though in quite different ways. Both are shat-

tering the institutional forms of religious life that came to birth during and after the Reformation. Both are uniting people who once
fought each other and dividing people who once felt united. Both
are creating new forms of religious association that are rendering
denominations, the most characteristic social expression of modern
Christianity, obsolete. Both emphasize the Bible and claim to be
recalling people to the Original Message, away from the errors and
idols of modernity. Both emphasize increased participation of Christians in political life. Both rely on leaders whose authority has more
to do with personal charisma than with academic degrees or ecclesiastical ordinations.

Yet despite these similarities, the differences between the burgeoning mass media religion of the United States and the fast-growing
base-community liberation Christianity in other parts of the world
could not be greater. The two open a schism in the church that runs
far deeper than the occasional bickering that still divides Catholics
from Protestants. Mass media fundamentalism, though it varies in
tone and tenor, presents a theology that celebrates patriotism, individual success, and a political spectrum ranging from moderately
conservative to the far, far right. The base communities on the other
hand, though they also vary immensely from place to place, exemplify a theology that affirms social justice, the rights of the poor, a
communal understanding of salvation, and a politics that stretches
from moderately reformist to revolutionary. Still, both movements
are strongly antimodernist; to understand them is to understand why
"modern religion" and its theological rationale seem fated for dissolution.

As I describe mass media fundamentalism and community-based
liberation theology it will become evident that my evaluations of the
two are not wholly symmetrical. During my research I came to believe that fundamentalism, at least in its early days, was putting many
of the right questions to modern theology, and that the current
comeback of fundamentalism, this time via television and computer
mailings, will probably contribute a good deal to the demise of modern theology. But I do not believe fundamentalism has much to offer
to a postmodern theology. Liberation theology on the other hand
will probably not play as large a role in the dissolution of modern
theology (in part because it occupies a social terrain where modern

religion never gained a secure foothold in the first place). Still, I believe it will supply some of the main ingredients of a postmodern theology, one that combines radical and traditional, premodern and modern elements.

In Part One we will examine recent American mass media fundamentalism understood against the larger background of the traditional religious rejection of modernity. In Part Two we will look at the liberation theology of the base communities of Latin America and elsewhere, also with attention to their wider history, that of religiously inspired political protest against modern social injustice. And in Part Three we will see something of the way the bottom and the edges are already making a postmodern theology visible.

PART ONE

Praying for the Children at the Gate: The Conservative Critique of Modern Theology

Will the veiled sister pray for
Those who walk in darkness, who chose thee and
    oppose thee,
Those who are torn on the horn between season
    and season, time and time, between
Hour and hour, word and word, power and power,
    those who wait
In darkness? Will the veiled sister pray
For children at the gate
Who will not go away and cannot pray:
Pray for those who chose and oppose
              —T. S. Eliot
               "Ash-Wednesday 1930"

1. "To Bring the Nation Back . . ." The Revival of Redneck Religion

I am fully expecting between now and the coming of
the Lord that this world is going to experience a
spiritual awakening unlike anything in the past.
There is going to be an invasion of God on this
planet, and changing of lives: real biblical evangelism. There is going to be a terrific harvest of souls
somewhere between here and the Rapture. I believe
that God's role for America is as catalyst, that he
wants to set the spiritual time bomb off right here. If
that is the case, America must stay free. And for
America to stay free we must come back to the only
principles that God can honor: the dignity of life,
the traditional family, decency, morality and so on.
I just see myself as one to stand in the gap and, under
God, with the help of millions of others, to bring the
nation back to a moral standard so we can stay free
in order that we can evangelize the world. And protect the Jews.

—Jerry Falwell

The maroon-robed eighty-five-voice choir moves in from the wings
and sits facing the congregation now gathering at Thomas Road
Baptist Church for the regular eleven A.M. Sunday service. It is July,
and the temperature in Lynchburg, Virginia, stands at 95 degrees.
But inside the church it is cool to the point of frostiness. "One thing
Jerry just can't stand is heat," my attentive hostess whispers as we sit

in the third pew from the front waiting for things to start, "so every-thing is air-conditioned. Still, it gets real hot sometimes, especially on the stage, what with the TV lights and all."

There is a brief pause between the adult Bible study class, which meets here in the main church auditorium at 9:45, and the tradi-tional eleven o'clock service, which is about to begin. There were nearly four thousand people at the Bible class, led by the youthful Dr. Ed Hindson, who in addition to serving as the Reverend Jerry Falwell's associate pastor at Thomas Road is also chairman of the Religion Department at Liberty Baptist College, head of its counsel-ing center, and associate dean of the seminary. He has just led the congregation through a lively forty-minute verse-by-verse commen-tary on Matthew 22 which he called "Jesus and His Critics."

The chapter tells of Jesus' encounters with Herodians, Sadducees, and Pharisees, and each of these groups, the teacher suggested, has its own contemporary equivalent. Thus the Herodians—(the Jewish supporters of the Roman-installed ruling dynasty in the Palestine of Jesus' day)—were likened to "those today who are obsessed exclu-sively with the political sphere" and "push for social change but neglect the things of the spirit." He equated the Sadducees—(the strict traditionalists of Jesus' day)—with modern religious liberals "who want to hang on to Christianity but jettison the supernatural element." Finally, the Pharisees were compared to the hyper-holier-than-thou Christian conservatives of today, those who take the bib-lical exhortation "Come ye out and be ye separate" so literally they will not even dine with people they consider in error.

In Dr. Hindson's interpretation of the text, Jesus bests all three parties of critics. He puts the Herodians to shame by eluding their trick question about whether it is right to render tribute to Caesar. Dr. Hindson wears a handsome three-piece brown suit and a tasteful tie—the leaders at Thomas Road all eschew double-knit clothes. He underscores his point by flipping a coin he has held while comment-ing on Jesus' answer ("Render therefore unto Caesar the things which are Caesar's; and unto God the things that are God's") out of the pulpit and onto the tufted powder-blue cut-pile carpet. The congre-gation chuckles appreciatively. He goes on to describe how Jesus refutes the Sadducees by exposing their theological and spiritual shal-lowness, and routs the Pharisees by turning the tables and asking them a question they cannot answer. Dr. Hindson concludes his exegetical tour de force by saying that he himself is not as impressed with the miracles and healings of Jesus as he is with the Master's "sheer brilliance," proof that we are dealing here not with a mere man but with God himself in human flesh.

During the Bible study the entire congregation listened with rapt attention, Bibles open, following the verses as the teacher commented on them. It had been an eloquent, if rapid-fire presentation. The discussion certainly left some opening for scholarly discomfort. The portrayal of the Pharisees as self-righteous prigs perpetuated a historically questionable Christian stereotype. Still it was timely, engaging, and understandable to the listeners. Furthermore, Dr. Hindson's presentation was far more self-critical and expansive than what one would hear at other self-designated "fundamentalist" Baptist churches. He had obviously consulted some scholarly commentaries. The criticism of the liberals was measured, and it was balanced by a critique of overzealous fundamentalists. Hindson was staking out his ground.

He was placing Jesus, himself, and the Thomas Road Baptist Church and its famous pastor in what might be called the "liberal wing" of American fundamentalism. Hindson obviously saw himself taking the same position Jesus did. Pastor Falwell's Bible teacher wanted to claim the ground the older generation of fundamentalists, those the folks at Thomas Road like to call "hypers," probably cannot occupy because they have withdrawn (like Hindson's "Pharisees") into a "self-righteous ghetto." They have become powerless to influence the culture or be politically effective.

To some observers this ground may appear to be a narrow strip of sand, hardly worth contending for. But as Falwell himself estimates, there are 110,000 local churches in the United States that would gladly call themselves "fundamentalist." These include a large number of "independent" and "Bible Baptist" churches—both old ones and the new crop of cinderblock edifices springing up all over the country, the little ones with the neon crosses. The pastors of many of these churches attended Bible colleges rather than seminaries, and many work during the week as electricians, salesmen, roofers, and farmers. These are the churches—some on the outskirts of town where real estate is cheaper, some in downtown areas—which mainline church members, including many in Lynchburg, drive by wondering who actually goes there. They also include thousands of churches that are fundamentalist but not Baptist. These churches represent a considerable segment of the American population, a segment that has not gone unnoticed by political organizers and fundraisers in recent years. Yet, largely because of the class and regional divisions in the American religious community, most ordinary Christians have only the vaguest idea of who fundamentalists are.

The Bible study class ends and the service itself is about to begin. Visitors to Baptists churches sometimes find it difficult to distinguish between the two. Both normally include songs, prayers, announcements, and a lengthy presentation that might be a "meditation," a sermon, a message, or a Bible study. At Thomas Road, however, it is easy to know when the service begins. The klieg lights are on, the microphone booms are positioned, and the pastor, standing behind the big white pulpit, is greeting not only the people gathered in this building but the "millions who are watching at home."

We are now on nationwide TV, and I sense a change in the congregation, and in the pastor too. Baptist church services always include lots of announcements—the time for choir rehearsal, prayer meeting, evening services. This one is no exception, but in addition to these standard items, Falwell also tells about a wedding he conducted the night before and reminisces about knowing the parents of the groom for twenty-five years. He mentions how much he enjoys "watching Christian young people meet, fall in love, marry and begin building Christian homes." It is all folksy and informal. He joshes a woman in the choir about her advanced age before presenting her with a large-type Bible. He makes a long plea for contributions to Liberty Baptist College. He announces that the wife of a male soloist has just had a baby boy (although "Brother Jerry" had confidently predicted a girl), calls for a second collection of money, this one to help send a student from Ghana who has been studying at Liberty Baptist College back home to preach the gospel there. The choir sings an anthem—technically well rendered but musically flimsy. A TV technician monitors the service on headphones. One of the cameras scans the congregation, and the large monitor screen, located on the wall just below the central balcony—directly opposite the pulpit so the preacher always knows what the TV congregation is seeing—dutifully records the rows and rows of attentive worshipers, most of the men in ties and jackets and the women in modest dresses that cover arms and backs.

The sermon begins. Brother Jerry is preaching today on Chapter 23 of Proverbs and the sermon is entitled "Guidelines for Christian Living." It is not a fundamentalist sermon in the classical style of Charles Fuller or Donald Grey Barnhouse. The list of virtues he commends—honesty, fairness, communication, listening well, hard work—would sound unexceptionable to almost any viewer. On the air this is known as the Old Time Gospel Hour, but there is no hellfire and brimstone, only a passing reference to the precious blood of Christ, hardly a mention of being born again. There is a response to a recent *Wall Street Journal* article ("although," the preacher says, "it is one of the best papers in the country"); an ambiguous defense of Billy Graham against people who "misquoted his remarks about religious freedom in Russia"; a criticism of Jimmy Allen of the Southern Baptist Convention for allegedly doctoring the video tape of a recent meeting in New Orleans. All this is within the improbable context of a commentary on Proverbs 23. ("Preaching is really not Brother Jerry's strong suit," a church member tells me the next day, "and he knows it. What he is is a pastor and a counselor . . . he still does all the funerals. And an organizational genius.")

The sermon ends with the traditional "invitation" to both those present and those watching to accept Christ as personal saviour. A few people come forward and are escorted to counseling rooms in the rear to talk with one of the pastors (there are sixty-three full-time paid staff members at Thomas Road Baptist Church). Then we are off the air.

It is about five hours until the evening service begins at 6:00 P.M. There will be four thousand people present for that too, and although Brother Jerry will preside, the message itself will be brought by a young evangelist who was one of the first graduates of Liberty Baptist College and is now leading revivals in California.

Everyone has come by car, and getting four thousand people out of the Thomas Road Baptist Church parking lot is no easy feat. Brother Jerry spends a few minutes shaking hands on the platform, then moves out the side door. He is driving his own Chevy Suburban and I sit on the seat beside him. He starts the engine and clowns with a church member by pretending to ram his Buick, braking just before the bumpers touch. Before we leave the lot he has a conversation with an associate about where to house an adolescent girl whose mother is ill and who does not want to stay with her father. The pastor zooms out of the lot and drives through Lynchburg waving. He seems to know everyone. He is the embodiment of the genial small-town Baptist pastor, that mixture of the saint, the glad-hander, the orator and raconteur, the friend in need, the moral exemplar.

But this small-town parson has just addressed several million people on television. He is said to raise over eighty million dollars a year for his various causes. He delights in the label "fundamentalist," but his fundamentalist critics call him a "compromiser."[1] Jerry Falwell personifies all the contradictions in the current fusion of American fundamentalism with mass media and its theological and political implications. He also raises questions about how a born-again, self-designated "redneck preacher," addressing millions of viewers from a pulpit in a renovated soft-drink factory, can be part of a ground swell of religiously inspired antimodernism. Antimodernism started many years before the fundamentalist renaissance and reaches out to include philosophers, poets, and culture critics who would be terribly uneasy singing "Are You Washed in the Blood of the Lamb?" at Thomas Road Baptist Church.

Jerry Falwell is not even the top television preacher. There are other video revivalists who are seen by more viewers and who raise more money. But as politically conservative religion made its unexpected reappearance in America, Falwell became the most widely touted of the new breed of evangelists. As a self-described Baptist "fundamentalist" he spared the media the difficulty of finding the proper theological label for him. To make sure no one misunderstood what he meant, Falwell once made a trip to Dayton, Tennessee, the site of the historic Scopes "monkey trial," the event historians used to say marked the beginning of the decline of fundamentalism. It was here that William Jennings Bryan, the "great commoner," the perennial presidential candidate, the religious and political populist, crossed lances with Clarence Darrow in the battle over evolution and the literal truth of the Bible. In the same courtroom Jerry Falwell posed holding a copy of a newspaper with the headline "Scopes Convicted: Fined $100." No amateur in the use of visual symbols,

Falwell was sending a clear message. What Hindson calls "redneck religion" is alive and well, and it is reaching millions of people who never heard of Clarence Darrow.

Born and raised as a Depression kid in a working-class family in Virginia, Falwell has a life story that is more exemplary than unique. His parents were not particularly pious and there are still members of his family who are notorious nonchurchgoers. Falwell likes to depict himself as the ornery kid who got saved, and the ne'er-do-well whose life was headed for perdition until the Lord turned him around on his personal road to Damascus. There is no reason to doubt his testimony. That it is virtually identical with that of thousands of other born-again Christians does not detract from its credibility. If anything it points to the power of religious traditions to shape life cycles in similar ways, especially in a region where such a tradition pervades the atmosphere.

After his conversion, Falwell quickly decided he was called of God not only to the Christian life but to be a preacher of the Word. After a few false starts, in 1956 Falwell set up his own independent Baptist church in a Donald Duck soft-drink factory that his congregation bought and renovated on Thomas Road in Lynchburg. From his new pulpit Falwell preached his version of Baptist piety, conservative politics, and sound advice on moral living. Among the main targets of his verbal polemics were preachers such as Martin Luther King and the antiwar ministers who mixed religion with politics. So far it was all going rather predictably.

Then Falwell had his second conversion. By the middle 1970s it dawned on him that if black activists and white doves could base their appeals on the Bible and use the churches in their efforts to effect political changes, conservatives and fundamentalists could do the same. For Falwell this insight did not come as a result of studying the previous waves of evangelical Christian involvement in politics —the antislavery and prohibition movements,[2] for example. Despite the Dayton trip, and like many other fundamentalist preachers today, he is not particularly interested in these precedents, perhaps because to delve into them might raise uncomfortable questions about how and on what side one actually gets into the political fray. The religiously inspired political movement Falwell personifies arose, ironically, not from a renewal of its own theological and social sources but as a result of Selma and the march on the Pentagon.

Another reason Falwell quickly became such a favorite of the press was that he was so unabashedly political. "I am," he says, "as far right as you can get." Moral Majority, which he established in 1979, is a nonreligious organization, Falwell says.[3] It has come into existence not to save souls (which is more properly the business of his Thomas Road Baptist Church and the Old Time Gospel Hour) but because "all the real volatile moral issues had become volatile political issues by the late seventies." It is "prolife, protraditional family, promoral" and "opposed to the illegal drug traffic and pornography." Also, Falwell adds, "We are pro-American, which means strong national defense and the State of Israel." Despite its nonreligious character ("nondenominational" might be more accurate), Falwell claims there are seventy-two thousand ministers among the organization's four million people.[4]

Falwell considers himself one of the principal architects of the revival of fundamentalism. In addition to his church and Moral Majority, Inc., Falwell·is the head of Liberty Baptist College, which he founded in Lynchburg in 1971. It now enrolls nearly four thousand students. He is also the chancellor of Liberty Baptist Seminary, which trains young people for the fundamentalist ministry. This position as an influential educator, along with his television contacts, has enabled Falwell to become a leader within the often severely divided community of Baptist fundamentalists.

In the summer of 1982 Falwell was buoyant and optimistic. The church, the college, and the seminary were all growing. Reporters and interviewers were descending on Lynchburg to seek him out. President Reagan had invited him to Washington for a meeting at which the President declared his support for a constitutional amendment to make prayer in the public schools possible again. Plans were underway for transforming Liberty Baptist College into Liberty University and for building a retirement village on the adjacent hillside.

It would be as misleading and inaccurate to consider Jerry Falwell representative of the conservative wing of the attack on modernity as to consider Ernesto Cardenal representative of the radical wing. Both men are volatile and flamboyant, and their styles sometimes embarrass the more cautious sectors of their respective alliances.

Still, both personify in a vivid and outspoken way the perspectives of a wider movement. Cardenal, with his flowing gray beard, "Ché" beret, and fatigues, embodies something larger; and one cannot visit Lynchburg without marveling at the thespian skills of Falwell and pausing to wonder how the fundamentalist-evangelical-neoconserva-tive coalition sticks together.

What are the essential features of the traditional conservative re-ligious critique of modern society and modern theology? What are the sources of its disaffection? How does American fundamentalist Protestantism relate to the other elements of the conservative group-ing? Finally, is there anything in this criticism to help us move beyond the present stalemate of modern theology? We turn to these questions in the following chapters.

2. Fundamentalism and the Tradition of Religious Antimodernism

"I perceive," said the Countess, "Philosophy is now become Mechanical." "So Mechanical," said I, "that I fear we shall quickly be asham'd of it; they will have the World to be in great, what a watch is in little; which is very regular, & depends only upon the just disposing of the several parts of the movement. But pray tell me, Madam, had you not formerly a more sublime Idea of the Universe?"

—Fontenelle
Plurality of Worlds, 1686

People who are fond of tradition have always complained about the times they live in. For thousands of years older people have worried about the younger generation frittering away what was most vital. Still, the fact that traditionalist indictments of novelty repeat themselves generation after generation does not render them meaningless. In our time in particular, such criticisms of the dominant patterns of civilization have achieved an eloquence and weight that require thoughtful reflection.

For the traditional religious critics of modern theology the central image of our age is that of a wasteland: desiccated, lifeless, desolate. At the same time it is frantic, contrived, plastic, unnatural, excessively technological, rootless and artificial. The emotion these critics express most often is that of sadness. Something has been lost; and what is lost seems to be religious: the sacred, the element of mystery in life, the transcendent, the spiritual dimension, a morality firmly grounded in revealed truth.

What are the sources of our current malady? The conservative critics list many, but they can all be summarized under the rubric "secularization," and this process is generally seen as the dismal outcome of two historical forces, the impact of scientific technology and the rise of impersonal urban civilization.

1. Science-based technology has made it more difficult for religion by subjecting us to such a dazzling display of its prowess that it lures people into thinking they can now solve for themselves the problems for which they once turned to God. There is still a prayer for rain in the Episcopal Book of Common Prayer, but most Episcopalians, though they might say the prayer, would rely on cloud seeding if their own fields were drying up. Science itself is not the culprit, so runs this argument, but its spectacular success has reduced the traditional deity to a mere "god-of-the-gaps" whose only job is to explain or do what science cannot (or cannot yet) explain or do better. The heavenly realm is progressively reduced with every new discovery and invention.

What the conservative critics of modernity dislike about the role of science in the modern world is the reverse image of the expectation trumpeted by the anthropologist Anthony Wallace, who says:

> . . . the evolutionary future of religion is extinction. Belief in supernatural beings and supernatural forces that affect nature without obeying nature's laws will erode and become only an interesting historical memory.[1]

One suspects that Wallace, unlike the religious critics, is not saddened by the religionless world of the future he describes. True, he concedes that religion as he defines it will not disappear in the next generation or two. It may take hundreds of years, and even then there may continue to be quasipsychotic cults. But "as a cultural trait," any religion that postulates powers beyond nature is "doomed to die out, all over the world." The reason for this unavoidable demise of religion, says Wallace, is obvious. "As a . . . result of the increasing adequacy and diffusion of scientific knowledge . . . the process is inevitable."

Neither the traditional conservative critics of the modern world nor the fundamentalists consider themselves enemies of science.

There are differences in emphasis. Cultural traditionalists might feel uneasy at finding themselves grouped, even remotely, with those fundamentalists who either oppose the teaching of evolution in the schools or demand that "scientific creationism" be given equal time. Fundamentalists believe that science rightly used, what they sometimes call "True Science," can help rather than hinder faith. Still, there is a deeply felt suspicion on the part of both that the impact of a certain kind of science has eroded the beneficial influence of traditional religion. Fundamentalist critics fasten on the theory of evolution as a negative influence undercutting the authority of the Bible. If God did not create the world in six days, then Genesis is mistaken. If one part of Scripture is untrustworthy, so is all the rest. Not only are we shamefully linked to furry, flea-picking apes, we are left morally adrift. The more sophisticated critics are nervous about the logic of this fundamentalist argument, and they regret its heavy-handedness. But they too are troubled by the place science and technology have assumed in the modern psyche. They lament the displacement of that sense of mystery before the Numinous, the feeling of awe that a whole school of scholars has identified as the principal source of religion at least since Rudolf Otto published *The Idea of the Holy* in 1917. Both parties agree, however, that one of the underlying flaws of the modern world is that the predominance it assigns to science and technology weakens religion, and that this in turn makes life less livable.

2. Conservative critics also make urbanization a main target: cities, they claim, are and always have been spiritual disaster areas. Conservatives fault modern religion for either not realizing how detrimental city life is or, worse, becoming itself a part of the problem. Bureaucracy is regarded as an urban excrescence. Some conservatives criticize the bureaucratic style of the World Council of Churches and the National Council of Churches. The remote "church bureaucrat" is a favorite whipping boy. The implication is that churches should oppose bureaucracies, not become them. Bureaucracy segments human contacts, it is argued, while real religion is possible only where there are deep, ongoing personal relationships that flower over a long period of time. People can be religious only if they share a web of personal entwinements that will see them through youth, maturity, and old age, strengthening them with its customs, its recurrent sacred seasons and its life-cycle rituals.

Again the down-home fundamentalist and the elite conservative
critics of modern theology overlap here, though neither feels fully
comfortable in the other's company. There is a common suspicion of
the city as the most concentrated location of the modern malady.
For the fundamentalist, either based in a small-town setting or carrying its ethos to larger cities, the antiurban sentiment sounds forth in
hymns about meeting the Lord "In the Garden" and tarrying with
Him "while the dew is still on the roses." It appears in the folk saying
that "God made the country but man made the city." Its historic
enemies were the city saloon and corrupt big-city machine bosses.

Educated cultural conservatives are more subtle. Morton and Lucia
White have shown in their *The Intellectual Versus the City* that there
is a powerful antiurban bias in the American literary and philosophical tradition which demonstrates the same disbelief in the compati-
bility of city life and human values that the more unlettered folk
express in songs about the God of roses and dewdrops.[2] The antiurban
element in the various criticisms of the modern world and of modern
theology's attempt to make a home in it reflects the conservative
belief that spirituality and city life do not mix. Urbanization is the
process by which the fast-paced multiplication of transient contacts
replaces the continuity of smaller-sized habitations: so cities will inevitably be secular, inevitably evil.

The antiurban sentiments of the critics of modern theology recall
another conviction which is shared by both the elite and the folksy
conservatives: that modern people have a more difficult time being
religious because they are cut off from nature. How can they sense
the natural pulsations on which religious feeling is dependent?

Despite similarities, there are significant differences between the
way fundamentalists and more traditional conservatives condemn the
modern world and its mistaken theology. Fundamentalists favor con-
spiracy theories. They impute the moral decay and ethical flabbiness
of the modern world to the conniving of secular humanists, who
have seized power in the universities, the schools, the media, and
even the churches. The fundamentalists are angry and ready to fight
back. They believe that science and possibly even the cities can be
retrieved from the infidels who now control them. But it will take a
mighty purging.

Traditional conservatives are sometimes angry too, but they are
usually less willing to single out villains and less apt to smell conspir-

atorial plots. Like the fundamentalists, however, they hold that the underlying malaise of today's world stems from its loss of faith. They complain that secularity, fed by mindless gadgetry and tasteless urban hypertrophy, has made our lives trivial and vacuous and our world a wilderness of hollow men, lacking depth or transcendence. The result is more boring than evil, however; less unrighteous than undimensional. The traditional critics are more upset by the loss of genuine passion than by adultery or pornography. They pray more for a restoration of ritual and hierarchy than for a born-again revival. But at bottom all the different varieties of conservatives agree: the awfulness of the modern world is a direct result of its insane inversion of the Garden of Eden. There God expelled Adam and Eve for trying to become divine. Here men and women drive God out in order to create an earthly paradise. And the shame of modern theology is that it has been unable or unwilling to prevent this disaster from taking place.

If science and urbanization have been the principal culprits in the creation of the modern world, when and how did theology become their accomplice? Every theory of how religion should engage with culture contains a critical history, an intellectual analog of a fall from grace. Religious antimodernism is no exception.

Conservative and traditional critics of modern theology differ about when this fall took place. In the past, Catholic theologians often cited the Reformation as the fateful turning point. They blamed the reformers for undermining the authority of religion by destroying the universal authority of the papacy and for compromising with one of the modern world's most influential inventions, the new sovereign states. Protestant theologians do not accept this theory and more often locate the "fall" with the rise of the historical-critical method and its subverting of the authority of the Bible.

More recently, however, since conservative Protestants and conservative Catholics have become allied in the campaign against liberalism, this has changed. Catholics have soft-pedaled attacks on Luther and Calvin. At the same time, some theologically conservative Protestants have accepted certain elements of the historical-critical approach to the Bible. This has enabled them to find favor with sophisticated conservatives who recoil from any hint of redneck antiintellectualism. Many conservative Protestants have virtually eliminated their traditional anti-Catholicism and have chosen to defend what they usually call "classical" or "orthodox" Christianity, a category which now also includes Catholicism. But these conciliatory moves have also strained the alliance. By softening their stands on the dangers of popery and the inerrancy of the Bible the Protestants have enraged the "real" fundamentalists for whom any concession on these fronts marks the first step down the road to modernism and heterodoxy.

Holding the right wing of the antiliberal alliance together is not easy, and the various conservative critics differ among themselves on where modern theology went wrong. But *that* it went wrong somewhere they wholeheartedly agree. They also agree that theology should relinquish its unseemly *affaire d'amour* with the modern world and go back to attending to the more enduring ideas it once cultivated, such as transcendence, mystery, and the sacred. Their hope is that the veiled sister will sense the mute longings of the children at the gate and that through her prayers, prayer itself may again become possible. This is no mean goal. But whether the fundamentalists, who have only recently joined the older conservative coalition, are entirely welcome in its halls is still questionable.

The love affair between conservative religion and the mass electronic media is the most significant recent religious event in the United States. This development came as something of a surprise to those scholars who had looked upon fundamentalism as a declining, marginal movement, mainly a residue of ignorance and regional isolation. To the established custodians of religious antimodernism, however—the poets and literary critics—it came less as a surprise than as an embarrassment. Preferring a more reserved and modulated tone, the traditional critics of modernity sometimes seem mildly disquieted by the fact that their newest allies are a cadre of fast-talking Protestant evangelists whose major means of attacking the scourge of modernity is network color television.

True, not all TV preachers consider themselves fundamentalists, but many do. The emergence of "redneck religion" out of its self-imposed cultural exile and into the public domain is an event of enormous portent for the future of religion. The more strait-laced antimodernists will have to adjust to their less restrained colleagues. The same preachers who forbade three generations of believers to attend movies, and who looked with suspicion on the negative influence of science on human morality, have now become the acknowledged masters of cinema's most successful offspring. They are making themselves heard by virtue of technologies that the most advanced laboratories have spawned.

Fundamentalism is a relatively new phenomenon in American religious history; it dates back only to about the turn of the century, and it emerged as a conscious counterattack on what its early leaders called "modernism," the attempt to adjust Christianity to science, evolution, and liberalism. The name comes from a series of booklets called *The Fundamentals*,[3] issued from 1910 to 1915, which delineated what their writers believed were the irreducible doctrines of the faith, the beliefs without which Christianity could no longer be called Christianity. These fundamentals of the faith included belief in the deity of Christ, the Virgin Birth, the bodily Resurrection of Christ, the imminent Second Coming, the substitutionary atonement, and—very emphatically—the verbal inspiration and inerrancy of the whole Bible.

When one looks at this list today it is not difficult to discern what the early fundamentalists were reacting against. Such items as the deity of Christ and the Virgin Birth have appeared in Christian creeds since the earliest centuries. But the fundamentalists' insistence on the inerrancy of Scripture (not just its religious authority) signaled their rejection of the historical-critical approach to the Bible. Previous generations had held to the authority of Scripture but not to its literal infallibility. Christian creeds had always included some reference to the Second Coming of Christ, but the fundamentalists' emphasis on the *imminent* Second Coming indicated their concern about the tendency of liberal Christians to embrace ideas of progress and to talk about the "building" of the Kingdom of God. For fundamentalists, human beings do not build the Kingdom. God alone will establish the Kingdom when Jesus "comes again in glory."

Falwell may be exaggerating only a bit when he claims there are well over a hundred thousand fundamentalist churches in America. His own background is in the Baptist Bible Fellowship, which he refers to affectionately as "the BBF." The BBF, with headquarters in

Springfield, Missouri, has thirty-five thousand churches in America, some of them even larger than Falwell's (and Thomas Road has a membership of eighteen thousand). But despite their numbers, fundamentalists have not played as influential a role in American public life as one might imagine. Not yet, anyway.

There are two reasons for this impotence. One is that fundamentalists are notoriously quarrelsome and internally divisive. They are "come outers" who tend to resolve disputes by splitting and separating. Their insistence on absolute doctrinal conformity and their sharp distrust of any authoritative hierarchy has led fundamentalist leaders into an acrimonious history of mutual condemnation and founding of new churches. Churches have split and new congregations formed as pastors argued over whether Christ will come again before or after the great tribulation, or just when the "Rapture"— the miraculous lifting of all living true believers off the earth and into heaven—will take place. (This fundamentalist belief explains a bumper sticker that some people find puzzling: "Warning: in case of the Rapture this vehicle will be empty.")

In addition to its tendencies toward splitting, fundamentalism has certain theological features that have led it to a posture of withdrawal and a suspicion of those who try to influence society. One is its imminent eschatology. If Jesus is indeed coming soon, then why bother? Every minute not devoted to reaching lost souls (who will be left behind by the Rapture and then go to hell if they do not repent) is a minute wasted—and a soul lost for eternity. The logic of Jesus-is-coming-soon theology is not that of long-range planning or of ameliorating stubborn social ills.

Yet the Reverend Jerry Falwell has set out both to unite American fundamentalism and to make it a force in the shaping of American public life according to what he considers traditional conservative values. His vision is to reverse its long history of secession and kidney punching and to begin uniting the large conservative wing of American religion. He hopes to start with fundamentalist Baptists and move out in increasingly larger circles to include other fundamentalists, and eventually to forge an alliance with conservative nonfundamentalist evangelicals.

The difference between fundamentalists and evangelicals may appear minimal to many people, but to both groups the distinction is immensely important. In the United States today "evangelical" generally refers to the historic mainstream of theologically orthodox American Protestantism, going back to the earliest settlers and founding fathers (minus the deists) and including Jonathan Edwards and Charles Grandison Finney, the leaders, respectively, of the first and second "Great Awakenings" of the eighteenth and nineteenth centuries. What confuses some people is that although this conservative theological stream has been present since the beginning, the use of the term "evangelical" to designate it is relatively recent. It started around 1940, when the National Association of Evangelicals was organized not only as a conservative alternative to the more liberal ecumenical associations that were then coming into existence (such as those that eventually produced the National Council of Churches), but also as a more moderate alternative to fundamentalism.

 The difference between fundamentalists and evangelicals is not by and large one of theology. Even Jerry Falwell concedes that. Both uphold the same doctrinal fundamentals. The difference lies almost entirely in the way the two relate themselves to liberal Christians and to society at large. Evangelicals generally see fundamentalists as narrow, intolerant, maybe even bigoted, and unwilling to engage in social action. Most evangelicals believe they are right to remain within such "liberal" denominations as the United Presbyterians, American Baptists, United Methodists, and others, whereas almost all fundamentalists insist that true believers should obey St. Paul's command to "come ye out and be separate."[4]

Falwell reflects the view of many fundamentalists when he excoriates what is often called "the New Evangelicalism" (which represents mostly younger and more politically progressive evangelicals, such as the ones who organized Evangelicals for Social Action and the Sojourners) for tolerating the "inclusion of Christ-denying, Bible-deprecating unbelief" and for encouraging an atmosphere of "conformity to society." The efforts of Billy Graham and other evangelicals to cooperate with liberal Protestants and Catholics, even in evangelistic campaigns, elicits no approval from Falwell. He believes that this "overtolerance" has "left the Evangelical movement in neutral" and "in danger of drifting into moderate Liberalism."[5]

These do not sound like conciliatory words from a man who wants to create an alliance between fundamentalists and evangelicals. Yet this is just what Falwell hopes to do, and the stakes are large. The fundamentalist-evangelical wing of American Protestantism is growing quickly today. Falwell claims that two hundred thousand students are preparing for various types of ministry in conservative Christian seminaries and Bible institutes, and that there are already fifteen thousand "Christian academies" (some enrolling children from kindergarten through high school), with new ones opening every day. Conservative Christian student groups like Campus Crusade and Intervarsity are drawing large memberships on campuses all over the country. There is an evangelical religious publishing boom. Conservative Christians virtually monopolize religious television and radio.

It is this enormous religious upsurge that Falwell wants to unite and to make more effective in the public realm. "The time has come," he says,

. . . for true Fundamentalists and sincere Evangelicals to rise above the excessive labeling and listing of people, groups and schools. . . . Divergent groups of Bible-believing Christians who hold to the basic tenets of the faith can cooperate together in order to develop a broadly united front against the real enemies of true Christianity. Let us once again focus the theological guns at liberalism, humanism and secularism.[6]

The Jerry Falwell most analysts do not see is Falwell the healer of schisms, the patient negotiator, the "ecumenical" reconciler within the fundamentalist camp. "People apologized to each other," he says, describing a meeting of fundamentalist Baptist chieftains he had brought together, "and even asked forgiveness. One of them said to another, 'I used to think you were a dangerous heretic and possibly even the antichrist. But now let's put that all behind us and pull together.' "

I once asked if he plans eventually to bring non-Baptist fundamentalists into the mix. He smiled tolerantly, as though I had no idea of the difficulties involved. Right now, he said, he cannot even bring in conservative pastors who are still associated with the Southern Baptist Convention, for this would arouse suspicions. That will be the next step, but for now, one small step at a time.

His vision of a Baptist fundamentalist *ecumene* must at present avoid the conservative churches that, unlike the ones he is now working with, remain within the Southern Baptist Convention (a denomination many Americans regard as itself the archetype of conservatism), because his constituency would regard them as too liberal. Fundamentalists accuse each other of compromise and deviation with far more vehemence than they expend on liberals. This may be because they see liberals as down for the count anyway. As Falwell said about the Equal Rights Amendment, the deadline for which had passed a week before I visited Lynchburg, "Never speak ill of the dead."

The most fascinating feature of fundamentalism as a branch of religious antimodernism is its ambivalence. It is at the same time more isolated from the modern world and more critical of it than liberalism. Liberals find little reason either to dismantle the modern world or to desert it. They are at home in it. Their program is to live within it and speak to it. Fundamentalists see it differently. Called to birth by the heresies of modern theology as well as the errors of the world that theology was trying to speak to, fundamentalism oscillates. Sometimes, like a Billy Sunday punching the devil in the nose, it thrives on the negative energy generated by its battle with "modernism." At other times it seems to live as though the modern world never existed, as though one could ignore the major intellectual and cultural currents of the past two hundred years. Fundamentalism has never been able to decide whether to gather at the river and await the Rapture or to invade the citadels of sin with the Sword of the Lord in hand. This explains why it gyrates between attacking the modern age and its false theology with every available weapon (including political ones), and then turning its back on this fallen age and waiting for the coming judgment.

We are living today in one of fundamentalism's periods of militant confrontation and interaction. The sword of the Lord is unsheathed and fundamentalists are moving out of their self-imposed isolation into the mainstream, whether their more decorous allies in the conservative wing of the attack on modern theology are ready for them or not.

3. True Reason, True Science, and True Faith: The Burden of Fundamentalist Theology

".... the ills of our times come from the cleavage
between faith and science ... and the beginnings
of this cleavage are to be found within faith itself."
—Fritjof Schuon
Stations of Wisdom

Few historians study fundamentalism as an important cultural phenomenon. There are no modern theologians who study it seriously as
theology. This is unfortunate. Two of the main characteristics of the
modern world to which modern theology has tried to speak are reason
and science. Modern theology's hope was to make religion acceptable
both to the modern mind and to the scientific sensibility. But now
both reason and science, which arrived in the modern world as its
darlings, have fallen from their previous positions of esteem. Theories
of the unconscious, such as those of Freud and Jung, have raised
questions about the omnipotence of reason. The growing distrust of
technology has eaten away at unquestioning trust in science.

A postmodern theology will need a new attitude toward both reason and science. Can fundamentalism help provide it? It has continued to question modern views of science and reason since its earliest
days. But whether it has much that is useful to say today is a question
that is difficult to answer because of modern theology's nearly total
rejection of fundamentalist theology as a subject worthy of serious
attention.

At first this rejection is easy to understand. Why should anyone be concerned about anything so obsolete as fundamentalist theology, for that is just how it is perceived by the vast majority of modern theologians. On the other hand, one might also ask why religious scholars will spend a lifetime studying Islam, in which the prescribed attitude toward the Koran is quite similar to the fundamentalist view of the Bible; or Hinduism, whose teachings on women, family, and sexuality are just as much at variance with contemporary American practices as fundamentalism is. Yet scholars certainly study them.

The reason why students of religion in mainline institutions have managed to ignore the reality of fundamentalism, a faith that has attracted fifty million people, may be a subtle one. It is well known in universities that rookie anthropologists often fall in love with "their" tribe. Those who investigate religious phenomena also tend to grow fond of their subjects, even to become defensive about them. This weakness is quietly tolerated if not exactly approved in academia, but it works against the sympathetic study of fundamentalists who, unlike Amazonian Indians or Tibetan Buddhists, have a history of conflict with liberal academicians. Here, fondness for the tribe might look like fraternizing with the enemy.

When theologians do pay attention to fundamentalism, they often misunderstand it. They tend to examine it as a somewhat bizarre variant of Protestantism. Most fail to recognize it not only as a theology but also as the faith of an identifiable subculture and as an ideology. The rudiments of a postmodern theology will emerge from Christian subcultures that have been in touch with the dominant liberal theological consensus of the modern world but have not been absorbed by it. The American fundamentalist movement qualifies as such a subculture. But will it be such a resource?

To try to answer this question, we must first dislodge a questionable reading of fundamentalism that often appears when students of religion acknowledge it at all. This reading has to do with fundamentalism's perspective on the proper role of science and the place of rational philosophical discourse in the world. It comes as something of a shock to scholars who begin to examine fundamentalism, believing it to be the religion of educationally retarded and semiliterate people, to find that, rather than despising science and reasonable discourse, fundamentalists tend to place considerable confidence in both. Professor Benjamin B. Warfield of Princeton Theological Seminary, one of the patron saints of fundamentalism, wrote in 1903:

It is the distinction of Christianity that it has come into the world clothed with the mission to *reason* its way to its dominion. Other religions may appeal to the sword, or seek some other way to propagate themselves. Christianity makes its appeal to right reason, and stands out among all religions, therefore, as distinctively "the Apologetic religion." It is solely by reasoning that it has come thus far on its way to its kingship. And it is solely by reasoning that it will put all its enemies under its feet.[1]

This sober fundamentalist respect for reason often surprises contemporary students of religion involved in the recent wave of mystical, psychological, and existential spirituality in which modern science and rationality are almost ignored. Theologians who do find this characteristic are likely to attribute it to fundamentalism's having been unduly influenced, as many "anti" movements are, by its opponent. It is claimed that fundamentalism has been marked by its life-long combat with "modernism." The scientism and rationalism of fundamentalist theology are seen as something that has rubbed off onto it.

Viewing fundamentalism as a subculture (as well as a theology) yields a more satisfactory explanation. However, like the religious and cultural artifacts of any marginated and dominated group, those of fundamentalism are also expressed in forms that should not be taken merely at face value; they are also ciphers or symbols that point toward larger issues. To uncover the real significance of fundamentalism's complex view of science we will have to dig a little deeper.

Liberty Baptist College, the fast-growing institution founded by Jerry Falwell in 1971, together with the Liberty Baptist Seminary, provide the intellectual core of the whole Lynchburg complex. The faculty is largely young and vigorous. The buildings and laboratory are brand-new. There is an upbeat frontier quality. The professors talk excitedly about the day Liberty Baptist will become a full-fledged university. There must have been a similar atmosphere among the eager young preacher-educators who founded a college along the banks of the Charles River in 1636.

Liberty Baptist College is an excellent place to reflect on the significance of the fundamentalist fascination with science and rational discourse. One finds both of them here, though there is a qualification. In rational discourse, for example, it is true that at the more popular level, say of tract distribution or radio preaching, fundamentalists tend to make their case by relying heavily on Bible quotation. At Liberty Baptist, however, the bright professors prefer to defend their position (to do what theologians call "apologetics") by relying on rational argument. The catalog of the seminary indicates this respect for the capacity of the human mind and the power of logical persuasion. Few liberal seminaries list courses in Apologetics, but Liberty Baptist Seminary offers three:

> APOL 500 INTRODUCTION TO APOLOGETICS
> Three Hours
>   This introductory course deals with the biblical basis for apologetics, methodology, and the relationship between faith and reason before turning to scientific and historical evidences. The relationship with theology and evangelism is also explored.

> APOL 505 HISTORY OF APOLOGETIC METHODOLOGY Three hours
>   A study of major apologists from New Testament times to the present, concentrating on the reasoning methodology used by each, including the formulation of a valid apologetic technique.

> APOL 560 COMPARATIVE RELIGIOUS APOLOGETICS Three Hours
>   A contrast between the truth-claims of the major world religions and the uniqueness of Christian theistic apologetics both in content and method.

Dr. David Beck, the professor of philosophy and apologetics at Liberty Baptist Seminary, who holds a doctorate from Boston University, is a staunch defender of reason. He rejects what he calls the "modern" notion that basic world views are ultimately intuitive and cannot be criticized or defended cognitively. Whether he is right or not, it is significant that he does not merely appeal to the authority of an inerrant Bible (which he does believe in) to make his case. Rather, he displays a confidence in the power of reasonable discourse to help settle basic philosophical issues. Professor Beck's style and his assumptions about what philosophy is and what it can do are reminiscent of the premodern and early modern philosophers. One could dismiss his position as obsolete, but it can be seen as keeping alive a once highly respected philosophical tradition which, given the decline and disarray of contemporary philosophy, may once again emerge (in a postmodern philosophical atmosphere?) as a viable possibility. In fact this may already have begun.

According to the contemporary French philosopher Jean-François Lyotard in his book *La Condition Postmoderne*, the main agenda of a postmodern philosophy will be the question of how—given the vast variety of "language games" and contradictory world views that emerged and gained acceptance during the modern period—one can begin again to ask meaningfully about what is really true and good.[2] It would be ironic if, when discourse about such subjects as God and truth and morality are once again common, conservative Christian philosophers found themselves back in the dialogue because they never gave up on it in the first place. Philosophical traditions like religious traditions cannot survive in books alone. There must be groups of human beings who perpetuate them. Roman Catholic theologians have done this in some measure, but so have those conservative Christian philosophers who swam against the modern current and now find that the tide may be turning.

There are differences between fundamentalist and liberal theological attitudes toward science. This is another area in which the failure to understand fundamentalism as a continuing subculture has led many observers astray. A reputation for closed-minded antiscientism among fundamentalists is partly a result of the Scopes trial. The ironic truth is that fundamentalist theologians are very much interested in the relationship between religion and science, while most liberals are not. Current liberal theological quarterlies carry virtually no articles on the subject, restricting themselves to the ethical issues raised by science-based technology. Consequently, liberals are surprised when "scientific creationists" appear demanding equal time in schools, or when a book dealing with science and spirituality such as Fritjof Capra's *The Tao of Physics* attracts a wide readership, or when college students and seminarians still raise questions about religion and science.

The debate between science and religion is not dead; it has assumed a different form. The Penn State physicist and lay theologian Rustum Roy argues in his *Experimenting with Truth* that it is one of the most disastrously neglected areas in contemporary theology. Rejecting both the idea that science and religion must clash inevitably and the liberal notion that they deal with separate orders of truth, Roy's discussion focuses instead on how they can complement each other as ways of knowing a single order of reality.[3]

Those who advocate the teaching of creation on an equal basis with evolution in the schools do not do so because they believe the Bible teaches creation. They do so because they believe creation can be established scientifically—"scientific creationism." However improbable it may seem, the creationist argument is an appeal to "true science." The conviction supporting their position is that science, rightly understood, supports and confirms religious belief—or at least *this* religious belief. This is not an antiscientific attitude. It expresses an idea of the relationship between religion and science which, though Isaac Newton held it, is no longer in fashion.

At Liberty Baptist College there is this same "premodern" vision of the relation between science and faith. It began when Dr. Gary Habermas, one of the faculty members at Liberty Baptist Seminary, presented me with a copy of a book he had written with a nuclear physicist about the famous "Shroud of Turin." The shroud is a gravecloth that turned up many centuries ago and carries the dark imprint of a human figure supposedly bearing the wounds the Gospels describe in their accounts of the crucifixion of Christ.[4] Some people believe it is the actual burial shroud of Jesus, and that the image was burned into the cloth by the explosion of energy and light that occurred at Christ's resurrection. Others think it is another pious forgery, like the two heads of St. Peter allegedly displayed in different churches in Rome. During the past decade teams of scientists have examined the shroud using recently developed methods for determining its age and the nature of the imprint. The book avoids making the blatant assertion that the shroud is the actual cloth in which Jesus was buried, but assigns this possibility a high level of statistical probability.

When I asked the coauthor what theological significance it would have if the cloth were proven to be the "true shroud," he told me it would constitute further proof of the resurrection of Jesus ("further," that is, in addition to both biblical and extrabibilical accounts).

This fundamentalist idea of science is the expression of a subculture that has refused to accept the modern division of labor by which theology was to deal with the inner life of faith and science with everything else. Oddly, "redneck religion" is closer to some of the outer edges of "new age" religious and scientific thought than most modern theology. The Shroud of Turin fascinates the same people who read books like Capra's and look for religious elements in new biology. All these movements taken together represent a protest—often confused and overcredulous—against the airtight compartmentalization of science and religion, something both the premodern and the postmodern mind refuse to accept.

Gary Habermas is a theologian who insists, against the consensus of modern thought, that laboratory science and empirical observation can play a role in illuminating religious truth. The Shroud of Turin is not one of the genre of miraculous phenomena that require faith as a precondition for appreciating them. Instead, it is a piece of cloth imprinted with an image any person can see. It has testable characteristics even the most empirical scientists cannot deny. Indeed, those who regard the shroud as evidence for the resurrection of Christ invariably emphasize how many skeptics and religious agnostics have worked on the investigation of it.

Granted, the shroud case may not be the best one for demonstrating a different relationship of science and religion. It requires considerable "decoding." Still this fundamentalist assumption about true science is similar to the one which informs the fundamentalist belief that "true reason" is also dependable, so that one can productively discuss even the most basic world views with a reasonable interlocutor. Both positions hark back to an era before theology and science were divorced and before the methodological skepticism of philosophy was itself elevated into a world view.

Fundamentalists could never accept Kierkegaard's idea of the "leap of faith." They hold that faith is a perfectly reasonable step, not a leap. Nor could they accept the late-medieval idea that "I believe because it is absurd" (creo quia absurdum est). For a fundamentalist, faith is decidedly not absurd. From a "sophisticated" fundamentalist perspective, the liberals who defended Scopes at the "monkey trial" against those who accused him of teaching evolution in violation of Tennessee law were mistaken in appealing to a division-of-labor argument. The liberals granted that the Genesis account of Creation might be "religiously valid" but insisted it was not science. For ordinary fundamentalists these liberals were wrong to "deny the Bible" and that was that, while scholarly fundamentalists would add that the critics of the Scopes verdict were mistaken at a more basic philosophical level in accepting such a dichotomy between science and faith.

Fundamentalists are misunderstood so often by their academic critics because the critics fail to see that fundamentalism is an enclave, a little world that has been preserved by a range of alternative schools, churches, colleges in which many of the assumptions of the premodern world still obtain. In the subculture of fundamentalism people talk and think differently. Like any subculture, fundamentalism challenges the dominant culture not so much in its explicit ideas but in its unspoken premises. Theologians at Harvard probably would not wish to argue one way or another about the Shroud of Turin and whether the empirical evidence points to its authenticity. Their assumption, shared with nearly all modern theologians, is that such evidence is irrelevant to the truth of the Resurrection. But if intellectual discourse thrives on the raising of troubling questions, it is precisely this assumption and not the argument itself that is important. And questions about really basic assumptions, the ones that are not generally raised because they seem so obvious they do not require debate, can be raised only by people who do not share the same subculture and therefore do not share the unspoken assumptions either. It is fundamentalism's relative isolation from mainstream theology that enables it to pose questions (albeit in ways that sometimes seem exasperating and even eccentric) no one within the mainstream would think of voicing.

Fundamentalism's fascination with science and reason suggests that at the theological level the most interesting challenge fundamentalism offers to modern theology is how we are to understand the *nature of faith*. Fundamentalists reject out of hand the modern theological notion that "there are no revealed ideas," and that faith is a personal encounter with God which carries with it no necessary cognitive content and needs no historical mediator. This modern view of faith reached its zenith in the works of Emil Brunner and Karl Barth, and became an acceptable Catholic position when Hans Kung wrote that he saw no important difference between Barth's doctrine of justification and what he himself believed the Catholic Church taught. Faith is seen as a relationship of trust and fidelity. It is a view that fits neatly into the characteristically modern concentration on the individual as the center of the reflection. It has the added advantage of securing the possibility of religious belief no matter what happens to the philosophical or political makeup of the world.

Fundamentalists (joined in this respect by many evangelicals) reject this view. As they do so, however, they find themselves—as we shall see later—keeping company with liberation theologians, though the two repudiate the modern view of faith for different reasons and in different ways. The fundamentalists insist that faith is not just a personal relationship (though it is that too): it also has a doctrinal content. God not only reveals Himself. He also reveals certain truths about Himself. Faith is substance as well as form.

Liberation theologians also insist that God's revelation has a content. The content is what Jon Sobrino calls "the faith of Jesus." It is this faith of Jesus which led him to identify himself with outcasts and to accept the painful criminal's death that choice entailed. This demand to "accompany the poor" is, for the liberationist, not something derived from the revelation. It is part and parcel of it. God is revealed as the *dios pobre,* and this is a content that is inseparable from the revelation of God itself. In a later section I will return to the liberationist critique of the modern view of faith. Here I want to explore the intriguing possibility that in clinging to their "premodern" position, fundamentalists may inadvertently supply us with a clue to the formulation of a "postmodern" definition of faith.

I began my inquiry about fundamentalism hoping that because it stubbornly retains its old-fashioned insistence on "premodern" modes of philosophical and scientific discourse, and even creates a subculture in which this discourse goes on, it could supply us with hints about the emerging "postmodern" view of the proper roles of philosophy and science. I eventually came to believe that it will not. But before moving on to explain why it will not, it is important to note that the view of faith shared in different ways by fundamentalists, evangelicals, liberationists and others on the outer edge of the modern consensus may also become a much more prevalent view in the postmodern world.

Fundamentalists are right to insist that faith must have a content, that the modern severance of faith from reason is abnormal. But they are wrong about what the content should be since they are not sufficiently aware of the historically conditioned character of their own movement. A postmodern faith will agree with the fundamentalists that ultimately people will not be satisfied with the separation of will and intellect, thought and feeling, affect and cognition which has informed the modern liberal understanding. The questions of what the content should be is a primary agenda item for a postmodern theology.

This point is discussed with considerable cogency by a brilliant French student of comparative religion named Fritjof Schuon. Schuon is no fundamentalist. He has acquired a reputation for sympathetic appreciation of Islam and of Asian religions that no fundamentalist ever could. He argues for a definition of faith that runs counter to the current modern view. "It has often and justly been said," Schuon writes on the first page of his *Stations of Wisdom,* "that the ills of our times come from the cleavage between faith and science." Schuon agrees with this diagnosis, but goes on to say that "the beginnings of this cleavage are to be found within faith itself . . . in the sense that faith has not been, or is not, adequately buttressed by . . . the sapiential order, or that in the minds of most people sentimental rather than metaphysical grounds have been dominant."[5] He believes that this neglect of the intellectual ("sapiential") element in faith meant that eventually the intellect, reduced to a kind of arid rationality, would turn against faith. That is exactly what has occurred.

What Schuon is advocating is not that faith be either buttressed or criticized by rationalism, but that intelligence should once more become "contemplative intelligence." Intellect needs to be reunited to faith so that human beings can understand both the truth of revealed traditions and the discoveries of science. For Schuon, the modern mind has reached an impasse that makes it dangerously incapable of dealing with its own world. It can be restored to its proper capacity only by understanding itself in the light of one of the great religious traditions, in which one can grasp "the immutability of the principles which govern the Universe and fashion our intelligence."

Schuon says that "the sacred Scriptures, far from being popular tales, are on the contrary highly 'scientific' works through their polyvalent symbolism which contains a science at once cosmological, metaphysical and mystical."

Fritjof Schuon's reasoning is a kind of "apologetics," which is similar in its strategy to conservative Christian thought. Instead of seeking to reinterpret religious ideas within the context of modern categories, Schuon wants to change the modern categories to make them more open to religious thought, beginning with the modern definition of "intelligence."

Fundamentalists and other conservative Christians might accept some parts of Schuon's argument. But he also brings into relief one of fundamentalism's most crippling "premodern" qualities, one that will surely prevent it from making any significant contribution to a postmodern theology. This is fundamentalism's inability to cope with religious pluralism, its insistence that it is not "sacred Scriptures" but one particular Scripture, not religious traditions but one tradition alone, that merits fidelity.

But Schuon fails to ask what caused the change in our understanding of faith from which such dire consequences have come. And like some other contemporary religious thinkers who draw on more than one religious tradition, Schuon fails to deal persuasively with the contradictory claims of truth that these different traditions advance.

Still, I predict that in a postmodern world in which science, philosophy, and theology have once again begun to communicate with each other, and in which politics and religion no longer inhabit different compartments of the human enterprise, the present unnatural separation between faith and intellect will also be transcended.

These "theological" questions also have a social dimension. None of this can happen until human communities arise in which the irrational dichotomies of modernity are overcome, something—as we shall see—that is already going on in the basic Christian communities movement in Latin America and elsewhere. We must now look at the political significance of the "coming out" of American fundamentalism. As we do so we will ask whether the evidence suggests that, given their present political posture, fundamentalists are likely to make a positive contribution toward fashioning the kind of world their religious vision implies.

4. Populist Piety:
Fundamentalism as Ideology

> If true Christianity consists in carrying out in our daily lives the teachings of Christ, who will say that we are commanded to civilize with dynamite and proselyte with the sword? Imperialism finds no warrant in the Bible. . . . Love, not force, was the weapon of the Nazarene; sacrificing for others, not the exploitation of them, was His method of reaching the human heart.
>
> —William Jennings Bryan
> *Memoirs*, 1925

American fundamentalism is a movement that began among urban intellectuals and was most keenly articulated by a Princeton scholar, Professor J. Gresham Machen. Why then did it come to find its home among rural white poor people and urban lower middle classes? The usual answer is that fundamentalism is the religion of the uneducated, that accepting it was largely a matter of cultural deficiency. I do not agree with this thesis.

Fundamentalism is not only a theology and a subculture, it is also an ideology. It interprets and defends the perceived life interests of an identifiable social group. Falwell and Hindson (using the familiar ploy by which blacks and gays and others have appropriated terms originally used as epithets against them) are largely correct to call fundamentalism "redneck religion." This also means that fundamentalism, like liberation theology, the religion of Native Americans, and some other theologies, is an *antimodern* ideology. For the small-town and rural poor who appropriated it, fundamentalism expressed their opposition to the powerful modern, liberal-capitalist world that was disrupting their traditional way of life.

An ideology is a cluster of ideas and values that provides a class or a nation or some human group with a picture of the world that can guide and inspire corporate action. As an ideology, fundamentalism contains an implicit image of what society should be like. Fundamentalists not only insist on preserving the fundamentals of the faith, they also envision a world in which these fundamentals would be more widely accepted and practiced. They want not only to "keep the faith" but to change the world so the faith can be kept more easily.

This requires a world in which science and philosophy would play roles quite different from those they have today. When fundamentalist scholars reject the modern idea that philosophy has little to say about worldviews, they are not just advocating a style of philosophy closer to the grand tradition of Plato, Aquinas, and Spinoza. They are also proposing a society in which philosophy would hold a more central role. When fundamentalists bring infrared photographs of the Shroud of Turin into play, they express a confused yearning for a culture in which scientists and theologians would work together in a common intellectual enterprise.

This vision of a common culture is held by nearly all the conservative and traditionalist critics of modernity. On the vital issue of how to achieve such a culture, however, fundamentalism differs from both theologically conservative evangelicalism and religious liberalism. Both of these accept in varying measure the modern reduction of the role of religion and theology. Although evangelicals differ sharply from liberals on what the content of the faith is, they tend to accept the modern world as the arena in which the theological task is to be done. The argument between liberals and evangelicals is about the message, not about the world. Fundamentalists on the other hand—as becomes paradoxically evident in their protestations about "separation from the world"—are more uncomfortable with the modern *logos* and more critical of it. Their idea of apologetics is not to translate the gospel into the mental categories of modernity but to change the modern mental categories so the gospel can be grasped. They are culture critics and political theologians despite themselves.

Its opposition to modernity places fundamentalist theologians closer to liberation theologians than either would like to admit. Both refuse to accept the modern world or the "modern mind." Both speak from the context of social groups that have not benefited from the modern liberal ethos but have felt it a threat to their well-being. Both believe that the most pressing task of Christianity today is not the refinement and redefinition of doctrine, not translating the message into the world's terms, but bringing the world more into conformity with the message.

The fact that fundamentalist and liberation theologians often come out on opposite ends of the political spectrum should not obscure this striking structural similarity between them. Karl Marx once said that up until his time philosophers had merely interpreted the world but what was needed was to change it. One might say that liberal and evangelical theologians have tried to make the Christian message credible to the modern world. Fundamentalists and liberation theologians are not interested in interpreting. They do not want to speak to and be heard by the world so much as they want to change it. Can the form of traditional religion represented by fundamentalism make a contribution to a postmodern Christianity? Its recent history raises some doubts.

There is something rather logical about American fundamentalism's habit of swinging back and forth between withdrawal into a subculture and highly confrontational efforts to remake the whole of society. It stems from the belief that the whole world, not just some religious segment, should reflect its sacred source. This is a view of society Paul Tillich once described as "theonomous" (as opposed to a "heteronomous" one in which religious values would have to be imposed). When one holds this view it is impossible to settle for the marginal role to which religion has been relegated in the modern world. One either tries to change the whole society to bring it into conformity (thus risking heteronomy) or one retreats to a smaller, more manageable subculture where a kind of minitheonomy is possible.

Harold Berman of the Harvard Law School has written:

It is supposed by some, especially intellectuals, that fundamental legal principles . . . can survive without any religious or quasireligious foundations on the basis of the proper political and economic controls and the philosophy of humanism. History, however, including current history, testifies otherwise. People will not give their allegiance to a political and economic system, and even less to a philosophy, unless it represents for them a higher, sacred truth.[1]

Fundamentalists in their own way support this theory of the relationship between religion and civil society. But will American fundamentalists be able to help shape such a society in the future? There are three reasons why this seems unlikely.

First, American fundamentalism is at once theology, subculture, and ideology, but not all components have equal weight. "When I was a boy in Virginia," says Jerry Falwell, "in a redneck society, patriotism was just a part of life." To his credit, Falwell concedes that racism was also a part of that life, but he believes he has overcome it. Thomas Road now has black members, and Falwell is proud that he has been attacked by the Ku Klux Klan as "an enemy of the white race."

But how many other values Thomas Road and similar fundamentalist churches stand for are derived from Christianity and how many from "redneck society"? Christians everywhere have to ask this question about their own cultures all the time. It springs from a recognition that although culture must be the bearer of religion, biblical religion also judges and purifies cultural values. Are fundamentalists ready to test the Christian bases of their nearly uncritical support of American foreign policy and the capitalist economic system? Are they willing to test these positions through careful study of the Bible and discussions with people who share the same faith but have a different culture?

There is evidence that some fundamentalists are ready to enter such a dialogue, and to alter their positions on some social issues (not theological ones) if they are persuaded. But many are not ready for such conversations. They have lived in the fundamentalist ghetto too long to want to emerge and converse.

The redneck ideology element in fundamentalism makes the mixture of culture and theology more volatile. The poor rural workers of America have not always been as well disposed toward big businesses and corporate capitalism as the leaders of American religious funda-

mentalism now seem to be. Jerry Falwell's friendly reference to the
Wall Street Journal in his sermon would not have pleased the "great
fundamentalist" William Jennings Bryan, who stood in the courthouse in Dayton, Tennessee, long before Jerry Falwell did, but who
also moved people to tears with his populist attacks on those who
would crucify the working people of America on a "cross of gold."
Some of his fellow fundamentalists have accused Falwell of betraying
the cause, of becoming a "compromiser." Bryan not only defended
the Bible from what he considered modernist attacks on it, he also
stood up for the disprivileged rural and ordinary small-town people of
America, the "moral majority" of his day, against the power of Wall
Street and corporate wealth. He even resigned as Secretary of State
when he could not in good conscience execute what his Christian
conscience told him was a warlike and belligerent foreign policy.

Although Jerry Falwell claims the mantle of William Jennings
Bryan (what else can the trip to Dayton and the courthouse picture
have meant?), in many respects he has discarded Bryan's populist
politics and become a supporter of the very people Bryan spent a
lifetime combating. In American political fundamentalism we can
trace the tension between the genuinely populist "poor redneck"
tradition and the upwardly mobile pro-big business element. Which
will eventually win?

If Bible study teachers in fundamentalist churches continue to
ponder the confrontation between Jesus and the "critics" he met in
his day, like the Sadducees and the Herodians, they are bound to
discover that these were not only "schools of thought" but political
movements. The difficulty Jesus ran into with the Sadducees was not
principally over doctrinal points. Rather it arose from the clash between the property-owning, politically dominant classes the Sadducees represented and the landless rural poor and urban rabble who
formed the majority of Jesus' movement.[2] If the "politics of Jesus"
rather than some unlikely combination of Eastern Establishment and
down-home booster politics ever begins to predominate, as it already
has on some occasions, then fundamentalism would make quite a
different impact on the national political scene.

Liberation theologians have generally not paid much attention to
fundamentalism. If they did, however, they would notice that the
"redneck" element represents an ambiguous but not entirely negative

dimension. Redneck politics in America has always been unpredict-able, given to alternating spasms of red-clay rebelliousness and easy accommodation to demagoguery. But it has rarely toadied to the modern equivalents of the Sadducees and Herodians for very long. How much influence it will have in the current coming out of polit-ical fundamentalism, and what that influence will be, remains to be seen.

My second reason for doubting whether fundamentalism can suc-ceed in making a contribution to a postmodern theology has to do with what might be called its "political apocalyptic" belief that the end of the age is near. This Christ-is-coming-soon eschatology not only discourages any kind of work for constructive change, it can also produce a kind of overheated fatalism: if the big bang is going to come, then let it happen soon.

In Lynchburg, however, though they talk about the Lord's immi-nent return, they are planning for the long haul. Liberty Baptist College will become a university. Nearby, on Liberty Mountain, a retirement village will be built. Falwell's scheme for reuniting the scattered fundamentalist tribes will require years of patient orchestra-tion. No one seems to expect it to be all over soon.

Out in the byways, however, it is different. When the novelist A. G. Mojtabai went to Amarillo, Texas, to see how the town was responding to Bishop Leroy Matthiesen's plea to his people to con-sider not working for Pantex, a local plant where nuclear weapons are assembled, she found that the major religious opposition to the bishop came from the Reverend Mr. J. Alan Ford. Ford is minister of the Southwest Baptist Church (which claims to be "Amarillo's fastest growing church," with two thousand members) and the local leader of Moral Majority. Ford believes the biblical books of Daniel, Ezekiel, and Revelation tell us what will happen in the near future: ". . . a Russian invasion of Iran. Russia will press its advantage in the Middle East . . . Russia will go to war with Israel." It is all there in Revela-tion and in Ezekiel. We live in the last days.

Another minister in Amarillo, the Reverend Mr. Royce Elms, leader of a local Pentecostal church, invited a visitor to examine Second Peter 3:10, which says "the elements shall melt with fervent heat," and verse 12, "Wherein the heavens being on fire shall be dissolved." Elms comforts his people by assuring them that although this catastrophe is imminent, there is also the Rapture. Real Christians will be caught up into the air to meet the descending Lord. It will all be instantaneous. "All through this, God is speaking through his word, telling us not to worry. If the Amarillo bomb dropped today, it wouldn't bother me one bit."[3]

In the regions and subcultures most influenced by fundamentalism, this sense that we are in the last days, coupled with a kind of vertiginous fascination with the prospect, is widespread even among people who do not attend church. When I responded to the friendly query of a young couple I met in a restaurant in North Carolina about what I was doing "so far from home," and told them I was speaking at a local church in favor of the nuclear arms freeze, they smiled. I was wasting my time, they assured me. They never went to church themselves, they said, but they knew the world was going to end soon by an atomic war, because "that's what the Bible says." They then went back to sipping their beer and watching television.

After her trip to Amarillo, Mojtabai described it this way:

The impression is unavoidable: some of the most ardent born and born-again Christians are writing Christianity off as something that didn't, couldn't work—at least, not in the First Coming. The conviction that mankind is bent on its own destruction, that goodness cannot succeed in a world so evil, the constant recourse to the Old Testament, and to the most bellicose sections, the turning for betterment to the dire remedies offered by the book of Revelation, the only light left to the Second Coming—all this strangely negates the "good news" of the Gospels and the First Coming.[4]

This ominous fatalism is not only a far cry from that of the Bible and what most Christians have believed over the centuries. It is also a very different message from the one conveyed in the jovial, smiling atmosphere of Lynchburg. The trouble is that spreading the bad news of imminent nuclear war can become a self-fulfilling prophecy. When fundamentalism ceases to proclaim the central kernel of the biblical message—that God calls human beings to repent, to change their evil ways, and that God's grace makes such repentance possible— then fundamentalism forgoes any claim to being a Christian or biblical theology. It has opted for a low-grade kismet, an it's-all-in-the-cards fatalism that produces a cynical sense of powerlessness. It has become a religious pathology.

Which of these two faces of the fundamentalist tradition will eventually predominate—the one that calls the nation back to righteousness or the one that closes the cyclone door and awaits the cataclysm? On the answer to this question hangs the future of fundamentalism's capacity to speak a healing word and to influence the shape of the future. If its fatalistic side predominates, then fundamentalism may become one more factor in depriving us of any future at all.

My third reason for doubting fundamentalism's influence on postmodern Christianity is its recent romance with the electronic media. Fundamentalism is a highly traditional religious expression. Television is a tradition-smashing phenomenon. Yet rarely has any religious movement embraced an artifact of modernity as enthusiastically and as uncritically. The top regular religious television shows (Rex Humbard, Pat Robertson, Jerry Falwell, Oral Roberts) are all more or less fundamentalist in orientation. Colleges and seminaries associated with the fundamentalist movement have some of the finest television equipment available to students anywhere. It is generally acknowledged that fundamentalist television is produced with a high level of technical competence. And this is only the beginning. Writing in the evangelical periodical *Christianity Today*, Tom Bisset, general manager of the Baltimore station WRBS-FM, says:

The Christian world is about to be future-shocked by an invasion of space-age multiple delivery systems. . . . Much of the technological hardware is already in place. Cable and pay television have widened the public's viewing options. Two-way cable systems, where both parties can see and talk to each other, have been tested successfully. A nationwide Christian media counseling service beckons. Videocassette recorders and video-discs will soon make it possible for a local Christian bookstore to offer concerts, revival meetings, or teaching sessions—video and audio—for the price of a record. Low-power television, soon to be in use, and UHF/VHF translators, already in use, augment broadcasting's ever widening delivery system. . . .

But even the wildest dreams would find it hard to anticipate what is coming in satellite and computer technology. Picture, if you will, a worldwide Christian satellite system pumping out 24 separate television signals and 24 separate FM signals to earth. That makes 48 new listening and viewing options available to anyone who is plugged into the right wire or who owns the necessary equipment. . . .

Every conceivable audio and visual need will be covered. Every taste in music, every unique ministry, every interpretive whim and wish—all can and will find their way to these highly specialized channels.[5]

Bisset fears a "gospel glut." What happens when a profoundly antimodernist attempt to reassert the primacy of traditional values utilizes a cultural form that is itself thoroughly modern and antitraditional? This is the tension between content and form, between message and medium, that occurs when the Old Time Gospel Hour goes out on network television.

The German Jewish writer Walter Benjamin took up this issue in an influential essay first published in 1936,"The Work of Art in the Age of Mechanical Reproduction." Benjamin was writing about art, but his observation, as he himself says, is equally applicable to religion. He argued that the mechanical reproduction of any work of art profoundly alters its meaning, makes it different in ways its reproducers can never anticipate. It was Benjamin's conviction that "the technique of reproduction detaches the reproduced object from the domain of tradition." This leads ultimately to "the liquidation of the traditional value of the cultural heritage," what Benjamin called the "decay of the aura."[6]

When one applies this analysis to religious phenomena, the change in meaning is particularly radical. For Benjamin, an essential feature of any work of art is the sense of distance and awe it elicits, a power he believed is also derived from the religious and spiritual purpose art originally served. It is this distance which gives it authority. Reproduction, in severing the object from its intended spiritual "location" and depriving it of its aura, at the same time robs it of its authority by making it too close, too available.

Jerry Falwell and other religious traditionalists who have embraced network color television, the ultimate form of modern mechanical reproduction, may have struck a mortal blow to exactly what they are trying to defend, the "old time Gospel" and traditional religion. The move from the revivalist's tent to the vacuum tube has vastly amplified the voices of defenders of tradition. At the same time it has made them more dependent on the styles and assumptions inherent in the medium itself. This explains the none too subtle shift one feels at Thomas Road Baptist Church when the adult Bible study ends, the big lights go on, and the entire congregation suddenly becomes the cast of a nationwide network show. It is hard, despite Jerry Falwell's consummate skill at bridging the gap, not to feel that one has been pushed further into the modern world and moved a notch away from the "old time" antimodernist intent of the message.

Religious television moves toward entertainment. Jerry Falwell still appears behind the pulpit, but Pat Robertson uses a setting copied from late-night talk shows. A succession of splendidly dressed guests tell the audience how the Lord has brought them success, health, money, power. The Gospel is reduced to a means of achieving the same modern secular goals the evangelist began by opposing.

The German social critic Jurgen Habermas sees a battle shaping up between what he calls "communicative life-worlds" and the more formally organized systems based on power and money steered by the media.[7] This is exactly the contradiction television-based political fundamentalism finds itself in today. In the contest between the System and traditional morality, Jerry Falwell and his followers fervently believe they are on the side of the angels. They believe they are defending the old-time moral values against the invasion of modernity. But the technical and organizational means they have chosen to fight the battle may be destroying precisely the religious resources most needed to save traditional morality.

Television, mass computer mailings, the latest marketing techniques are not neutral tools. Embedded in them are a set of attitudes and values that are inimical to traditional morality. They extend massification. As Habermas says, capitalist modernization transfers more and more "social material" from the "life-worlds" into realms of action controlled by large outside systems. This process previously left religion, education, the family alone, and concentrated instead on more overtly economic sectors like banks and factories. Now, "the system's imperatives," says Habermas, "are attacking areas of action which are demonstrably unable to perform their own tasks if

they are removed from communicatively structured areas of action."[8]
Network television and computer mailings are not "communicatively
structured areas of action." They are powerful anticommunicative
forces, engaged in shoving more and more of those human activities
which used to go on in small "life-worlds" into the insatiable maw of
the modern system.

The contradiction between traditional religion and the mass media
seems unavoidable. The deepest contradiction lies in the question of
the nature of a genuine religious community. One real strength of
the newly emerging Christian base communities in Latin America
and elsewhere is that they foster the face-to-face groupings human
beings need so badly. The television evangelists do not. Despite their
efforts to include viewers through letters, telephone calls, and a
folksy style on camera, something essential is missing in a television
congregation. By buying into the mass-media world so heavily fundamentalism may have unintentionally sold out to one of the most
characteristic features of the very modern world it wants so much to
challenge. If the devil is a modernist, the TV evangelists may have
struck a deal with Lucifer himself, who always appears—so the Bible
teaches—as an angel of light.

Just before I left Lynchburg I stopped in to visit the national
headquarters of the Old Time Gospel Hour, in a converted ware-
house next to a supermarket. Inside, rows of volunteers take incom-
ing calls on banks of telephones. The atmosphere is brisk, friendly,
efficient. Earlier in the day I was there Falwell had appeared on
network television talking about President Reagan's decision to seek
an amendment to the United States Constitution that would permit
voluntary prayers to be said in the classrooms of public schools. He
interviewed Senator Jesse Helms of North Carolina, a supporter of
the amendment, and offered a "Kids Need to Pray" bumper sticker.
He also asked viewers to call in their opinion on the subject to his
toll-free number. The volunteers were receiving continuous calls,
nearly all of them supporting the amendment. By calling and giving
their names and addresses, of course, they were also supplying the
Old Time Gospel Hour with thousands of prospective new donors.
But some volunteers were also engaged in a kind of hi-tech counsel-
ing. Typists sat at word processors sending out a stream of prewritten

letters to troubled and questioning viewers all over the country. The age of mechanical reproduction, I thought, has come not just to art but to prayer and the cure of souls as well.

In its nearly a century of life American fundamentalism has weathered many attacks. It has been a scandal to liberal intellectuals and a stumbling block to skeptics. But it has always been irascible, full of a certain feisty vitality. Beaten back into its corner on many occasions it has always emerged again, picking up stones to sling at the Goliath of modernism. But will the subtle whirr of computers and Nielsen ratings succeed where contempt, condescension, and even persecution have failed? Fundamentalists and other conservative Christians have something important to say to a world that has grown rightly sick of modernity. But there are very few people who want to live in a society in which the values of a particular subculture are unloaded onto all of us in the name of Jesus.

Fundamentalists have had a record of turning defeats into victories, and vice versa. When William Scopes was convicted for teaching evolution, it was a victory for fundamentalism. It quickly became evident, however, that because of the immense publicity the case received, it had not been a victory at all, but a defeat. After the trial fundamentalists retreated again. Now with television and computer mailings available they smell a new victory, much bigger than the one they achieved at Dayton, Tennessee. But for some of the same reasons this victory could turn into another defeat, perhaps this time for good.

5. Fundamentalism and Postmodern Theology

> In view of the lamentable defects of modern life, a type of religion certainly should not be commended simply because it is modern, or condemned simply because it is old. On the contrary, the condition of mankind is such that one may well ask what it is that made the men of past generations so great and the men of the present generation so small.
> —J. Gresham Machen
> *Christianity and Liberalism*, 1923[1]

We have examined the current renaissance of fundamentalism in the hope that—given the dead-end modern theology has now reached—such a strongly antimodernist religious movement might offer some clues and resources for a postmodern theology. We have concluded that it probably will not. Why, then, in a search for a postmodern theology, would anyone pay any attention to a religious movement that seems so past-oriented and bereft of any ideas for a future theology?

The theologies and religious movements out of which we can hope for a postmodern vision share the characteristics of being both highly critical of the modern world and its theology and also strenuously engaged with it. Whatever else one might say about American fundamentalism it clearly shares these two qualities.

J. Gresham Machen of Princeton Theological Seminary was perhaps fundamentalism's most brilliant advocate. Machen exemplifed the Christian theological rejection both of the modern world itself—

which he found vulgar, mechanized, increasingly dominated by "experts," and lacking in artistic creativity—and of modern theology, which he condemned as a betrayal of the historic faith. He rejected theological liberalism not just as a mistaken interpretation of Christianity but as another religion completely. "The great redemptive religion which has always been known as Christianity," he wrote in *Christianity and Liberalism,* "is battling against a totally diverse type of religious belief, which is only the more destructive of the Christian faith because it makes use of traditional Christian terminology." [2] For Machen, the confrontation was of sufficient seriousness that there could be no compromise. The churches could not contain the two parties. One cannot serve both God and Mammon. Either the liberals or the fundamentalists would have to go. "A separation between the two parties in the church," he insisted, "is the crying need of the hour."

"The church," Machen also wrote, "is perishing today through the lack of thinking, not an excess of it." He insisted that ideas were important and that what is today a matter of academic speculation "begins tomorrow to move armies and pull down empires." So telling were his arguments that the most secular periodicals commended him even when they disagreed. Both the *New Republic* and the *Nation* published articles in 1923 suggesting that the fundamentalists had logic on their side and that if the modernists wanted to redefine the faith they should at least start new churches or denominations in which to do so. Even the stalwart nontheist Walter Lippmann wrote in 1929 that Machen had formulated "the best popular argument produced by either side in the current controversy." Lippmann did not agree with Machen's conclusions; he believed that mankind was going to have to go it alone. But he did believe that Machen had correctly delineated the choice between historic Christianity and modernism, and that liberal theology only muddied the waters. "We shall do well," Lippmann wrote, "to listen to Dr. Machen."

Machen's work represents what is important about fundamentalism: its insistence that there is something essentially incompatible between Christianity and modernity, that any attempt to adapt the Gospel to the modern world view can lead only to disaster. By the same token, they were curiously tolerant, even enthusiastic, about those features of the modern world they did not see as inimical to

Christianity. Machen himself, for example, believed that individualism and *laissez faire* economics were good, and he spoke out publicly against legislation abolishing child labor. Still, the underlying philosophical stance of the fundamentalist intellectuals pitted Christianity against modernity and modernism in an unambiguous manner.

American fundamentalism has become in some respects the opposite of what it set out to be. Beginning as an intellectual movement that quickly developed a grassroots following but had articulate scholarly defenders, it has become an elite-led phenomenon which—with some important exceptions—displays relatively little interest in intellectual questions. Starting as a ferociously antimodernist movement, it has recently embraced some of the most questionable features of the modern world its founders despised. The question of how and why this happened suggests that in the history of fundamentalism there may be a cautionary moral for other antimodernist religious movements.

Fundamentalism is an offshoot of the tradition of antimodernism which has fought against the modern world since its inception. As an identifiable movement, however, fundamentalism has come into history only relatively recently, not so much as the guardian of an ancient heritage but as one of the shrillest outcries within this wider and more modulated complaint.

The conservative religious critique of the modern world and of modern theology does have a certain poignancy that elicits sympathy even though its diagnosis seems wrong. Although the tone of the fundamentalists is often censorious and even self-righteous, it is easy to share some of their revulsion at the way modern theology has so easily accepted the premises of modernity. Many religious conservatives are sad. What they seem to be saying is that the lost souls of the modern tundra are more to be pitied than censured, that they may even hunger and thirst for righteousness but somehow the thinned-out atmosphere stifles their cries. It is not that the children at the gate are callous scoffers. They want to pray, but cannot.

The focal thesis of the conservative religious critics of modern theology is that since the modern world is a spiritual disaster area, theology should never have come to terms with it in the first place. The modern age is the crook and modern theology is the moll. The portrait of the spiritually parched modern desert these conservative critics paint can be detailed with plenty of evidence. The fundamentalists lament the runaway divorce rate, the pornography plague, the banning of God from the schoolhouse, the rise in homosexuality. The more sophisticated critics decry the erosion of taste, the decline of language, the disappearance of civility. The political neoconservatives talk about the specter of totalitarianism and the demise of the work ethic. Yet almost all the critics agree that the underlying cause of all these symptoms is the disease of secularization, what the fundamentalists call "secular humanism." Though the different schools of conservatives use different terms to describe it, they all agree that there is a spiritual source to the moral, social, and political decay.

Nearly all conservative critics agree that ours is a *uniquely* fallen or deranged age, that it was easier to be religious at some other time. The vocation of religious teachers and exemplars—especially in the biblical tradition—is to call the nations to righteousness, to expose sin and folly, to uphold the moral law. That is nothing particularly new. What is to be questioned is the apocalyptic tone, the suggestion that we are worse off in these respects than anyone else has ever been, that the modern world is peculiarly cursed and damned.

Believing that one's own age or nation or tribe is *sui generis* is characteristic of most ages and cultures. Sometimes we place ourselves at the apex of civilization, at other times at its nadir. This claim to uniqueness is not unique. Are we uniquely less capable of being religious? How we answer this question will go a long way in helping us to understand the inner meaning of the tradition of religious antimodernism.

The evidence suggests that we are not as different as the traditional religious critics of modernity, including the fundamentalists, think we are. A professor at a midwestern university always begins his course on comparative religion by screening a film made a few years back showing the religious rituals of a preliterate people living in remote central New Guinea. The movie begins with the village religious specialists, sometimes referred to as medicine men or witch doctors, preparing the turf and the ritual objects for the ceremonial dance. The rite begins with vigorous drumming, animal sounds, and much spirited gesticulating. The students watch spellbound. Here is a real primitive tribe, an unspoiled culture in which everyone is still linked to the ancestral myths and to each other, in which skepticism and ennui have not made their fatal mark. Then the camera slowly pans to the figures just on the edge of the central ritual action. Some are moving slightly, some chanting, others mainly watching. As the camera moves back we also catch glimpses of other figures moving about in front of the surrounding shelters, stirring kettles and poking at fires. They seem almost oblivious to the grunting and jumping going on in the inner circle. Now the camera moves back even further. On the outer edges of the ritual center we see men and women chatting, laughing, searching each other's heads for lice, and in general paying almost no attention to the ceremony. Finally the camera focuses on one older man who is perched on a large tree stump on the periphery of the village square. Unlike those near him, he is at least watching the ceremony. But his attitude seems somewhat negative. He looks at the dancers with his bottom lip thrust out and his brow furled; he wrinkles his nose, puts out his tongue, turns his shoulder away. A moment later he jumps down from the stump and for a few brief seconds engages in a kind of obscene caricature of the dancers, then walks off camera shaking his head. The movie ends with a distant freeze shot of the old man, his backside covered only by a wispy garland of leaves and feathers, going off to find something else to do.

The myth of the Noble Savage dies hard, as does the legend of the good old days. Despite a plethora of evidence to the contrary, many members of the modern tribe still persist in thinking of our own epoch as uniquely damned. If we have trouble finding a purpose in life, sustaining friendships or family ties, or discerning any significance in history, we cannot help suspecting that other people had it easier in this respect. Surely the early Christians were not troubled by doubt and uncertainty. Surely medieval people lived embedded in an unshaken symbolic universe. Surely our grandparents, or at least our great-grandparents, came more easily to the consolation of faith. But above all, the noble redmen or unspoiled tribal people, even if they suffered from hunger, cold, and lice, had something we do not have. The movie shown to the undergraduate class often startles them. It suggests that in this particular village one can find not only the analogs of the priests and holy people of other cultures but also the rough equivalent of skeptics, scoffers, and agnostics. If a skilled investigator could somehow interview the villagers shown in the film, what would be discovered? Would it be found that different individuals—depending on age, gender, temperament, and other factors—have different attitudes toward the tribal myth? Might it also be found that some are bothered by the degree to which this or any other ceremony involves them? Might there even be New Guinean children at the gate who would like more than anything to be in the inner circle but somehow just cannot bring themselves to it? Maybe the Great Gap is not as wide as it appears.

For many modern Christians the medieval age carries the nimbus of an eon when one could be swept along on a firm tide of piety. It was a time, many wish to believe, when the culture was so steeped in the stories and legends of Christianity that both the simple and the sophisticated could drink at the same well of faith. Monks chanted, nobles sought the advice of prelates, artisans busied themselves constructing floats for the miracle plays and peasants in the fields humbly crossed themselves when the angelus sounded at the end of the day.

How much this idyllic depiction has to do with the reality of medieval life is something of a question. The English historian John Carroll describes a somewhat different scene. "The picture of medieval man as closely integrated into his church, a pious believer in its comprehensive moral code, and as a result very secure in his view of the universe and his place in it," he writes, "fantastically glamorizes the anarchic reality." Most of the more competent and self-conscious religious people of the day, Carroll says, withdrew into monasteries, leaving the masses with little guidance or instruction. The consequence is that contemporary accounts of church life often compare the people at worship to unruly schoolboys who would "jostle, nudge, spit and swear." Carroll's conclusion, something of a disappointment to modern travelers who visit Notre Dame or Maria Lach, is that "overall the age seems to have been characterized by great religious indifference."[3]

Carroll's description should help to disabuse moderns of the notion that our time is singularly fated to sacral malnutrition and spiritual vacuity. Nor, according to Carroll, did things change much as the medieval age gave way to the Reformation period. The simple, close-to-nature Elizabethan village was "filled with malice and hatred, its only unifying bonds being the occasional episode of mass hysteria which temporarily bound together the majority in order to harry and persecute the local witch."[4]

There is hardly a historical period in which our wishful images are not contradicted by harsh facts. One thinks of the Pilgrim Fathers, those decorous models of Puritan piety, solemnly marching through the snow to the meeting house, muskets on their shoulders. Within a few years of their arrival in the virgin wilderness however, the preachers were already proclaiming that skepticism, heresy and, later, even witchcraft were rampant. The proportion of the population belonging to churches was lower during the colonial period than it is now. By the early 1700s Jonathan Edwards considered America in a state of religious bankruptcy, and a hundred years later the great revivalist Charles Grandison Finney had the same impression.

Whatever may be wrong with the modern soul, and much is wrong, the unprecedented quality of our current spiritual desolation has been exaggerated by its conservative interpreters. We are unique in only one important respect, and that is one which, despite their preoccupation with the devastation science has caused, they almost never mention: the advent of nuclear weapons with their capacity to end human life on the globe. Ironically, the conservative critics do not dwell on this awful nuclear uniqueness. They leave it mainly to the radicals.

Much of the confusion surrounding the issue of whether or not the modern world allows us to be religious springs from conflicting definitions of what "being religious" means. Many conservative critics, although they are reticent about admitting it, are actually complaining not about people being *less* religious but about a change in the *way* people are religious today.

One tactic used by those who portray today's world as peculiarly irreligious is first to identify religion with something that is obviously less present in the modern world—a high degree of social integration, for example. Having answered the question in advance, they lament the difficulty we have in "being religious." To equate religion with something the modern world does not have in order to prove the modern world is not religious is hardly convincing. Religion is not declining in significance or influence today. A look at Iran and Latin America and Poland (or at American TV), confirms its growth.

The common conservative assertion that the modern world is less religious than any previous one cannot be accepted as self-evident.

One wonders also why the conservative critics fail to see that it is possible for people to live amid social disintegration and still be religious. Indeed there are some classical saints who believed that no one could achieve true holiness without extended periods of isolation, loneliness, dark nights of the soul, and the experiencing of a certain lag of spiritual substance. One might even construct an argument, perhaps based on St. John of the Cross, that the hardness and chilliness of the modern world decried by the conservatives should elicit a deeper and more authentic spirituality than the imagined warmth of the Christian Middle Ages.

If the evidence does not support the contention that the modern world is uniquely incapable of religious faith, then why do the critics persist in believing it is?

The British anthropologist Mary Douglas suggests an answer. Writing in *Daedalus* magazine about the blindness of so many scholars to the obvious presence of religion in today's world, she suggests it may be a case of psychological projection. Intellectuals see the modern world as a difficult one in which to be religious mainly because they have such a difficult time being religious themselves. Douglas holds that the modern world is not as different from the premodern one as is often thought. She believes we have created our idealized picture of spiritually superlative premodern people as an expression of what we wish we were; in reality they were, alas, very much like us, some of them pious but others "as mobile, footloose, and uncommitted as any modern academic."[5]

Douglas' observations about the relation of religion to the modern and the premodern are helpful as we anticipate the role of religion in a postmodern world. She identifies the power of science-based technology as one of the principal features of the modern world, but she does not believe this necessarily makes it harder for people to be religious. Without specifically mentioning the nuclear threat, she contends that if religion needs some minimal quota of awe on which to thrive, modern science has given us much to be in awe about.

As for bureaucracy, Douglas believes it is an essential human adaptation to increased population. It actually helps us preserve some genuine personal relationships by permitting us to deal with the large numbers of people we meet in urban life in a less exhausting way. Urban life enables us to be more selective about those with whom we share the personal aspects of life than we could be in a small town.

A distinction has to be made, however, between urban life and bureaucracy. At one level, modern cities are characterized by seg-mental, bureaucratic procedures. At another, however, there are neighborhood fairs, local bars, clubs, ethnic communities, and hundreds of other nonbureaucratic modes of interaction. Most of these are carry-overs from premodern forms of social life. The danger of bureaucracy is that it dilutes the sense of personal responsibility. Still, bureaucracy does serve some essential purposes, and if it is not instituted, some other equally effective method must be found to enable us to deal with large numbers of people without needing to bare our souls to each and every one. The "depersonalized" quality of bureaucracy does not preclude our deepening the contact if we choose. To argue that there is some essential contradiction between religion and bureaucracy, whatever the evils of bureaucracy, is to define religion in a peculiar way, one that makes it difficult to explain why millions of people who work in highly bureaucratic jobs today seem to be devoutly religious.

It is also hard to give real credence to the complaint that our difficulty in being religious stems from our living in cities and being cut off from nature. This charge restricts religion solely to the context of nature mysticism. Such identification of piety with closeness to the natural order is questionable in that religions have flourished in urban areas for millennia (albeit maybe not the kind of religion nature romantics yearn for), and that Christianity in particular spread most rapidly in its earliest years in the crowded urban centers of Alexandria, Corinth, and Rome. The British historian Owen Chad-wick in his book *The Secularization of the European Mind in the Nine-teenth Century* says that the second quarter of the nineteenth century was "an age of rapid revival of religion in all the countries of western Europe," and that it was also "an age of rapid movement from coun-try to town." "We cannot assume without further enquiry," he con-tinues, "that if you are living in a town you are more likely to lack a feeling for the sacred."[6]

The city today does not prevent people from being religious. From the shipyard masses of Gdansk to the burgeoning Baptist churches of

Houston to the sects in the slums, or *favelas*, of São Paulo and the cremation ghats of Benares, religion appears to thrive, not expire, on crowding and density. Although some people find God in the sunset or the blades of grass, others encounter the divine in man-made cathedrals lit only through dark-blue rose windows, or by turning a prayer wheel or by marching in a demonstration or even by switching on the TV. Some critics may not like the God they find, but to claim that none of this is religion is to claim something insupportable.

Let us not project our own spiritual limitations onto the modern world, for it is not the world which prevents us from being religious. The kind of world we live in shapes the manner and mode of our religiousness.

The assertions by religious conservatives that our modern age is uniquely incapable of faith are not lies or self-deceptions but cries *de profundis* from those who utter them. They are not attempts to describe the world so much as they are a prayer, a reaching out for God. Paradoxically, it is evidence of the modern world's capacity for faith. As all the great saints have known, recognizing one's own spiritual thirst is the first step in discovering the fountain of life. Can it be that the secularization the religious antimodernists deplore, even when it is not a projection of their own unsatisfied spiritual aspirations, is a bird of dawn that sings only during waking hours but retreats when night falls, sleep comes, and even the most allegedly secularized computer programmer becomes a painted shaman capable of mystical flight and magical transformation?

The spiritual Saharah theory of the modern world that religious conservatives advance does say something about the modern world, but it does not say what they think it says. Something is indeed wrong, but what is wrong is different from what they believe. Their *cri de coeur* tells us something important. It must be understood neither as diagnosis nor prescription but more as the groan issuing from the wounded victim who does not know why he hurts.

The reason the religious antimodernists can inspire us but cannot help us make the move they themselves seem to want so badly is that they tend to ignore the mundane forces that went into the making of the modern world and, therefore, of the modern religious vision and modern theology they so thoroughly dislike. In reading these critics, despite their complaints about machines and cities, one gets the feeling they are talking about some metaphysical plague or inner rot. But the coming of any new historical epoch with its characteristic religious values is the victory of the classes of people who are the principal bearer of those values. Historical eras do not descend like the materialization of a Zeitgeist. The dominant manners and morals of any given period begin as the life style of a minority that eventually comes into power and puts its stamp on an entire age. This is what happened with the modern age. The people who brought the modern world into being ended the rule of feudalism and became the dominant strata in the period of capitalism; this group is the bourgeoisie.

The modern age appeared in history as the creation of that class which also created the capitalist economy. The one would not have been possible without the other. "Modernity" is at its core the world view of the entrepreneurial class which seized the tiller of history from the weakened grip of its feudal forerunner. The current fundamentalist wing of the conservative critics, unlike its more populist forerunner, is willing to defend capitalism, usually referring to it as "our way of life" or "our free enterprise system." It even does so in the name of Christianity.

The more classical cultural conservatives, however, find this kind of advocacy gauche, and prefer to avoid the subject. To be heard defending capitalism still appears "bourgeois," so most do not mention it or else view it as a minor feature of the age they so despise. But not to grasp the centrality of capitalism in the emergence of our age is to miss something crucial. It is also to misread the history of modernity's tangled relationship with theology. It is at just this point that the radical critique of modernity departs from that of the conservatives and takes the next step.

PART TWO

"How Shall They Possess the Earth?" The Radical Critique of Modern Theology

The middle of the night. The little lights
of the dispossessed shine on the shores.
    Their tearful reflections.
Far, far away laugh the lights of Rio de Janeiro
and the lights of Brasília.

How *shall they possess the earth* if the earth is owned
    by landowners?

Unproductive, prized only for land
speculation and fat loans from the Bank of Brazil.
    There He is always sold for Thirty Dollars
        on the River of the Dead.
    The price of a peon. In spite of
    2,000 years of inflation.
                —Ernesto Cardenal,
            Epistle to Monsignor Casaldaliga, 1974

Blessed are the meek, for they shall inherit the earth.
                —Matthew 5:5

6. Foreigners in Consumer City:
The Rise of Revolutionary Christianity

A New order. Or rather
a new heaven and a new earth.
New Jerusalem. Neither New York nor Brasília
A passion for change: the nostalgia
of that city. A beloved community
   We are foreigners in Consumer City
The new man, and not the new Oldsmobile.
             —Ernesto Cardenal

While conservatives have criticized the modern world and its religion from the right, an equally vociferous attack has come from the left. The history of the radical protest against modernity is also a long one, but, like the conservative critique, it has become particularly strong in recent years, especially in those parts of the globe sometimes known as the Third World.

The life and poetry of Ernesto Cardenal exemplify this revolutionary Christianity. Not a theologian, Cardenal represents the mystical and monastic stream of Christian history. Not a political or social theorist, he has been an eloquent advocate of nonviolent change, a revolutionary, a political refugee, and a minister of state. As a Nicaraguan he lives his life at the very center of the history he incarnates. It would be hard to think of a better exemplar.

In 1957 Cardenal was spending his days praying and studying as a novice at the Trappist monastery in Gethsemane, Kentucky. His spiritual director was Thomas Merton. Cardenal, then thirty-two years old, had been born into a privileged family in Granada, Nicaragua, in 1925. Like Merton he had studied at Columbia University (1947–49), sampled the bohemian life, and tried his hand at poetry. After a shattering personal religious conversion in 1956 he had followed Merton's example and chosen the monastic path. But unlike his mentor, no matter how hard he tried Cardenal could not reconcile himself to the solitude and social isolation of the Trappist life. Coming from a large family he missed having children and married friends around. His mind returned incessantly to the friends he had left behind in Nicaragua, living under the increasingly repressive rule of the Somoza family whose position was secured by the *guardia nacional* that had been organized, trained, and armed by the United States. Merton understood all too well how Cardenal felt the tension between the *vía activa* and the *vía comtemplativa* as a fissure in his own soul; Merton had felt it that way himself. But finally, unlike Merton—though at his advice and with his support—Cardenal left Gethsemane and returned home.

At first he concentrated mainly on his poetry, but he soon began to pour his immense spiritual energy and poetic talent into the growing popular opposition to Somoza. Even in a country entering a revolutionary civil war, Cardenal's dreams of monastic and contemplative life stayed with him. The memory of Gethsemane persisted. Ordained in 1965, he fulfilled a long-standing dream by founding a new kind of monastery on an island in Lake Nicaragua the following year. He called it Our Lady of Solentiname. It was to be a monastic community in which some of the restrictions on a shared spiritual life that he had chafed under during his months in Kentucky would be shed. It would include married couples and single people, children and adults. In the old tradition of Benedictines, its members would labor and pray and study. In Solentiname they worked mostly as farmers and fishermen. But for Cardenal, perhaps more in keeping with the medieval than with the more recent practice, the monastery would not be a sanctuary to which one retreated from the world but an open community participating fully in the life of society.

The new monastic community thrived. The people built cottages, shared their goods, studied the Bible under Father Ernesto's guidance. For ten years Cardenal lived at Solentiname in relative tranquillity, writing poetry and giving spiritual guidance to the families who made it their home.

But then it all changed. The contradiction between the serenity of the cloister and the turmoil in the rest of the country came to Solentiname itself. What Cardenal had not foreseen was that in a nation ruled by a dictatorial regime, no such "beloved community" could be allowed to exist indefinitely. In neither its capitalist nor its communist forms has modern society been capable of nourishing the life of small independent communities. Their very existence is seen as opposition.

First suspicion, then surveillance, then cracking down occurred at Solentiname. The members of the new community at first responded nonviolently. Cardenal, a revolutionary activist in the 1950s when his poem "Zero Hour" was published, had subsequently renounced violence. He had been schooled by Merton and was a friend and admirer of another priest-poet, the pacifist Daniel Berrigan. But the attacks continued and finally the members of the community had to decide whether to arm themselves to defend their fields and their families against the *guardia nacional*. For Cardenal it was an anguishing decision that he puzzled over for years. In 1972, while he was still urging a peaceful social revolution, to be accomplished mainly by example, he wrote a poem called "Nicaraguan Canto" which he dedicated to the FSLN, the guerrilla movement that was already active in the northern hills. In the early 1970s Cardenal himself remained reluctant to support armed insurrection. By 1979, however, he had decided to do it.

In casting his lot with the revolutionaries, Cardenal knew that he was risking the understanding and friendship of many lifelong acquaintances and colleagues. When he learned of his friend's decision to approve of arming in self-defense, Daniel Berrigan wrote an eloquent "open letter" pleading with Cardenal to remember that violence is never justified, that not even the highest moral principle can outweigh the loss of life of a single child. Cardenal did not respond, at least not publicly. Perhaps the reason he failed to do so was that at about the same time, after an FSLN raid on a barracks in nearby San Carlos in which members of the community took part, the *guardia* closed in on Solentiname, killed several of the residents, and drove the others, including Cardenal, into exile. The soldiers tore up miniature paintings done by the residents, smashed the home-made furniture, wrecked the boats and farm implements, and burned down all the buildings except the church, which they transformed into a barracks.

Later, when he finally responded to Berrigan's plea, Cardenal agreed. There was indeed no principle in the world that was worth the life of a child. He added, however, that the principle of pacifism had to be included, that the members of Solentiname, and with them many of the poor people of Nicaragua, had finally and reluctantly resorted to arms to defend children and others from murder.

When I met Cardenal in Mexico in February of 1979 he seemed alternately frantic and depressed. He was once again separated from his people, this time, however, not as a Trappist novice but as an exile. He smoked nervously and crossed and uncrossed his legs as he talked about Solentiname, now in ashes, and about Nicaragua, which was, although neither of us knew it then, living through the final bloody months of its revolution. Cardenal still expressed a horror for guns and bombs and violence. He told me about the bishop of the Nicaraguan city of León who had stared in disbelief when he saw Somoza's planes dropping American-made white napalm on his town, then went on the telephone, dialed the office of an international press agency, and told them in a voice shaking with emotion that they had to inform the world about this "unequal battle between David and Goliath."

The next time I saw Cardenal, two years later, David had won. A coalition of rural and urban guerrillas and middle-class professionals, led by an armed group named after César Augusto Sandino (the organizer of an insurgent group who was killed by the Somoza family forty years earlier) had defeated the *guardia nacional* and assumed governmental power. Somoza had fled and Cardenal had been named Minister of Cultural Affairs. We talked in the office of his ministry in a house in Managua that had once belonged to Somoza himself. Chuckling, Cardenal showed me the dictator's luxurious sunken Roman bath, now used by the staff to wash up at the end of the day. He seemed amused at the irony of the whole thing. A mystical poet and contemplative heading a government ministry. A monk who never wanted to lead a parish because he hated administrative detail sitting at a desk next to a telephone and a file cabinet. He admitted, though, that he enjoyed some things about the job—like organizing poetry workshops for the police and the soldiers and starting an indigenous university for the Miskito Indians in the eastern part of the country. Still, he said that his fondest hope was to return some-day to Solentiname, perhaps this time with a company of men and women drawn from many different nations and religious traditions; to repair the cottages and fix the furniture; to rebuild the boats and mend the nets; to start over. He seemed wistful.

Since our previous meeting Cardenal had become the first Central American to receive the Peace Prize of the German Publishers' Association. In the *laudatio* he delivered for Cardenal, the German Catholic theologian Johannes B. Metz made Cardenal a kind of living embodiment of that form of Christian protest against modernity one might call the "radical vision." Metz said that Cardenal's entire career could be seen as a risky attempt to overcome the divisions and contradictions that slice up modern society—between religious and secular, the communal and the individual, luxury and misery.[1] Metz did not use any German equivalent of "holistic" or "synergistic," two currently popular English terms for what the members of the community at Solentiname were attempting, but he might have. They were not only trying to close the chasm between religious and secular life; they were also attempting to overcome the rifts between producers and consumers and between the cloister and the city.

Having tried to be a Christian as a monk, a poet, a rebel, an exile, and now a cabinet officer, Cardenal has most recently faced a series of hard new choices. The threat of invasion from Honduras on the north finally persuaded the revolutionary government of Nicaragua to move thousands of Miskito Indians from the border area and resettle them farther south. Once the Indians were gone, troops destroyed their huts so they could not be used by infiltrators. Although he agreed that the removal was necessary, it still pained Cardenal. The poet who had once written a "Homage to the Indians" was now part of a government which had to resettle Indians; and even if it was for their own safety, the bitter irony of it cannot have been lost on the man who once wrote angrily about the destruction of the Pataxo and Tapaiamas, and the "crackling of huts in flames."[2]

It is never easy to go from being a prophetic poet to being a minister of state with responsibilities to a government, especially one threatened by invasion and destabilization. Such a jarring transition puts theories about reuniting politics and spirituality, contemplation and community, to a severe test. Cardenal felt the test as one that was trying not only his ideas but his personal vocation as a Christian.

He thought about leaving his post, and the pressures placed on him and the other priests holding public office in Nicaragua to resign, made the trial even more taxing. But he decided to stay on his assignment. The rebuilding of Solentiname would have to wait.

Cardenal's story can be read as a painful lifelong struggle against modernity. As surely as T. S. Eliot or Evelyn Waugh ever did, Cardenal recoils against what the bourgeois world has become. As Metz said in his *laudatio,* Cardenal yearns to revive the "dialogue with nature" which was interrupted in European and American history by the appearance of capitalism and the worship of productivity. This part of his vision can best be seen in the lyrical descriptions of birds and natural settings that appear in his poetry and in the satisfaction he finds in his educational work with the Indians. Cardenal, however, is committed to more than the reintegration of the ideas of politics and poetry, the sacred and the profane, even nature and art. He is committed to nurturing an actual community where people bring these separated spheres back together, providing one small building block for the new culture that will reunite religious, political, and personal lives. The vision he once cherished for Solentiname has now become one for Nicaragua itself.

The trajectory of Cardenal's life reveals why a monk became a guerrilla. It also uncovers something about the mood—somehow both traditional and revolutionary—of his whole continent. The story has a distressingly similar plot throughout Latin America. Corporate farming of luxury foods and export crops for profit pushes subsistence farmers off the land, reducing them to either urban rabble or seasonal rural employees. Small farmers try to defend what is left through peasant leagues and church-sponsored cooperatives. Those in power become fearful and try to stem the discontent. Repression follows; then self-defense; then rebellion. By the time the first shots are fired, the people who began as defenders of a traditional order they saw being uprooted have become revolutionaries who recognize that the old values will have no chance until they can find expression in a new political structure. Cardenal is a living example of Péguy's famous adage that religion always begins in mysticism and ends in politics. What Cardenal would add, however, is that the reason for the politics is to make the mysticism possible again.

7. Questionable Concordat: The Radical Ruptura from Modern Theology

> ". . . every theology is political, even one that does not speak or think in political terms. . . . When academic theology accuses liberation theology of being political, thus pretending to ignore its own relation with the political status-quo, what it is really looking for is a scapegoat for its own guilt complex."
>
> —Juan Luis Segundo
> *The Liberation of Theology,* 1976

Like their conservative counterparts, the radical critics of modernity view the contemporary world as a spiritual fiasco. [1] For them, however, the evidence of the failure is not that the children at the gate cannot pray, but that they cannot eat. They cite the great divided cities of the Third World gleaming with luxury hotels and three-star restaurants in the center and festering with garbage pits and acres of jerry-built shantytowns around the edges. Their poets are Neruda and Cardenal rather than Eliot and Stevens. They bewail the dissolution of the mystical in consumer city, but they believe there are identifiable historical sources for modern unbelief and ennui. Their principal emotions are not loss or sadness but anger and hope.

The radical critics look upon the modern world as a blasphemous denial of the justice of God and a negation of the Christian message of "good news to the poor." This is the fundamental sacrilege. They view with suspicion those forms of theology that have too easily come to terms with the modern world. [2]

For the radical critics of theology's acceptance of the modern world, the wrong turn did not come with the Reformation, as some Catholics argue, or with the historical criticism of the Bible as conservative Protestants claim. It came, rather, during the nineteenth century, when one by one the theologians who had been holding out against the philosophical ideas associated with the Enlightenment gave up the battle and accepted the new situation. It came with the victory of modern theology. [3]*

For the radical critics, modern theology arose during the period when the victorious bourgeois revolutions of the eighteenth and nineteenth centuries were systematically depriving religious institutions of the powers they had exercised earlier. The attack on the power of the churches, which the bourgeois revolutionaries saw as the citadels of the *ancien régime,* was accompanied by an assault on theology itself in the name of Science and Reason. It was an onslaught aimed at the intellectual and the institutional levels of religion. The bourgeoisie wanted to establish both their political power and their ideology.

In the radicals' version of the history of modern theology, the victorious bourgeoisie continued to fight. They did so not only by whittling away the political power of churches but also by developing an impressive series of legal, political, and scientific theories that were indifferent to whether God existed or not. Pierre Bayle tried to create a political philosophy independent of religious underpinnings. The English philosopher Thomas Hill Green feared that the historical criticism of the Bible would cut morality loose from its moorings, so he tried to design a form of Christian ethics that would not be dependent on the events of biblical history. Both Immanuel Kant and Bishop Butler attempted to fashion systems of ethics that could

---

* There is something very Catholic about the way the radical critics read history as a combination of ideas and institutions interpenetrating each other. Their viewpoint is "ecclesial." They contend that one cannot appreciate the changes in religious thought and theology that took place during the eighteenth and nineteenth centuries without seeing them in the light of the events that shaped religious institutions, the relations between those institutions—churches—and the contending parties around them. Cardenal and the liberation theologians live in a world where prelates and theologians stayed on speaking terms with each other longer than they did in the Protestant world; so they are skeptical of historians who present the history of theology as a succession of ideas that influenced each other like colliding billiard balls. They always remind us of the political clashes of the period, which altered dramatically the role of religious institutions.

repose on reason alone. Theories of evolution and of progress began replacing the doctrines of Creation and of Providence; and the "social contract" theory of government was developed to render religiously based theories of political power obsolete.

The elusive process scholars call "secularization" proceeded. Religious institutions were shorn of temporal power in large measure because the new ruling classes believed that their power had been used to bolster the old order. "Secular" theories about the origin of the human species, the legitimacy of political authority, and the reasons for morality challenged theologically anchored beliefs.

The defenders of religion returned the fire. Bishops, popes, theologians challenged the new ideas. The struggle was a vicious one, but nowhere was it purely a battle between church and state, or a "warfare between science and religion." Various political factions sided with or against the church when it served their interests, and the church herself developed skilled politicians. The doctrine of papal infallibility, debated for decades but finally enunciated in 1870, exemplifies this mixture of political and philosophical currents. Though phrased in theological idiom, it had as much to do with political power as with religious truth. It was an attempt by the Catholic Church to curb sovereign states from encouraging national churches in order to exert political control over religion within their borders.

As the radical critics read the history of modern theology, the "confrontational" stage of religious response to the new world did not last long. Beginning with the Protestants, followed by the Catholics, theology eventually caved in. The "modern mind" won. Except for a few holdouts, theologians, who were often members of social sectors that benefited from the bourgeois order, soon moved from battlefield to conference table. They stopped opposing the modern world. Theologians found ways to accept and lend religious credence to the ideals and theories of the dominant tradesmen and entrepreneurs. Religious laws against usury had already been discarded. Catholic theologians decided that the Papal States, for years defended both theologically and militarily as essential to the pope's spiritual independence, were not that indispensable after all (a convenient finding since they were wrested from the pope in 1870 by armed invasion). Modern science was also accepted little by little. Protestant pietists taught that since faith was strictly an affair of the

heart, no conflict either with the state or with science could possibly
arise. Other Protestant theologians, carrying Luther's doctrine of the
"two kingdoms" a giant step further, happily turned over the secular
realm *in toto* to the state. The climax of this process was the idea that
eventually came to dominate modern theology and to elicit the most
vociferous criticism from the radicals: the autonomy of the whole
secular sphere.

The arrangement was never airtight. Catholics clung to the theory
that the papacy was an equal actor on the international stage with
the right to enter into treaties—concordats—with other sovereign
entities to guarantee the inherent rights of the church itself. Protestant theologians continued to speculate on the divine sources of the
elegance and symmetry that the scientists discovered when they sur-
veyed the spacious firmament on high. Both Catholic and conservative Protestant thinkers continued to insist that reason rightly
understood still led the way to the divine.

But these were largely rear-guard actions. The tidal current of the
nineteenth century established nearly everywhere the separation of
church and state, the emancipation of reason from the yoke of
dogma, and the freedom of science to do whatever its method suggested. Politics, science, and technology became allegedly neutral
areas outside the scope of churchly influence or theological criticism.
Just as papal nuncios attached their signatures to concordats with the
new national states, delineating the rights and privileges of each
party, so Catholic and Protestant theologians negotiated the intellectual equivalents of these contracts with the reigning ideologies.
There were always political and intellectual clashes, but mostly the
strategy of conciliation was successful.

But the question radicals now ask is why did the theologians come
to terms? What did the church get for its conciliatory attitude? What
was its *quid pro quo* for ceasing to oppose a new governing class that
was still viewed with suspicion precisely by those segments of the
population, the rural and urban working classes, that continued, for
a while, to be religious? Religion received the provision within the
concordat that brought modern theology to birth. Reality was "par-
titioned," divided between faith and reason, science and religion,
sacred and profane, much as the pope had once divided the New
World between the Spanish and the Portuguese. It was an offer
theology could not refuse. [4]

It seemed a fair exchange. The state would not interfere in matters having to do with heaven or the soul. In return, religion would keep its nose out of "this world." Ironically, as Gustavo Gutiérrez points out, the modern doctrine of religious toleration was made possible only by a sweeping retreat from what "religious" means. [5] The implications were devastating, for now reason ruled and the question became that of what place faith should occupy. The world was governed by alliances of national states which expected loyalty. The economy was managed by financiers who insisted the market needed no religious or moral direction since it was already steered by a benevolent, if invisible, hand. In effect, the church with its different theologies and the "modern world" with its various ideologies and institutions became two parts of a single unified religio-social system. The only worldly task left for theology now became the exploration of the forms of coherence between these two planes. Its job was to make the rough places smooth and keep the joinings welded. Disputes arose, of course, but they were border skirmishes. By and large the terms of the theological concordat continued to obtain, just as the détente between the churches and those classes and states that governed the modern world continued. To question either one became tactless. It put the questioner outside the sphere of reasonable discourse.

There was a certain difficulty with the concordat, however: it did not permit theology to figure out what the churches should be doing in the modern world. What was their "mission"? At one time the church had sought to guide economics by teaching that there was a "just price," and to minimize armed conflict by delineating what was and was not a just war. This pastoral and prophetic function was declining. The churches were left with little to do in this world but to comfort, console, and prepare people for the next one. Making money and making war could proceed without the inconvenient restraints of morality sanctioned by religion.

It was not that religion was banned from dealing with morals or "social ethics." Individual Christians could not avoid being engaged in such activities as long as they lived in this world. But the guidance the churches now gave was intended to help these individuals be kind and honest within the established modern structures. Moral advice was proper but only as long as the terms of the concordat were respected. When churches and theologians did become interested in worldly issues, as evidenced by the pope's Social Encyclicals or the Protestant Social Gospel, their teachings usually deferred to the power of the classes that had established the right to govern. They rarely complained about societies dominated by small financial or political elites. What they pressed for was not a change in the structure of domination itself but for some modification in how those who ruled would do so. People with property and power should exercise compassion. The rights of those below should be respected. Just as feudal lord and vassal had once accepted their lot, so now entrepreneur and employee, mill owner and migrant worker should strive together for the health of the commonweal.

Viewed from one angle the new church-and-society arrangement seemed to work well. After experiencing some painful losses, religion staged a comeback, at least among the growing middle classes, as the nineteenth century approached its midpoint. But, modern theology did have an Achilles' heel.

The defect in the modern concordat was that it left out most of the people in the church and most of the people in the world. It had been negotiated behind closed doors and then announced to the plebeians. It ignored the vast populations of ordinary working men and women of the industrialized nations whose lives were massively altered, often for the worse, by the very world the modern theologians were now embracing. [6] It disregarded women and racial minorities (both dramatically missing from the encyclicals and the Social Gospel). It overlooked the vast majority of the people of those countries outside Europe and North America whose role in the new era was to supply customers and commodities for the nations the modern ideology declared to be more advanced. These excluded groups make up most of the people who are the church; it is the perspective from which the radical critics write. Radical critics see that modern theology has failed because by accepting the intellectual and political rulers of the modern world as its interlocutors, and by agreeing to the contract that turned the economic and technical spheres over to allegedly autonomous inner dynamics, it forfeited its ability to say anything to the margin. But it is from the margins that the postmodern world is coming to birth. A radical break, a *ruptura* from the whole tradition of modern theology, was needed. [7]

This then is the story of the rise and fall of modern theology as seen from the perspective of its radical critics. Based on a shaky compromise between the historic Christian Gospel and the political and ideological requirements of the echelons that came to dominate the modern world, it excluded from its purview those sectors of that world which its secular rulers had already banned from cultural and political power. Consequently the world of modern theology could endure only as long as its pattern of domination and debarment lasted. It should not be surprising then that in the last decades of the twentieth century, as the corporate edifice of modernity has begun to crack and peel, its religious nimbus and theological rationale has also begun to come unstuck. Nor should it be surprising that the most dramatic evidence of this ungluing should come not in the Protestant churches, which had, on the whole, adjusted more easily to modernity, but in the Catholic Church, which had never completely made the adaptation in the first place. [8] It is appropriate therefore that we should visit this time not an independent Baptist church like the one in Lynchburg, but two local Roman Catholic congregations—one in Latin America, to witness the seedbed of the current revival, and one in the United States, to ascertain how far the movement has spread. It is especially important that we look into a "typical" Catholic parish in the United States. Given the nearly legendary conservatism and strictness of the American Catholic Church, if hints of a postmodern theology and religion are appearing even here, then they must be seen as something more than passing fads. Let us go then, first to La Chispa and then to Hyannis.

8. La Chispa and St. Francis Xavier

Only from the ground up, from the popular movements, from the popular Christian communities, is it
possible to see what is lasting, profound and irreversible in the Latin American historical process, as well
as what is alive and creative in the church.
—Gustavo Gutiérrez
"La Fuerza Historica de los Pobres," 1978

Today the human race is passing through a new stage
of its history. Profound and rapid changes are spreading by degrees around the whole world. . . . Hence
we can already speak of a true social and cultural
transformation, one that has repercussions on the
religious life as well.
—*Gaudium et Spes*
Second Vatican Council

Padre Muñoz expertly wheels the rusting blue VW along the rock-
strewn road through billows of suffocating dust. Born in Spain, he
has been working for twenty-two years in Central and South America. The "base community" is in a tiny *pueblito* called La Chispa
("the spark"). It has been meeting for four years. [1] Most of its members live and work on a large sugar hacienda. The others do subsistence farming or try to grow corn for the market. The hacienda
enterprise is prosperous but the people are poor. The closest doctor is
in a village two and a half hours away by car on a dry day. There is
no school. The water must be carried nearly a mile. About one fifth

of the children born in the settlement die before their first birthday. The diet is beans, cornmeal tortillas, chicken on occasion, and local fruit in season.

There is no church building, but when we arrive the members of the base community are already gathered in a thatch-roofed hut with a freshly swept dirt floor. Not counting the children who wander in and out, there are about twenty people. They greet Padre Muñoz with obvious affection. The group meets two or three times a week, but he is able to get here only once every few weeks. When he is not present they sing and pray and discuss their common problems. Sometimes they select delegations to go to the local government office or to meet with the landowner's representative. When they feel safe to do so they talk about the rural workers' union they are trying to organize with people of similar base communities from other haciendas, but in this country even talking about such things can be dangerous. At every meeting one of the literate members reads a passage from the Bible and anyone who wants to comments on it. Before they close they pray for themselves and for people they know who are sick, in jail, or in any other kind of difficulty.

We drink some tea, eat fresh tortillas and wild pears. The meeting begins. Padre Muñoz sits in the large circle. Someone else reads the passage for the day. Everyone is listening intently. Most of the people cannot read the text, but the words we are hearing were once a part of an oral tradition; two generations of Christians heard them repeated from mouth to mouth before Luke gathered them and wrote them down, probably around A.D. 90. Even after that they circulated in oral form. There is more than one way this little clump of Christians at La Chispa is like an early Christian congregation.

The passage read is the section at the end of the Gospel of Luke in which Jesus is meeting with his disciples in the upper room just before his arrest. It has become an important passage in many theologies because it includes the "words of institution" by which Jesus initiates the sharing of bread and wine that has developed into the communion service and the mass. When the time comes to discuss the passage, however, the people of La Chispa have some unexpected things to say.

Ana begins. Why, she wonders, did Jesus allow Judas to eat with him and the rest of the disciples and to listen to their plans when he seems to have known that Judas was going to sneak out and tell the police where he was?

Guillermo suggests that this is just like the meetings they have of the clandestine group that is planning the campesinos' union. You never know if someone is a spy, but even if you suspect someone is, you always hope he will see the error of his ways and side with us instead of them. You have to take some risks. Maybe this is what Jesus was doing.

Pepe mentions that all the disciples seemed worried about whether they could stick it out with Jesus. They kept asking, "Lord, will I betray you?" We really need each other's help a lot, he says, not to give in to all the pressures and bribes the government uses to get us to betray each other.

Ana is not completely satisfied. She feels one has to be more careful, not take too many chances. She looks pensive and intent.

Guadalupe remembers that Judas got thirty pieces of silver for "ratting" on Jesus (she uses the Spanish slang phrase), but she says that is just the trouble. When you need to buy seed before it rains, or your baby needs medicine, sometimes you will do almost anything to get money. Her voice rises in anger. That is just how they keep us divided, she says. Maybe Judas thought he needed the money, but still that was no excuse for what he did.

Elena, who once went to a catechism class many years ago, remembers that later on Judas hanged himself and also recalls that this is a mortal sin. She asks Padre Muñoz about it. He responds by asking the group what they think sin is.

Ana has a swift reply. For years, she says through set teeth, people have told her that the worst sin is not being married the way the church decrees, or having impure thoughts. Thank God, she says, now we have this group and we can read the Bible and find out how much nonsense that was and what Jesus really said. For me, she says, sin is seeing what's wrong in the world, how the supervisors treat the field workers, how the children are ignored when they are sick—and then not doing anything about it. Her brow furrows.

Guillermo agrees. The worst thing, he says, is the way all this talk about sins and sins and more sins used to make us feel so damn bad we didn't think we could ever do anything right. What the church never got around to telling us "until just recently," he adds, smiling at Padre Muñoz, is that when we follow Jesus we get a feeling that we *can* do something. We have his *fuerza*.

Pepe says that the fact the other disciples were still with Jesus at this point, although they ran and hid later, shows how much strength they got from being with him. He says he gets a sense of the same *fuerza* from this group and from the people he meets from other similar ones, in San Carlos and Culiaca.

Guillermo now recalls that this is the supper at which Jesus initiated the mass, or so he has heard. What does the padre think? Was this a sacrament?

Padre Muñoz has said very little so far. Speaking softly now from his stool in the circle, he says that, yes, this was a sacrament. But, he continues, it was Jesus himself who was and is the main sacra-ment. And the church, he says, the people of God, like us gathered here in La Chispa, is a sacrament. We have to be a visible sign of God's presence in the world, to show the world what God wants.

Pepe says he thinks God wants people to live in peace, to have enough to eat, not to have to worry night after night about repaying the money you've had to borrow. But, he says, some people tell us that as Christians we should not get into all these political things . . .

Ana interrupts. That's just what they said about Jesus, too, she sniffs. Nothing ever changes.

The discussion continues for over an hour. Padre Muñoz speaks only occasionally, to respond to a question or raise another one. Once in a while a child who has fallen down runs in to be comforted. A dog wanders through, a chicken explores the floor for scraps. Eventually the meeting ends with a time of prayer in which several people pray aloud. Padre Muñoz says a benediction and people cross themselves.

The members of the group were all eloquent and sharp. No one seemed shy. Each spoke with conviction and vigor, and everyone listened carefully to the others. "So much," says Muñoz, "for the myth of the mute, listless campesino." He did not celebrate mass at La Chispa this time but does so often. There is a supply of conse-crated hosts on hand and they are often distributed during services. But Muñoz says he does not want to perpetuate an infantile depen-dence on a clerical class. He believes it is very important for the church to begin returning to the people the resources and powers that have been wrongly vested for centuries in the clergy. Otherwise, he says, the church becomes an unintentional replica of consumer society, in which the people's ability to take care of themselves is expropriated—the terms have become a little more Marxist.

Padre Muñoz has learned much from another Spaniard now living in Latin America—he is Ignácio Ellacuria, whose best-known book has appeared in English with the title *Freedom Made Flesh.* [2] Ellacuria builds his pastoral theology on the very Catholic idea that the presence of God in the world cannot simply be proclaimed (as some Protestants would have it) but must be made visible. It must be mediated, fleshed out. For Ellacuria, the church should be the tangible sign of God's presence (as Padre Muñoz had said at La Chispa), a sign of that which it teaches. For Ellacuria (and Muñoz), what the church embodies is Jesus himself. The padre emphasizes that just as Jesus was misunderstood because he used political language ("the kingdom of God") to point to a much more comprehensive reality, so will the church be misunderstood today. God's salvation includes both heaven and earth, both time and eternity, both this life and the next, he says. But since so many people today—like the members of this base community—were raised on the mistaken idea that God cares only for their souls, the church must become political, with all the misunderstandings that will bring, if it is to be an adequate sign of the total sweep of God's salvation. If this produces martyrs, as it already has, it is a sure indication that the church is succeeding in some small measure in fleshing out the message God sends in the life of Jesus.

Padre Muñoz is a liberation theologian who communicates with the people not by correcting their theological ideas but by living among them. He does so by encouraging them to delve into the Bible —especially the Gospels and the prophets—on their own; by using the vast resources of the Catholic theological tradition to enliven their weary battle against injustice. During the few hours he has between meetings with many base communities, he reflects with his fellow theologians on the questions that have been raised; he reads, studies, prays, and then cranks up the blue VW for another sortie. He says he is writing a book on the sacrament of confirmation interpreted from a liberation perspective. He will finish it, he says, in two or three years, "if someone doesn't shoot me in the meantime."

La Chispa is not unique. Hundreds of thousands of these tiny human synapses meet all over Latin America. There are awesome risks for many members of base communities in countries where infiltration and *agents provocateurs* abound.

The base community at La Chispa is not just twenty people rapping. It is twenty people reappropriating a cluster of stories and a moral tradition that have survived the onslaught of capitalist modernization and are now beginning to provide an alternative to the officially established system of values and meanings.

A CHURCH ON CAPE COD

The Roman Catholic parish of St. Francis Xavier in Hyannis, Massachusetts, is certainly no base community. A typical small-town church, it serves the growing year-round population one finds in any coastal village on Cape Cod today. The church building is built in white frame New England style. A statue of its patron, St. Francis Xavier, the "Apostle of the Indies" and the first Jesuit missionary, stands in a flower garden in the neat grass lawn. The parish encompasses not only Irish, Portuguese, and Italian ethnic Catholics who have moved from Boston over the past decades, but also the more indigenous old Yankees and black Cape Verdians who have lived there for generations. This mixture of races and cultures has made it a lively hodgepodge of many of the different traditions (the Hispanic excepted in this case) that make up American Catholicism. It is in many ways an "average parish," neither *avant-garde* nor retrogressive. Still, even a casual visitor to St. Francis Xavier cannot help notice that something is happening in the American Catholic Church which could hardly have been foreseen two decades ago.

On a cold spring day in March 1982, the ample parish house of St. Francis Xavier sheltered a hundred chilly residents and visitors from nearby towns and villages who had marched down the main thoroughfare from the town hall carrying placards opposing the policy of the U.S. government in El Salvador. Many of the marchers were parishioners of St. Francis Xavier, but members of several other churches were present as well. The local Unitarian pastor and a Presbyterian minister sipped coffee from Styrofoam cups along with teenagers in shiny, bulbous down vests and older people in sturdy boots and knit scarves. Tables of literature opposing nuclear arms and military aid to Latin America stood near racks of Catholic tracts and pamphlets. There was a slide show on Central America made available by the diocesan office.

The following day at the ten o'clock "family mass" at St. Francis Xavier, a bearded young priest assisted by two older deacons presided over a festive celebration in which four children read the lessons and a nun strummed a guitar while a choir of fifth-graders sang the *sursum corda* and *credo* in English. The priest gave a sermon on caterpillars and butterflies, artfully relating the image first to the Gospel reading about the seed that must be placed in the ground and die if it is to bear life, and then to the crucifixion and resurrection of Christ. At the end of the service every child received a large red, green, or violet paper butterfly with a string attached so it could be strung through a buttonhole. Some of the adults who appeared at the coffee-and-danish gathering after the mass also wore butterflies.

The lively admixture of politics and caterpillars, nuclear pacifism and guitar masses at St. Francis Xavier recalled a line by Father Allan Figueroa Deck, S.J., in his foreword to the American edition of *Basic Ecclesial Communities*, by a fellow Jesuit, Alvero Barreiro. Father Barreiro is a professor of systematic theology at the Pontifical Catholic University of Rio de Janeiro. The book deals with the explosion of small grassroots Christian congregations which has occurred in the Catholic Church in the past twenty years, not only in Latin America but in Europe and other parts of the world as well.[3] In his foreword, Father Deck says that these local Christian cells are already having their impact on U.S. Catholics and other American Christians, and that "a new stage in the history of the North American Catholic Church is in the making." The transformation, he says, is a gradual one, but it is changing the Catholic Church "from one that in this century won national acceptance and even respectability to one that now, in these very different and emerging circumstances, dares to challenge the national and international structures of injustice, selfishness and complacency of which our nation is undeniably a part."[4]

Father Deck's description of a U.S. Catholic Church leaving behind its quest for respectability to accept the risk of challenging "national and international structures of injustice" may sound a bit like pious wishful thinking to some Catholics. They would complain that despite a new wrinkle here and there, and an occasional critical pronouncement, the U.S. Catholic Church is still the same old outfit underneath. Others may find his words true and regret them. Demonstrations opposing American foreign policy in a Catholic parish house? Whatever happened to the blend of Roman piety and patriotism most Catholics who are now over fifty grew up on? What happened to those rousing anti-Communist speeches at communion breakfasts and Legion of Mary meetings?

The coastal town in which St. Francis Xavier parish is located is Hyannis; and the white frame church building is the one at which John F. Kennedy, his family, and their entourage used to appear, fresh from touch football games and sailing trips, for Sunday mass in the early 1960s. It was through news photographs taken in this parish that millions of Americans became accustomed to seeing a president of the United States attend a Roman Catholic mass. In one sense, it was at St. Francis Xavier that American Catholics finally found the "acceptance and even respectability" their ancestors had been denied for generations. It is difficult to imagine how John F. Kennedy, who initiated the American involvement in Vietnam, took responsibility for the Bay of Pigs, and visibly winced when church people, especially Catholics, mixed religion and politics (in public), would have felt about the weekend's activities in his old parish. His children, now in their twenties, would not be surprised at all.

There can be little doubt that something has changed at St. Francis Xavier. William Halsey suggests in *The Survival of American Innocence,* his recent book on the history of American Catholicism in the twentieth century, that like many other Americans, Catholics have also lived through a certain loss of innocence about the inflated "promise of America."[5] But Halsey believes there is a difference. For a number of generations Catholics in the United States had become used to forgoing meat on Friday, attending special schools, being absent from community Thanksgiving services, hearing it whispered that they were somehow not as dependably patriotic as other citizens. Then came John F. Kennedy and John XXIII; so now, with such disabilities behind them, Halsey contends, American Catholics feel relieved yet uncomfortable. They became attached to being different. Might this ambivalence allow for a different kind of "difference" to emerge, a willingness to swim against the stream again, but on different issues?

If the change in the American Catholic Church, and at St. Francis

Xavier in Hyannis, is that Catholics are learning to be different in a
different way, the question then becomes: How will this new difference express itself? American Roman Catholics, unlike their Protestant neighbors, belong to a closely knit world church which is bound
to impinge on their way of being Catholic in America. In this world
church the most important change unfolding now is the vastly increased influence and visibility of Third World Catholics and the
mushrooming of local level, lay-led base communities. Not all the
changes at St. Francis are attributable to liberation theology or the
base communities movement, but Father Deck believes that many of
them are, and I believe he is right.

9. A Church of the Poor? The Birth of the Basic Christian Communities

> The poor know that history is theirs and that if today they must cry, tomorrow they will laugh. That laughter turns out to be an expression of profound confidence in the Lord—a confidence which the poor live in the midst of a history they seek to transform. It is a joy which is subversive of the world of oppression, and therefore it disturbs the dominator; it denounces the fear of those who tremble and reveals the love of the God of hope.
>
> —Gustavo Gutiérrez
> "La Fuerza Historico de los Pobres," 1978

> We invite all, without distinction of class, to accept and take up the cause of the poor, as if they were accepting and taking up their own cause, the very cause of Jesus Christ.
>
> —The Catholic Bishops of Latin America
> Puebla, Mexico, 1979

The past three decades have seen an explosion of small face-to-face groups in churches of all denominations around the world: prayer and healing groups; "marriage encounter" sessions; adult discussion hours; Bible study groups; *cursillos* or short religious courses; women's and men's fellowships; and "consciousness-raising" efforts. But not all small church-related groups are base communities, and not all base communities are small.

The term "base community" displays, in some measure, all three of the following characteristics:

1. Although they may have been initiated by clergy, and priests or nuns may continue to share in the leadership, they have a significant degree of lay control and direction, an ethos which is more egalitarian than the one found in most congregations and parishes.

2. There is an internal liturgical life of singing, prayer, the sharing of bread and wine, sometimes informally but often in a eucharistic fashion. The base communities are places of festivity where the historic images of biblical faith are celebrated.

3. Study and critical analysis of the real life "secular" situation in which the participants live in the light of the Bible's message becomes a basis for political engagement by the community and related groups as well as individuals.

Even if we count only local Christian base communities that exhibit all three of these characteristics, it is impossible to be sure how many there are, but the total is probably close to two hundred thousand. (Some estimates put the number in Brazil alone at eighty thousand.) They continue to multiply. Base communities still constitute a distinct minority in the world church, but the most active and committed minority.

Something of major proportion has changed in the Roman Catholic Church in the United States since the days of Camelot-in-Hyannis. A Vatican Council was held, and its impact was enormous. Without it there would probably have been no guitars and no vernacular mass at St. Francis Xavier that morning. The conviction has been growing that something else has begun to happen as well, something that better explains the antinuclear weapons pamphlets and the El Salvador demonstration.

The Catholic Church has become more "catholic," more reflective of its many-cultured global constituency, more aware that millions of its members are poor. Its European and American branches have begun to be influenced more by its Asian, African—and especially its Latin American—branches. It has absorbed new theologies, new types of political involvement. It has witnessed the massive emergence of a whole new form of local Catholic life, the base communities that some observers believe could eventually replace the parish structure.

The influence of the Latin American Church on its North American sister is one of the most curious twists of recent religious history. It was planned to happen the other way. In the early 1960s the North American Catholic hierarchy, prodded by Rome and concerned about the spread of Protestantism and socialism south of the border, mobilized a massive "mission to Latin America." During the next fifteen years, thousands of priests, nuns, and lay people, along with hundreds of millions of dollars, poured from Boston, Detroit, and Los Angeles into the villages and cities of Peru, Brazil, Guatemala, and their "sister republics." It was the most ambitious single foreign missionizing enterprise the American Catholic Church had ever attempted.

The mission to Latin America became controversial. Many Peruvians, Colombians, and Brazilians resented what they perceived as a heavy-handed effort to shape them up according to a "gringo" model and to keep them securely within the U.S. sphere of influence. For their part, many of the young missioners were appalled by the squalor they discovered and the role North American businesses played in perpetuating it. Living with poor people and conversing daily with angry campesino organizers, many North Americans lost their political innocence. When they returned after their terms of service or after having been deported by repressive regimes for allegedly meddling in politics, they became, in effect, missionaries to the United States. Within a few years there was hardly a religious order or a diocese without its inner cadre of "conscienticized" veterans of the *favelas* who joined other civil rights and antiwar activists in emphasizing social justice. They urged their bishops to use their domestic clout to influence American policy in Latin America. This has happened, and the result can be seen in the Catholic bishops' firm opposition to the American government's current policy in Central America. The great "mission to Latin America" had become a mission to the United States and had helped bring changes in the U.S. Catholic Church more profound than any the original mission had caused in Latin America.

Other things had happened in the worldwide church as well. The little Catholic church in Hyannis has been swept along in a larger history. On September 11, 1962, Pope John XXIII gave an address over Vatican Radio. It was one month before the opening of the historic Second Vatican Council he had called for on January 25, 1959 (to the consternation of the Roman curia, who thought they had elected a caretaking pope they could easily control, and for whom a council could only mean expense, change, and trouble). In that talk, expressing his hopes for what the council might accomplish, the Pope said: "With respect to the underdeveloped countries, the Church appears as it is and wants to be: the Church of all the people and, in particular, of the poor."[1]

On the face of it, this was a curious statement. In most of the "underdeveloped" parts of the world, with a few important exceptions, the church was clearly, "in particular," the church of the privileged and powerful, not of the poor. Although the lower classes might, as in Latin America, constitute the majority of baptized people, church schools and universities in Asia, Africa, and Latin America were more often organized to serve the children of elite families. Most priests were assigned to areas where the parishes could afford to pay the bills, while many less affluent sections of cities and impoverished rural areas rarely saw a priest at all. In Europe as well, the Catholic Church was hardly the church of the poor. The loss of the poor and of urban working classes from both Catholic and Protestant churches during the nineteenth century was the most important religious/demographic event of the period.

Among the industrial nations, only in the United States was there an exception to this exodus, and it was due to a number of factors peculiar to the American situation. One was that blacks, who constituted a large part of the rural working class, had already left mainline Protestantism in protest against their banishment to balconies and back pews, and organized their own churches and denominations, mainly Baptist and African Methodist Episcopal. Also, because of the fissiporous nature of American Protestantism and the tendency of mainline denominational leaders to support management during controversies with labor, lower-class whites often formed their own churches, many of them independent Baptist, Holiness, and, later, Pentecostal. Among the immigrant urban poor, Catholicism was the main religious institution, so in late-nineteenth- and early-twentieth-century America, the Roman Catholic Church became a church of the poor in America, not by choice but by historical circumstances. By the time of the council, however, the Catholic Church in America could hardly be thought of as the "church of the poor," as the Kennedy family itself demonstrated.

While speaking of a church "in particular, of the poor," Pope John XXIII also said he was summoning the council to effect an *aggiornamento*—a bringing-up-to-date of the Catholic Church. Everyone had some idea about what was out of date with the Roman Church and how it should be changed. There were advocates of allowing priests to marry; of translating the mass into vernacular languages; of instituting democratic governance through parish councils; of opening up dialogue with other religions; of accepting Protestant churches as fully Christian and therefore relaxing rules on ecumenical worship and mixed marriages. This was the liberals' agenda for the council. Their main hope, especially as far as the American bishops were concerned, was that the Catholic Church would take a clear and unequivocal stand for religious liberty. Monsignor John Courtney Murray was the Americans' erudite spokesman.

There was another group of bishops and theologians who had a different agenda in mind. This group held that what the church needed to do was not to open itself to the liberal currents of the modern world (though they agreed that was important) but to find a way to repair the demographic disaster, to reverse the exodus from the church of the poor and the working classes. The central challenge facing the church was how to escape from its reliance on the privileged strata of the society and become a church in which the poor once more felt at home. This goal for the council, as opposed to the "liberal" goal, was advocated especially by French theologians who had been influenced by the worker priest movement of the post-World War II years. The most eloquent advocate of this program among the bishops was Cardinal Lercaro, Bishop of Bologna, Italy. Cardinal Lercaro said on March 3, 1963:

> We will not respond to the truest and deepest demands of our time, nor to the hope of unity shared by all Christians if we treat the theme of the evangelization of the poor as one of the many themes of the Council. It is not a theme like others; in a way, it is *the* theme of our Council. If it is accurate to state, as has been done

several times, that the purpose of the Council is to conform the Church to the truth of the gospel, and make it capable of responding to the problems of our time, we can claim that the fundamental topic of this Council is, precisely, the Church as a Church of the poor.[2]

In the contest between those who supported a "liberal" agenda for the Vatican Council (including most Americans) and those who wanted to make the church the home of the poor, it was clear from the outset that the "liberals" would win, and they did. Despite some passing references to the poor in several of the documents, the real energy of the council went into the debates about ecumenism, reform of the liturgy, and religious liberty. The "up-to-date" qualities they succeeded in bringing into the church—such as vernacular services and ecumenicity—had been operative for decades in Protestant churches, and had failed in most of those churches to solve the problem of the loss of the poor. The council had succeeded in making the Catholic Church more attractive to the same educated middle-class people whose questions and criticism liberal Protestant theology had been trying to answer for over a hundred years. But Cardinal Lercaro's hope that "the center and spirit of all the doctrinal and legislative work [of the council would] be the mystery of Christ among the poor and the evangelization of the poor" was not fulfilled.

At Vatican II the Catholic Church decided to move into the modern world. But its decision came at a time when millions of people, many of them Catholics, were beginning to raise angry questions about what that modern world had done to make them hungry and workless. Vernacular masses were not the answer.

Cardinal Lercaro had gently warned his fellow bishops that if they tried to reform the church as the "sacrament of Christ" and to bring it into real contact with the modern world without facing the "mystery of Christ among the poor," they would founder. To that extent the council failed.[3] The fulfillment of the Cardinal's hope had to come not from the bishops but from the excluded masses of the poor themselves. It came from La Chispa and San Carlos, in the form of the basic Christian communities movement.

There is some disagreement on just how the basic Christian communities got started. Since they have become so significant in the current history of the Catholic Church, some Catholic historians naturally want to trace their origins to Vatican II. But given the failure of Vatican II to work out a theology that would enable the church to be present among those most alienated from it, it is hard to find any clear connection between the council and the spectacular rise of these communities in the past twenty years. Nevertheless, some observers think there is an indirect connection. The council did promote biblical studies, and this sometimes brought people together in small groups. Also, when John XXIII's encyclicals, especially *Pacem in Terris* and *Mater et Magistra,* lent papal legitimacy to the church's becoming an agent of justice, those involved felt the need to deepen this commitment through worship and theological reflection. Still, these changes mainly touched the middle class.

Some trace the source of the Latin American base communities not to the council at all but to the frightened, defensive strategies of a Catholic Church panicked by the spread of Protestantism and socialist-inspired trade unions in the late 1950s. It was then, during his last years as Pope, that Pius XII sent Father Lombardi to Latin America to save the continent from these two perils. Lombardi energetically swept across the continent setting in motion plans for "pastoral renewal." His strategy was based on the conviction that the Catholic Church in Latin America was suffering from an acute clergy shortage. There was no thought of changing the church into a church of the poor.

In some ways Lombardi's work was a success. By the early 1960s, "God's Microphone" had eighteen hundred "Courses for a Better World" under way in Brazil alone. The First Pastoral Plan of the Brazilian bishops, issued in 1965 and intended to last five years, speaks of basic Christian communities as already existing and views them as the main instrument through which the renewal of Brazilian Catholicism was to take place. The hierarchy also made use of the media by distributing transistor radios (some of them designed to receive only the diocesan stations) to rural areas. On Sundays, in small villages where no priest was available, people gathered around the radio to follow the mass celebrated by the bishop. In one diocese alone, Natal in Rio Grande do Norte, in poverty-stricken northeastern Brazil, there were already fourteen hundred such "radio communities" by 1963.

Meanwhile, another priest, Father Rossi, who was working in a parish in Rio de Janeiro, Barra do Pirai, met an old woman who complained to him that at Christmas the three Protestant churches were all brightly lit up and full of people singing carols while the local Catholic Church was dark and empty, "just because we had not succeeded in getting a priest." Rossi responded by starting a program to train lay catechists in every village to do everything permitted a lay person according to canon law. Local catechist and radio community movements merged and grew spectacularly. Soon the radios were shut off and, under the leadership of the growing number of lay catechists, people began singing, praying, studying the Bible, and discussing local political issues and problems. After ten years of rapid expansion, the first nationwide gathering of what by then were called *comunidades eclesiales de base,* or "CEBs," was held in Vitória, Brazil, in 1975. Representatives of several hundred CEBs appeared. The meeting had hardly begun when it became evident that the hierarchy had initiated something it could not control. Father Leonardo Boff, who attended the Vitória meeting as the adviser of one of the CEBs, writes that as it went on he knew that something "of unsuspected dimension" was taking place. "A church was coming forth from the people. It was a true *ecclesiogenesis.*"[4]

Subsequent events have supported Boff's observation. From a clerical attempt to shore up a rickety ecclesial apparatus a movement arose which has become a source of renewal of both Church and society in Latin America. CEBs, also called the "grassroots communities movement," had spread almost exclusively among the poorest people, either in rural villages or in the most crowded slums of the cities. Cardinal Lercaro's hope that the church would reincorporate the poor was being fulfilled in the base communities. The Vitória meeting demonstrated that the base communities were not particularly interested in countering Protestantism or socialism. From the outset, the local communities included people who did not consider themselves Catholics. The political activities they engaged in grew out of their reflections about their lives and departed from the line laid down by the papal encyclicals. By the late 1970s their critics were accusing the base communities of Protestant and socialist tendencies. It seems that in the early 1960s, before he was forced into exile, Francisco Juliao, the eloquent Catholic lay preacher and organizer of the Brazilian peasant leagues, was holding a rally in Pernambuco, a large agricultural town in the northeast. Some priests and nuns, worried about Juliao's socialist politics, had organized what they called a "White League" to oppose him. As Juliao spoke, on signal the church bells began to ring and the procession of Saint Peter and Paul began to wind its way through the area, sabotaging the rally.

Juliao, however, could not be deterred. Instead of retreating or fighting back, he preached to the people in the procession itself, telling them that if Peter and Paul were alive today they would not like their effigies carried around on people's shoulders but would join the peasants in their fight against hunger. As old-timers tell the story now, Francisco said, "We must remain together, hand in hand. Alone you are but drops; together we will become a powerful stream." He then signaled those at the political rally to follow him in *joining* the religious procession. They did, and the incident has become symbolic of the fusing of the base communities with the popular protest into what has become, in many places, a single "powerful stream."

The next critical moment in the history of the Latin American base communities movement occurred in February 1979, when the continent's bishops gathered in Puebla, Mexico, for their third assembly (the previous one had been held in Medellín, Colombia, in 1968). When it became known that the new Pope would come to Mexico and address them, the base community members throughout South America began to worry. As one observer said, commenting at the time on the speeches Pope John Paul II made in Mexico:

> At Puebla the base communities lived holding their breath until the last session, afraid of some unexpected Wojtylan statement in his alternating of "one hot and one cold" which characterized the papal speeches. The major risk was when John Paul II first arrived and was speaking before 4,000 invited guests "of class" in the Cathedral and stated that the church does not come forth from "the people or from any other rational category." Everyone knew that there was a club of bishops who were calling for a formal rejection of the base communities.[5]

The lay representatives of the base communities who were present in Puebla had reason to worry, especially those from El Salvador,

Guatemala, and other countries where military regimes were actively persecuting them. They knew from their own experience that even the slightest hint from the bishops that they did not approve them could have been seized upon by those regimes as an excuse to break them. Human lives were at stake.

There was also another reason. The Latin American base communities were too busy with issues of hunger and repression to get involved in an inner-Church debate with the bishops. Since the communities had not provoked a contest between local and hierarchical leadership, it was important that the small group of bishops who were out to "get" the base communities at Puebla not be permitted to do so. Otherwise, the CEBs would be drawn into a distracting ecclesiastical fracas.

It was well known that at Puebla there was a large minority of bishops, especially those from Brazil and from rural areas elsewhere, who were strong supporters of the base communities; and others, mainly from Argentina, who were strongly against them. Most bishops were undecided. Cardinal Baggio of the Roman curia, whose experience with the Italian base communities had made him their sworn foe, had placed Vatican delegates in key positions in the conference. To make sure that the base communities were dealt with before the new Pope could get around to forming his own opinion about them, Baggio assigned no fewer than five curial representatives to the Puebla commission that would deal with them. Then he made himself president of the commission.

Baggio was a careful strategist. He and his curial associates used the commission meetings to try to persuade the Latin American bishops to be cautious. Their base communities might seem innocent enough now, but they would go down the path of defiance and disobedience. A parallel and ultimately schismatic church was appearing which should be stopped. The commission prepared a negative report on the base communities to present to the full assembly.

At the same time, however, the bishops who had had favorable exposure to the base communities in their dioceses were quietly persuading their uncommitted colleagues that the communities should be roundly supported. The bishops did their work well. When the schema prepared by Baggio's commission disapproving the base communities was brought before the full assembly it was nearly unanimously defeated. Of the 288 votes cast by the bishops, only 25 were in favor. A substitute schema that explicitly supported the base communities was passed. A movement which had started as an idea in the minds of some priests but had gone on to become a "mighty stream" on its own had now survived an attempt by Rome to bring it back into line. The base communities, at least for the moment, had a new lease on life.

However mythical the stories of the early days of the base communities are, and however precarious their standing vis à vis Rome may be, everyone now agrees that they have become something which far exceeds anything their founders had in mind. As one writer says:

> . . . the intention of the church machinery in giving life to the base communities was to shake up the margins and move them toward the centralized power, [but] this time the mechanism went crazy and moved away from centralized power. The base communities bounced back against the . . . vertical structure and dismantled it.[6]

The origins of the base communities will probably always be shrouded in legend and dispute. Still, the emergence of these new forms of church life at the local level, first in Latin America and then elsewhere, constitutes a change in the Catholic Church that may be even more influential than the Vatican Council in shaping the future of Christianity.

10. Upending the Pyramid: Christian Base Communities in Europe and the United States

> The basic Christian communities mark a switch from a church resting on the point of a pyramid, in the person of a bishop or priest, to a church resting upon the base, the community of believers.
> —*Pro Mundi Vita*, September 1976

In October 1982 more than twelve hundred persons representing nearly all the close to three hundred Christian base communities of Italy met in Rome in the shadow of St. Peter's Basilica for their Sixth National Congress. Those in attendance included parish priests, nuns, and some worker priests. It was predominantly, however, a gathering of laity. The representatives talked mainly about how to become personally involved in action for peace and in social service to the needy. Colleagues from dozens of similar base communities in El Salvador, Poland, Nicaragua, Brazil, France, Belgium, West Germany, Holland, and Spain were also present. Speaker after speaker insisted that these communities were not a schism or a splinter group, but an integral part of the church, working, as one said, "to carry ahead a stalled renewal outlined in the Council twenty years ago." Another speaker, Giovanni Franzoni, encouraged the delegates to continue to work on the four "crossroads" at which the groups now found themselves. These four crossroads are those with the institutional Catholic Church, the various Protestant communities, the working class, and those persons in the society, like the handicapped, who suffer from being lost on the margins.[1]

The congress in Rome marked what one of the speakers called "ten years of grassroots communities." Such dating, however, can only be approximated. Genuine base communities, as opposed to standard parish renewal groups, probably began in Latin America. By the middle to late 1970s they were appearing all over the Catholic world. All began to combine the elements that had come to characterize the CEBs of Brazil: a more informal and participatory style of liturgy, often led by lay people; a rediscovery of the Bible, especially its prophetic and critical elements; vigorous engagement in the politics of peace, disarmament, and hunger.

The base communities of Europe differ markedly from those of Latin America, but in one respect they are similar. Both believe that information is power and that unless base communities all over the world set up alternative channels of communications they can easily become isolated from each other and die. The difference is that the Latin American groups have come to this realization only recently, while the European ones saw it from the start.

For the members of those European base communities who were aware of the fury of hierarchical disapproval, the news that their Latin American colleagues had actually been commended at Puebla came as a relief. It also aroused some anxieties. Would the Puebla decision now make the Latin Americans more dependent on the approval of the bishops? What would happen, some of the Europeans wondered, if someone in Rome, even the Pope himself, started a systematic effort to appoint bishops in Latin America who would destroy the base communities, or curtail their political involvement, or domesticate them into conventional parish renewal groups? The Europeans urged that communications links be set up between themselves and the Latin Americans. "It is absurd," wrote one member of an Italian base community, "for the Latin Americans and us to limit our knowledge of each other to filters such as the *Avvenire* and the *Osservatore Romano.*"

This preoccupation with information and direct international contacts points to the differences between the European and the Latin American base communities. Some of the differences can be explained by the fact that the European CEBs did not, as a rule, emerge from poor and working-class districts but from middle-class ones.

One of Italy's best-known base communities is "St. Paul's Outside the Walls," which claims over two hundred participants and was founded by Franzoni. Its social composition is typical:

> A good portion were definitely high school and university students; blue jeans, beards, and clean shirts identified them. Many of these were from the immediate parish, others from afar. The dress of some others—but especially the correct use of language, the gray hair, and the smooth, callousless hands—marked the presence of engineers, school teachers, a well-known anthropologist, managers of the state industry (with salaries in the four thousand dollar a month bracket, after taxes), and numerous employees of the state television company. These contrasted vividly with the few unemployed and blue collar workers in the meeting hall.[2]

Yet the St. Paul's base community exhibits the familiar combination of informality in worship, lay leadership, Bible study, and political engagement.

In 1980 there were reported to be 276 base communities in Italy; but they do not have it easy. Perhaps because the Vatican is closer, perhaps because some continue to meet in regular church buildings where the hierarchy can watch them more easily, Italian base communities have experienced much more opposition from the bishops than most of the Latin American ones have.[*]

The movement in Italy is also ecumenical, although, as in most parts of Latin America, there are so few local Protestants that the issue is not a burning one. Nonetheless, when the National Congress of Christian Grassroots Communities met in Verona in April 1980, Paolo Ricca of the Waldensian Theology Faculty of Rome was a featured speaker. The Waldensians trace their origins to the "Poor Men of Lyons," founded by Peter Waldo (a contemporary of St. Francis of Assisi) about 1178. Thus Waldensians antedate the Protestant Reformation by nearly four hundred years. Ricca startled his listeners when he said:

---

[*] In a widely reported case in 1969, the base community at Isolotto on the outskirts of Florence was forced to leave the church building by police dispatched by the bishop. The people have continued to meet every Sunday for the Eucharist in the open square in front of the church building, and it has now become one of the best known CEBs in Europe, in part because it publishes a news bulletin for and about European grassroots Christian communities.

One could say that Protestantism was born because Catholicism did not reform itself, at least in the sense in which the reformers intended it. One could even say that today Protestantism should not exist, and Catholicism should not exist as it is. We should have just one reformed Catholic church and that is all.[3]

In Holland, a country where there is hardly a slum to be found, the grassroots Christian community movement began with middle-class people and they continue to populate it. From the outset the Dutch base communities tended to be ecumenical, despite Holland's historic confessional separatism. In the 1960s some Christian movements began to focus on theological study and political action. Then in 1970 one of these groups, which called itself "Septuagint" (the name historically attached to the first Greek translation of the Hebrew Scriptures), circulated a "discussion paper on critical and active communities." The slightly stilted name of the group suggests that the Dutch base communities appeal to a somewhat sophisticated audience; the paper, which was intended to spark the creation of other such groups, was successful. By 1973 the first copies of an information letter for "grassroots groups and critical communities in the Netherlands" appeared, and on May 11, 1978, the first nation-wide congress of Dutch base communities convened in the Dominican church in Amsterdam.

The Dutch assembly was a historic one, corresponding to the one in Vitória, Brazil, in 1975. Representatives of forty-one groups were in attendance.

There are student communities, neighborhood groups and critical communities with five or ten years of growth in commitment behind them. Some have a strongly Catholic or Protestant background, others are ecumenical even in their composition. One group lays the emphasis on liturgical renewal, another on political action, and often the two emphases are closely bound up with each other. Joint study by the members of the group is central. The early stages of some groups have been marked by hard and painful conflict, whereas others have been launched in a more harmonious context. Among the groups there are some that have moved from dissatisfaction with the existing society, and a focus on injustice, to a new style of Bible reading, while other groups found in the Bible the inspiration to grasp the need for a critical standpoint with regard to society.[4]

Despite their heterogeneity, all the Dutch groups, both Catholic and Protestant, shared a conviction that the hierarchies of their respective churches were turning back from the spirit of renewal of the 1960s and early 1970s; a measure of freedom from institutional church control would be necessary if they were to fulfill what they called their "vision and program."

Nonetheless, the Dutch base community movement refuses to become another church. When it was invited to become an official member of the National Council of Churches of Holland the movement politely declined, saying, "It must be explicitly stated that the grassroots movement does not wish to be a new church institution. It is a cooperative association of groups of Christians critical of church and society—a linking of experiences, insights and forces aimed at our common priorities."[5] The decision not to accept this invitation meant that the leaders of the official Catholic and Protestant churches would have to continue to cope with them as "internal" sources of criticism and inevitably of conflict.

Like base communities everywhere, the Dutch communities are strong on Bible study. The study they engage in, however, is different from the inward-turning Bible discussions among some Protestants, for example. As the manifesto of the movement says:

> In the history of Christianity, the Bible has been used in different, mutually incompatible ways. It is often interpreted as a book full of dogmatic pronouncements, or as a description of a bit of factual history. As a rule, it functions as an instrument for the defense of the existing order. Within the grassroots movement, a break is being made—often with difficulty—with this way of handling the Jewish and Christian tradition. The rediscovery of the liberating power of the biblical writings is a central experience of people in the grassroots groups and critical communities. Many people find that their eyes are opened to the political and social dimensions of the biblical message by seeing injustice, oppression and social conflicts. Given this political broadening of awareness, new questions arise concerning church and faith.[6]

For these Dutch base communities it is precisely the challenge of their being largely middle class which they hope their study of the Bible will help them see in critical perspective. Hence they insist that the "reconciliation" of which the Bible speaks should not be used to gloss over conflict, that it requires a conversion on the part of comfortable Christians, a conversion that will enable them to open their lives to the mentally ill, the physically handicapped, the poor and other disprivileged peoples. These groups also emphasize the idea that biblical "salvation" means "an exodus in which all forms of injustice are left behind, as are all relationships whereby people are pressed into service and demeaned." In the early 1980s the Dutch base communities became actively involved in the European campaign against nuclear weapons.

Outside Latin America, perhaps the most impressive wing of the base communities movement is found not in a Catholic milieu but on the stern Lutheran soil of Communist-ruled East Germany. Writing in the liberal American Catholic journal *Commonweal* in 1982, the Irish journalist Peadar Kirby reports that the churches there have begun to provide something the Germans call *Freiraum*. The word signifies a "space," an open place for people to discuss their experiences candidly with each other, the only place in fact where it is possible to disagree publicly with the omnipresent state ideology.[7]

Consequently, Kirby says, many of the young people he met in cafes agreed that the churches are popular with the young. One priest even told him that some atheistic parents "are worried when they see their children going to church." This network of discussion groups now appearing in the churches is usually called the *Basengruppen* the exact German equivalent for *comunidades de base*. Nor is it surprising that these base communities provided the context out of which the Berlin Appeal calling for disarmament in both East and West Germany was issued in early 1982. The response of the East German government was the same as that of the repressive Latin American regimes. The Reverend Rainer Epplemann, a Lutheran youth pastor from East Berlin, whose name headed the Berlin Appeal, was immediately arrested and held for two days (a somewhat easier fate than that of many of his Latin American equivalents).*

* I worked in East Germany in 1962–63 as what was then called an "ecumenical fraternal worker." Already, something like the *Basengruppen* had begun. Small face-to-face

In the United States many different kinds of groups identify themselves as "base communities." Those emerging among Spanish-speaking immigrants are often derived directly from the Brazilian or Mexican models. They are frequently initiated by priests with years of experience in Latin America. There are other groups that are base communities only in name.

Kate Pravera, who has studied these different kinds of communities in the United States, divides them into three types.[8] Some result from efforts at parish renewal and are usually instituted by a hierarchy. Others boil up out of discontent with the existing church, with its social timidity, its unwillingness to give women equal leadership status (even when they are ordained), or its lack of receptivity to lay participation. These communities are usually organized "from below" or outside existing church institutions. Third, there are communities brought together around an experience of collective oppression or discrimination in the outside world. The last two types of groups can be organized from either above or below. But however they get started, their history suggests that, like the Latin American base communities, once begun they quickly assume a life of their own.

Pravera is skeptical about just how useful the Latin American model is for the United States. She has suggested that the combination of grinding poverty, popular religiosity, and political repression out of which the Latin American base communities grow does not exist to the same extent here. She might also have added that the religious pluralism in North America also makes the growth of base communities of the Latin American type unlikely here.

Yet there do seem to be possibilities for a U.S. equivalent to the base communities movement, as the current multiplication of small groups combining liturgical celebration, Bible study, and political engagement all over the country promises. The danger with these groups, Pravera feels, is that unless they consciously link themselves

---

Bible discussion groups were being organized all over the country, groups in which people sang and shared food and exchanged ideas about what was then an even more repressive political atmosphere. I recall meeting quietly with a small group of Christian schoolteachers who came together for weekly Bible study, discussion, and mutual encouragement in the apartment of one of them, which was located on Leninallee, the showplace street of the city.

to other groups outside their own immediate contexts, they can all
too easily become pious little clubs.

> Replete with lay leadership, democratic decision-making structures
> and even nonsexist liturgies, U.S. basic Christian communities
> that are not comprised of the poor or marginalized stand in danger
> of creating a parallel church of the prosperous.[9]

The churches are always evolving new institutional forms. The
question now, though, is whether the small Christian groups emerging in the United States will shake the church out of its lethargy or
allow themselves to be coopted into insulated enclaves while the
larger institutional church remains unchanged. The American base
communities will become a source of real reformation only if their
existence begins to confront the church with Cardinal Lercaro's theological issue of how to respond to "the mystery of the presence of
Christ in the poor."

11. The New Nuclei

> The single most important fact in the 20th century
> in Western society is the fateful combination of wide-
> spread quest for community—in whatever form,
> moral, social or political—and the apparatus of po-
> litical power that has become so vast in contempo-
> rary democratic society.
>
> —Robert Nisbet

St. Francis Xavier parish in Hyannis, Mass., is much different from
the parish it was twenty years ago when Pope John XXIII called for a
council to renew the church and make it, "in particular, the church
of the poor." Father Allen Deck believes that the changes one sees
in such a typical parish are attributable in large measure to the base
communities and the atmosphere they have engendered in the worldwide Catholic Church.[1] If he is right, then what happens in Hyannis
and in thousands of other "typical" parishes depends in part on what
happens to the base communities.

Something momentous is happening in the unfolding of these new
forms of Christian social existence. What we see appearing *in ovo* in
the base communities, for all their fragility and tentativeness, is a
new mode of Christian presence in the postmodern world. Neither
the Latin American base communities nor the European ones can be
copied elsewhere. Base communities must be rooted in a particular
locale. Still, eventually such base communities may well replace the
characteristic religious structures that developed during the modern
period—such as the exclusively "religious" parish, the national denomination, and the audience-style congregation.

The German Catholic theologian Johannes B. Metz believes

that in the base community movement, Christianity is undergoing a "second reformation" that will eventually alter the churches at least as much as the Reformation of the sixteenth century did.[2] In Metz's view the new reformation will affect Catholics and Protestants differently. For Catholics it will be a reclaiming of freedom, including freedom of dissent inside the church. But Metz, unlike his colleague Hans Kung, does not put so much emphasis on this "intraecclesial" freedom. He is talking not about the modern libertarian ideals of freedom ("liberty") but about the biblical idea ("liberation"). In this version, freedom comes from actual life chances, which are more often than not dictated by economics. For Protestants, Metz thinks, the new reformation will result in the recovering of "grace in the senses." By this he means that Protestants have tended to be suspicious of any concrete or historical "mediators," and have emphasized strongly that only the Word of God can channel such grace. This attitude can be seen in the characteristic Protestant reluctance to acknowledge that the bread and wine of the sacraments are themselves bearers of grace. Most Protestant theologies (with the important exception of Lutheran ones) have defined them more as reminders of a grace that, present only in the incarnation itself, or the preached word, does not suffuse earthly sensuous vehicles. Metz believes this is changing, that the Third World churches, especially those that have shaken off European and American domination as the base communities have, are already beginning to reclaim this freedom of dissent and this more "sensuous" idea of grace.

For Metz, there are two other important features of the present reformation in the Third World that prefigure the "postmodern" quality of this movement. The first is a new type of community which places the person within a skein of relationships that is neither an archaic tribal form nor a continuation of modern individualism. Sometimes described with the overused term "solidarity," the base communities demonstrate a style of common life which is chosen (unlike the premodern communities in which one simply found oneself). What is chosen is a corporate rather than an individual approach to the universal human problems of economic security, aging, finding a meaning in life. These communities are fashioning a new form of "life together."

The second feature Metz sees in the base communities is "the fusing of mysticism and politics." This sounds odd to the "modern" ear, for the separation of church and state—the severing of mysticism from politics—is regarded as one of the great achievements of the modern bourgeois world. The re-fusing of the two conjures up images of Caesaro-papism, inquisitors and theocracies, something the modern world is well rid of. For Metz, however, the most serious defect in modern theology is its "privatization," its consignment of God and religion to the inner subjective world of the individual. The task now is to "deprivatize" (Metz's word) the faith. Religion must be released from subjectivity, and theology needs to reclaim its political role. Metz believes that the base communities, because they do not exercise their political mission through the coercive structures of political domination, are demonstrating how to deprivatize the faith without going back to the *auto da fe* or the stocks and pillories.

We have already pointed out that despite many differences, there are certain structural similarities between the CEB movement and the recent emergence of media-based North American fundamentalism. Their main differences have to do with the formation and destruction of human community. Media religion in the United States does not encourage the development of small face-to-face communities. The CEBs do. Media religion appeals to a homogeneous mass audience of isolated individuals. It is consumer religion. It probably contributes to the uprooting of the already fragile small groups that exist in and around American churches by pulling people into the undifferentiated mass that makes up a television audience.

On the other hand, both media religion and the base communities seek to involve people in political activity. The base communities almost always begin by coping with small local issues, working their way slowly up to larger ones. They decide what to do by democratic discussion. Media religion takes on big national issues (which do have important local implications), but cannot by its nature encourage participatory decision making. The signal comes from the top down.

At first glance, it appears that both in the new high-tech media religion of the U.S. with its alliance to conservative political forces, and in the base communities of the Third World with their ties to unions and peasant cooperatives, the modern divorce of religion from politics is being left behind. But the similarity is only on the surface. By starting at the lowest level and drawing people into genuine decision making, the base communities are actually rebuilding the nuclei of a *polis* in places where it had never developed or where it had been destroyed by political repression. Media religion in the United States, on the other hand, is essentially depoliticizing. It is contributing to the further consumerization of politics, its transformation into the marketing of candidates and issues.

The attitude toward political participation in the base communities is premised on the belief that every human being is both *homo religiosus* and *homo politicus*. To sever the two is unnatural and produces a kind of schizophrenia in the individual, as well as the trivialization of faith and the abandonment of society to the toughest powermongers, untrammeled by spiritual restraints. Metz sees in the base communities evidence of a way to transcend the modern chasm between mysticism and politics without reverting to a Constantinian establishment of religion. The secret is that the base communities do not work from the top down, through the institutionalized power of the state and the ruling classes, but from the bottom up, as those without power gather and try to effect change.

Some people believe that Metz's hope for the base communities are inflated, maybe even a modern equivalent of the search for the noble savage. I do not think so. Metz realizes that CEBs cannot be imported into the "first" world, but he is convinced they can inspire changes in first world churches. Still, we need to ask how much of what he writes about them is the wishful thinking of a European who like so many before him wants to find salvation coming from the most oppressed. Is there any real evidence that the changes he is talking about are really taking shape in the base communities?

Arnaldo Zenteno, a Mexican priest who has studied base communities in his own country and in Brazil, takes a measured but hopeful view. Among his findings there is at least one that confirms Metz's vision of a form of church life which overcomes the modern dichotomy between mysticism and politics. In Mexico the most striking quality about the base communities in poor areas is that they depart from the modern, middle-class idea of the "religious parish."[3] The communities Zenteno studied there had features of local self-help, protest, or political action groups and were at the same time cells of

Christian worship and study. They pressured the government about such day-to-day issues as poor garbage disposal, inadequate bus service, or police corruption. They held study courses on family life, the causes of unemployment, and the marketing of handwork. They sponsored street theater and neighborhood festivals. In some ways they resembled a combination of an adult education center and a 1960s Saul Alinsky-style community organization. But unlike those groups, base communities do not hesitate to cooperate with other such organizations on a provincial and even national level or to plunge into partisan party politics at times.

In Brazil, as another observer, Clodovis Boff, reports, although the base communities have an enormous political potential, they have yet to make effective use of it. Other writers about Brazil agree that the power of the base communities there is still largely incipient but believe that when the military repression has run its course they may provide the seedplot for a new, democratic society there. They use the term *basismo* ("baseism") to suggest a popular, grassroots form of democracy they hope the base communities will someday help make possible.

But base communities, despite some similarities, are not just self-help clubs or community organizations or political cells. They are *"comunidades eclesiales,"* churchly congregations. They concern themselves with theological study and religious celebration; it is not possible to separate the "religious" from the "secular" dimensions of their work.

The religion of the base communities Zenteno studied is centered on making known the life and teaching of Jesus, especially the reign of God as a reality. As Zenteno says, this "religious" ethos of the base communities proclaims that the meaning of human life is to be found in the struggle for God's reign and that this has to do "not with a reign only in heaven or in the next life, but a reign of God that is arriving here and that becomes the utopia or the ideal for which Christians struggle and which they try to make real in a more fraternal and just life."[4]

The Mexican base communities also engage in what Zenteno calls "denunciation" or "prophetic criticism" of the "socially organized meaninglessness of human life." The mixture of political, existentialist, and religious language Zenteno uses provides an important key to understanding the base communities as incorporating elements of both the traditional and the radical critiques of the modern world. Often those who work with the base communities are just as concerned about the erosion of the "meaning of life" as conservatives are. But they see the sense of defeat, ennui, and directionlessness that the conservative commentators also decry as arising from political rather than metaphysical factors. They describe the interior life of base communities as a form of "testimony," a demonstration on a small scale of the quality of human and spiritual life that God offers to everyone. They stress especially the restoration of the sense of corporateness that is rebuilt in the base communities in the face of the emphasis on competition and individual success injected into traditional culture by capitalist values. "The new relations that are coming to be within the base communities," says Zenteno, "are an announcement of the new type of relationship we are seeking at a wider level."[5]

Theologically, the base communities look on themselves, to use Karl Barth's famous description of what the church should be, as "provisional demonstrations of what God intends for the whole world." The members of the base communities understand the political actions they undertake not as secular tactics, and not as steps toward a progressive construction of the Kingdom, but rather as "signs."

Zenteno harbors no romantic illusions. Both in Mexico and in Brazil he finds that utopian thinking about the reign of God sometimes introduces a perfectionist bent that prevents concrete political engagement rather than facilitating it.[6] He has noticed that as base communities grow, they face all the problems that other church groups (and all human groups) inevitably do. For example, those who originally constituted the community are reluctant to share leadership with newcomers. A special "insiders" language tends to develop. As they grow in numbers the communities lose some of their original simplicity. Zenteno found that although women take far more responsibility in the base communities than they do in most regular parishes, men still tend to dominate. He also found evidence of continuing clerical control, often quite subtle, in some base communities. Finally, he found, especially in Brazil, that the poverty and police harassment so many communities experience take their toll. It is not always true that faith thrives on persecution. People get tired and discouraged, even in base communities.

Still, despite their weaknesses and difficulties, Zenteno believes the Latin American base communities are the clearest sign of "the continuing presence of Christ in our history." He is particularly encouraged by the appearance of new networks of communication among the base communities, since this permits a horizontal form of information sharing to grow, one that does not rely entirely on the hierarchy.

It seems ironic that the explosion of Christian base communities has taken place mainly in the Catholic Church with its centuries old hierarchical tradition, while the advent of media religion has occurred in a culture marked more by the Baptist tradition of local congregational autonomy. But will the Latin American base communities be able to retain their egalitarian and participatory style? Will they fall prey to elitism or indirect clerical manipulation? Will they be reabsorbed into traditional hierarchical structures or kept as handy refuges, safety valves to draw off the energy of the dissenters and free spirits who will not stay in line?

One of the features of the base communities that makes it difficult to evaluate them is their ability to merge the protest rally with the religious procession. It is precisely this polyvalent quality which is their most significant characteristic. This is true of the Christian base communities of the non-Western world as well as those in Europe, where they merge subtly with peace, human rights, ecology, and other groups.

The polyvalent character of the base communities is also their most problematical feature. They are lively mixtures of elements drawn from the Methodist Bible class, the old-style Protestant prayer meeting, the local political club, and the Catholic mass. They are still searching for a form, a theology, and a world view. All this has sometimes led them into a set of attitudes and a style of political action that is more pre- or antimodernist than postmodernist. Base communities sometimes fail to make the necessary distinctions between the humanly destructive and unjust qualities of contemporary society that should be destroyed and those qualities that, however unappealing, are essential to a world as populous, complex, and interdependent as ours. This is one reason why Christian base communities in Europe and the United States should not try to emulate the ones in rural Brazil or Mexico. The justice and liberation that "first world" Christians are looking for must be created in their own milieu.

The basic Christian communities are still slender threads, but they represent the most promising response Christianity has made so far to the challenge of the transition from a modern to a postmodern world. Jürgen Habermas, the German social theorist, observes that the enlargement of the capitalist world market in the past two decades has brought with it the massive intrusion of rational administrative controls into more and more sectors of life.[7] The result is that people have begun to sense a threat from the system to the most fragile and vulnerable points of life. Activities that used to be more spontaneous, more lackadaisical, or more patterned by custom and tradition are now subjected to elaborate rules, standard procedures, and measurable techniques.

Nearly everyone senses the force of this invasion. Poor people, wherever they live, generally first feel the impact economically. Their small farms are devoured by vast agribusinesses. Their food costs more. They have a hard time finding work. Better-off people notice it not so much at the bread-and-butter level but as administrative procedures begin to disrupt family and neighborhood life. Thus base communities in different parts of the world will understandably fight back at different levels, depending on where they feel the pinch. But it is important nonetheless that both should realize the single world system of profit enlargement and consumer culture that is making itself felt in both situations.

Habermas' observation can help base communities learn how not to throw out modern complexity and personal responsibility along with administrative tyranny and injustice. With this distinction in mind, we can give hearty thanks for the appearance of face-to-face groups and counterinstitutions in postmodern life, because only such formations can counter the brave new world of what may be called "total administration"—a society in which the individual has no control over the economic and political forces that direct his or her life. At the same time we must continue to recognize that such staggering problems as the depletion of natural resources, the poison-

ing of the air, and the threat of nuclear annihilation are vast, complex, and global. They will not be solved by isolated local
communities alone.

Part of the way personal subjectivity emerged in modern life was
through the growth of complexity. Complexity, like density, is not
essentially bad. Density in a living space can contribute to its richness
and texture. Some of the most sought-after residential areas in the
world are among the most dense (Beacon Hill in Boston, Rittenhouse
Square in Philadelphia, Copacabana in Rio de Janeiro). The same is
true for complexity. Many men and women today thrive on it and
seek out intricate, many-faceted jobs and leisure pursuits. It is the
overlapping complexity of modern society that creates the interstices
and unforeseen possibilities that make a truly personal life possible.

It would be unfortunate if the promise of the base communities
were lost because the people within them mistook the intrusion of
total administration—which must be resisted—for the needed and
welcome complexity of a humane postmodern world. The two are
not the same. The confusion could sap the strength of Third World
base communities if they allowed themselves to become only tiny
islands of warmth and failed to address the systemic forces that determine how people live. The same thing could happen in Europe and
the United States if the base communities there became hypnotized
by a fantasy of Third World simplicity or failed to create new forms
of common life that nourish both complexity and spontaneity, both
face-to-face dialogue and global responsibility.

The Christian base communities today are weak and precarious.
One hesitates to hang such hopes on such frail vessels. Yet as these
new nuclei continue to spring up all over the world, one cannot
escape the feeling that the Spirit is at work.[8] People seem to be
reassembling the parts of human living that modernity succeeded so
well in segmenting. When one looks at the people among whom all
this is happening, it is hard to forget Jesus' statement to the disciples
of John the Baptist who also wondered whether they could allow
themselves to believe what they saw going on. In answer, Jesus told
them that the only proof he could offer that this was the work of God
was that "the deaf hear, the lame walk, and the poor hear the good
news."

12. Liberation Theology: The Voices of the Uninvited

But he said to him, "A man once gave a great banquet, and invited many; and at the time for the banquet he sent his servant to say to those who had been
invited, 'Come; for all is now ready.' But they all
alike began to make excuses. The first said to him, 'I
have bought a field, and I must go out and see it; I
pray you, have me excused.' And another said, 'I
have bought five yoke of oxen, and I go to examine
them; I pray you, have me excused.' And another
said, 'I have married a wife, and therefore I cannot
come.' So the servant came and reported this to his
master. Then the householder in anger said to his
servants, 'Go out quickly to the streets and lanes of
the city, and bring in the poor and maimed and blind
and lame.' And the servant said, 'Sir, what you com-
manded has been done, and still there is room.' And
the master said to the servant, 'Go out to the highways and hedges and compel people to come in, that
my house may be filled. For I tell you, none of these
men who were invited shall taste my banquet.' "
—Luke 14:16–24

Gustavo Gutiérrez, sometimes known as the father of liberation the-
ology, is a diminutive and bespectacled Peruvian Jesuit of Quechua
Indian descent. His first book, *La teología de la liberación*, subtitled
Política y salvación, was published in 1971. It was translated into

English in 1973 and became the single most widely discussed theological book of the decade.[1]

Gutiérrez does not like to be thought of as the founder of the most energetically contested current of theological thought to appear in this century. He insists that the theology of liberation is not all that important; that what is significant is the reality of liberation itself, of which both the base communities and the theology are servants and vehicles. "In the last instance," Gutiérrez writes in *A Theology of Liberation*, "we will have an authentic theology of liberation only when the oppressed themselves can freely raise their voices and express themselves directly and creatively in society and in the heart of the People of God, when they themselves account for the hope which they bear."[2]

Liberation theologians are in no sense antiintellectual. They are fiercely aware of the importance of ideas and they constantly emphasize the right of oppressed peoples to think for themselves. Still, one of the striking features of liberation theology is that its principal representatives attach as much weight to the historical process and the religious communities from which the theology arises as they do to their own theological ideas. There are at least two reasons other than mere modesty for this attitude. One is relatively modern, the idea of *theory and praxis;* the other is quite traditional, the notion of *consulting the faithful.*

Liberation theology is first and foremost a "theology of praxis." It is a style of theology, perhaps the first, based on the conviction that all human thought is a form of action. It grows out of the continuing interaction between reflection and engagement, theorizing and doing. It is not what is often called "applied theology," since this term suggests a package of ideas that is manufactured at one level for distribution at another. Liberation theology, although its practitioners utilize some recent European and American methods, was not invented in the libraries of seminaries and then disseminated to the masses. It is not a "trickle down" theology. These theologians spend hours with people who are engaged in difficult and dangerous political tasks, like those in La Chispa. Thought and action stimulate each other. Ideas grow out of reflecting on these tasks in the light of the Bible. They are then sifted and reinjected into the brew. What the members of the base communities are doing is the praxis of which liberation theology is the theory. The two go together.

The more traditional reason why liberation theologians pay so much more attention to the actual religious communities with which they are working than most other theologians do comes from the old Roman Catholic idea of *"consulting the faithful."* Consulting the faithful is part of the Catholic teaching that both Scripture and tradition are valid sources of theology, a tenet that in histories of dogma is often counterposed to the Protestant emphasis on *sola scriptura.*

The word "tradition" covers many things: libraries full of commentaries, stories handed on from generation to generation, the accumulated liturgical practices of the centuries. Luther and other reformers complained that tradition could become such an excrescence that it might obscure and disfigure the Gospel, and that only the Bible itself should be invested with final authority. In this sense, there is some element of "protestantizing" among liberation theologians. Their books and articles rely a great deal on biblical sources and rarely cite the early church fathers, Thomas Aquinas, or even more modern Catholic theological sources.

There is another sense, however, in which Latin American liberation theologians do reflect the importance of tradition, seen in their practice of "consulting the faithful." Here tradition means that theologians and church leaders are obligated to make themselves aware of what the people believe and do as an essential element in formulating theology. Catholic and Protestant theologians often fall into relying on other intellectuals as their principal interlocutors. "Consulting the faithful," at least in theory, builds an element of exchange into the process of theologizing. In the case of liberation theology, this exchange seems to operate in practice as well as in theory.

It has been argued that the single most informative and revealing element of any theology is its ecclesiology, its understanding of the nature and the function of the church. Any viable theology must include both a "doctrine" of the world and a doctrine of God, both a "logos" and a "theos" component. The difficulty is that one can examine either one of these elements in any theology without necessarily learning anything about the other or how the two are related. In studying an ecclesiology, however, both the "God aspect" and the "world aspect" have to be implicit, by definition. Examine any "doctrine of the church," however simple or complex, and you will discover an implicit doctrine of God and an implicit theory of the nature of the world.

The reason why its ecclesiology is the key to understanding liberation theology is that its view of the church is derived in considerable measure from the empirical reality of the base communities themselves. It is not an "empirical theology" in the sense of earlier Protestant theologies that tried to construct a system by analyzing individual religious experience. Rather, it is empirical because it is woven from both the ancient Catholic ecclesial tradition and from "consulting the faithful" in the base communities.

THE "WORLD" IN LIBERATION THEOLOGY

Liberation theology is biblical and experiential. The theologians get the "logos" or "world aspect" of their theology both from their direct experience in the CEBs and from the biblical and traditional teachings on ecclesiology. From these two sources they derive a picture of the world as the theater of both human and divine action; as a place where sin expresses itself in patterns of institutional injustice more than in individual failings; as a drama in which the principal actors are not single persons but corporate entities—classes and social groups. Liberation theology postulates a world marked by collective conflict, but moving toward both spiritual and terrestrial salvation in a kingdom of God that will eventually come to be "on earth as it is in heaven."

For the liberation theologians and the CEBs with which they work, the world or *logos* element of their ecclesiology is primary. This is a clear example of what theologians might call a God-and-history centered ecclesiology as opposed to an "ecclesiocentric" (church-centered) one. The church is one part of a total history and God is present in the whole, not just in the church. Christ tends to be seen as Lord and Liberator of history rather than merely as Founder of the church. The Spirit "blows where it will" and is not restricted to official channels. This world-centered theology has ancient roots. It is based on the biblical doctrine of creation and the stories of God's covenants with all of humankind as well as with Israel. It comes to classic expression in the sweeping theologies of history of the prophets Jeremiah and Second Isaiah, the poet of the Babylonian exile. It stands closer to the Augustinian than to the Thomistic strand of Christian theological history, which makes it at once thoroughly "Catholic" and also more available to Protestants, most of whose theologies are also more Augustinian than Thomistic.

In view of this history-centered approach, it is not surprising to find that when a liberation theologian like Gutiérrez turns his mind to the theological significance of the Christian base communities, he does not start by reviewing the ecclesial documents that have sought to promote them. Rather he begins by describing the actual history out of which they have arisen.[3] Lest this be misread as some kind of reductionism, however, we should see clearly that for Gutiérrez, God is working through this "secular" history both to liberate men and women and to call forth a new type of church life. The context is what he calls the "eruption of the poor" into the history of Latin America, the noisy arrival of those who for so long have seemed quietly absent. The immediate background of the rise of the base communities and of liberation theology is the disruption caused by the unwillingness of racial minorities, impoverished classes, and marginated cultures to remain quiescent. This upheaval is central to the recent history of Latin America. The base communities are made up of people who hear the gospel announcement of God's liberation from sin and bondage; who respond to that message in concrete historical actions; and who celebrate the story and the promise in sacrament, in song, and in political action. This all takes place, moreover, not within a special religious sphere, but in the day-to-day life of ordinary people in family, work, and politics.

Liberation theology shares with some other theologies the idea that the church is not primarily an institution. It is above all a "people of God" (a phrase that came into wide use in Catholic theology after the Vatican Council). As a people, furthermore, the church does not achieve its identity solely from its own origin and inner history (Gutiérrez would call this "ecclesio-centrism"). Rather, its identity arises in an "I-and-Thou" interaction with the world outside the church. Its identity is essentially "dialogical."

The eruption of the poor in their attempts to free themselves from poverty has not merely "set the stage" for the emergence of the base communities. Rather this eruption is an expression of the presence of God within the tumult of real human history. Nor is this eruption some passing "bad moment" (as those in power fondly hope), after which everything will go back to normal. It is not caused by small ideologically motivated elites (the "outside agitator" myth). It is a popular ground swell involving whole sectors and strata. People who once accepted their lot with fatalism and acquiescence now believe there are discernible reasons why they suffer, and they believe they can do something about it. This is a "conversion," a massive *metanoia* of thousands of people from a "kismet" view of history to a biblical one, characterized by freedom and agency.

It is significant to recall here that one of the most disturbing elements we found in the renaissance of political fundamentalism in the United States, especially in its popular variety, is almost the opposite of the theological shift in perspective now occurring in basic Christian communities. While a belief that the future is already determined, derived from a fatalistic reading of Daniel and Revelation, is paralyzing many North Americans, at the same time millions of Latin American Christians are leaving behind their traditional paralysis and coming to a conviction, also drawn from the Bible, that they are not fated to some already determined future, but can act and make a difference.

This passage from acquiescence to anger, from accepting systemic poverty to fighting against it, is what is meant by the "becoming present" of those formerly absent. It has also taken place in the church. The parallel is instructive. Just as the underdogs no longer accept with docility the place and function set for them in the society as a whole, so now they want to be in the church on their own terms, with their own language, customs, and hopes. It is also a question of how the church must change to make them full participants. If the media evangelists of the United States, whatever their intentions, are creating consumers of a mass-distributed religious commodity where small, participatory congregations once thrived, the base communities are doing the opposite. They are creating participation where once there was inertia.

The base communities are the vehicles for the hopes and demands voiced by newly militant Christians. Consequently they have aroused considerable hostility and suspicion. Some bishops and clergy, as became evident at Puebla, oppose them. Some critics go so far as to ask whether they are really authentic Christian congregations at all. For liberation theologians, this question of whether or not the base communities are churchly or Christian is the ecclesiological question par excellence. It can be answered only by going to the heart of what they believe Christian theology is about, namely "Christology," that aspect of theology which deals with how one is to understand the significance of Christ—to be authentically Christian a church should reflect and embody the life and ministry of Jesus Christ. It should be, to use a classical phrase, an "extension of the Incarnation." Since the base communities are suspect because they are made up of poor people who are involved in conflict, the question of whether they are Christian raises the question of how Jesus dealt with conflict and poverty.

Jesus' career was marked by conflict; he was crucified for pressing his confrontational approach to unjust power.[4] Most of the time the kind of conflict the base communities become involved in is nonviolent, though—in keeping with traditional Catholic theology —the use of violence as a last resort and in self-defense is not ruled out. The point is clear: If Jesus lived a life of conflict, the base communities can hardly be unchristian because they become involved in conflict too.

To liberation theologians the issue of poverty seems equally obvious. Not only was Jesus poor, but in the second chapter of the Epistle to the Philippians, as Gutiérrez points out, St. Paul writes these well-known words:

Let your bearing towards one another arise out of your life in Christ Jesus. For the divine nature was his from the first; yet he did not think to snatch at equality with God, but made himself nothing, assuming the nature of a slave. Bearing the human likeness, revealed in human shape, he humbled himself, and in obedience accepted even death—death on a cross.

—Philippians 2:5–8

Christ actually gives up the power and privilege associated with deity and becomes poor in order to reveal the love of God. The

Greek word used for this self-emptying of Christ is *kenosis,* and some liberation theologians argue that since it is the mode of Christ's own being in the world it should be a mark of any truly Christian church. It seems self-evident to them that since the base communities are made up almost entirely of poor people or those who side with the poor, the burden of proof of whether or not they are Christian rests with their critics.

An objection sometimes raised by liberation theologians outside Latin America, especially by women theologians who are aware of the subtle forms of domination that persist in many time-honored ideas, has to do with *kenosis.* This "self-emptying" image of God perpetuates a concept of condescension in which all the inherent dignity is on the divine side and none on the human side. God stoops to the essentially worthless human condition to bring salvation; but the idea of an inherent human powerlessness and dependency continues. When used as a source of ecclesiology, it is argued, *kenosis* says too much for the church and too little for the world.

Some women theologians insist that what they and other dominated peoples need to hear are not further assurances that deliverance will come from an outside source; rather, they need to hear that God can strengthen and undergird their own struggle, that they are not devoid of power or potential—as the sexist culture tells them they are—but are capable of standing up.[5] God is not the St. George who saves the hapless maiden by slaying the dragon, but the One who supports and inspires her to slay it herself.

Many biblical scholars believe the whole *kenosis* passage quoted above is in any case an earlier gnostic hymn which was incorporated into the Epistle either by Paul or by a later editor. This could explain why the passage reflects a theology—the gnostic one—which did not in fact put a high value on the creation, the world, or the earth. In its neoplatonic form this theology depicted God as the center of light with gradually diminishing rays extending out, ever less luminous and less real. It is not a theology that attaches much value to the grimy stuff of day-to-day history.

Furthermore, there is no evidence that Jesus was a rich man who assumed voluntary poverty, or that he divested himself of political power. Jesus seems to have come from an artisan family, to have drawn his followers mostly from the lower classes and the despised callings—fishermen and tax collectors. His choice was not to lower himself to an inferior station but to become a defender and representative of people with whom he already had close ties.

These are all good reasons why liberation theologians would do better to avoid using the theologically questionable notion of *kenosis* in interpreting the nature of the church, and of the place of the poor within it. It is true that in many areas of Latin America and elsewhere, members of religious orders have closed elite schools and moved into slum areas to express the "preferential option for the poor" that Latin American bishops called for at their conference in Medellín, Colombia, in 1968. But to suggest that "the church" divest itself of privilege in order to identify with the poor perpetuates the mistaken idea that the clergy is the church. It obscures the fact that those with whom priests and nuns live already are the church, the "people of God." Even the phrase one hears today, that "it is the poor who evangelize the church, and not vice versa," still contains a vestige of the old church-equals-clergy idea.

There is another facet to the dispute about whether the base communities can be viewed as authentically "churchly." Why would Catholics above all have any difficulty accepting both poverty and conflict as legitimate expressions of Christian existence? It would seem odd for a church that has canonized St. Francis of Assisi and St. Francis de Sales to be suspicious of Christians because they are poor. It would seem equally strange for a church that honors Joan of Arc and Louis IX of France (leader of one of the armies of the Crusaders) to rule people out because they engage in conflict. Somehow it seems to be the combination of poverty and conflict that upsets the critics of the base communities.

Liberation theologians deal with this challenge from a christological perspective too, but they also view it as a practical question: How are the poor to be present in the church? Can the "erupting poor" and not just the docile poor be in the church? Do they have to change, to stop being poor or stop engaging in conflict, to be in the church?

The key to understanding the view of poverty in liberation theology is that it is seen more in biblical than in medieval terms. In the Middle Ages poverty was often viewed as an "estate," a human condition which providentially provided the rich with an occasion for charity. In the Bible, on the other hand, being poor is always the result of oppression. It is not a fact of life but a result of the sin of the powerful, a cause for God's wrath, and God uses the poor to judge the rich. This means that accepting poverty as "natural" is a form of unfaith. It is exactly the fatalistic "kismet" idea which conversion to the biblical perspective calls into question. Going from acquiescence to resistance is a mark of conversion for a poor person in Latin America today. It is the outward sign of inner grace. "Conversion" becomes not just a matter of changing one's ideas but of changing one's life.

This tendency to deal with theoretical/theological questions as practical/policy issues characterizes the liberation approach to all the standard theological issues. It is "practical theology," not because it is developed in order to be "put into practice," but because it is a kind of thinking that is called forth when one faces issues that demand responsible choices. For this reason liberation theologians welcome the debate caused by the eruption of the poor in the church. It raises the question: If in order to assume the form of Christ the whole church everywhere must in some sense become poor, then just how is this going to happen?

One answer is being supplied by the base communities. In them, instead of asking how to help the church become poor, the poor are asking: How do we make the church our church? But it is the same question. A church which permits the erupting poor to take part in shaping it will change. It will "become poor," not in the self-emptying or condescending way the nonpoor might once have envisaged, but in the way the poor actually cause it to happen. In Latin America, the *kenosis* idea of the church is being undermined not by theological discussion but by a *fait accompli*.

This will mean big changes in churches. In Brazil it already has. Reports from some areas there say that in parishes where large numbers of poor people, with a base community approach, have begun to set the tone, some of the middle-class people who formerly attended have begun to drop out. A form of "class conflict" is appearing in the church. In writing about the ecclesiological significance of the base communities, Gutiérrez points out that for privileged people the church is often felt to be a place of rest and meditation. It is like one's home (or at least the modern middle-class ideal of the home), where one retires from the fray. For the "erupting poor," however, the church is more like a place of work, where there is a task to be done, a mission, a project to be undertaken. This attitude is some-times unfamiliar and threatening to more comfortable Christians. But the "pastoral question" is whether the poor should be required to leave this combativeness behind because it makes other people edgy. Liberation theologians think not. God welcomes the angry poor into the church on their own terms, rather than on the terms of those who have set the tone of church and society until recently.

There is another essential quality to "being poor." It is the recog-nition that being poor is not a matter of individual shortcomings or lack of personal gumption. Being poor means being a member of a class or race that has been made poor as an entity. This awareness of the collective quality of poverty and of its structural causes is also integral to being poor. Therefore, to require that the "erupting poor" put aside this awareness as a condition for being in the church is to require them to stop being poor (or to stop erupting) before they can become full participants in the church.

For liberation theologians this would be clearly illegitimate, similar to the requirement in some sectors of the early Christian church—a requirement St. Paul opposed—that converts should be circumcised before becoming Christians. In fact it would be worse than that. The Gospels are full of stories of how the wealthy must perform self-surgery before following Jesus. The rich young ruler had to "sell all." Zaccheus the tax collector had to make restitution. But the poor are always welcomed and favored just as they are.

The base communities are supplying an answer to the question Cardinal Lercaro hoped the Second Vatican Council would under-take: How can the church change itself not only to regain the lost classes but to be open to the classical Christian doctrine of the pres-ence of Christ among the poor? It is important to note here that the theological interpretations of the base communities we have just been reviewing are not recent *ad hoc* inventions or jerry-built justifi-cations. They hark back to an ancient belief, found especially in mystical theology, that it is through the weak and defenseless people of the world that Christ touches the strong.

Today the base communities of Latin America and their theology are under widespread attack from both inside and outside the Catholic Church. Few religious leaders today would argue that the poor should accept their lot as God's will and be thankful for the lesson of humility it teaches. Even fewer would be willing to tell poor people that their condition is God's just punishment. There are many, however, who, while conceding that the poor belong in the church along with everyone else, and even granting them the right to be discontented, would insist that group conflict or collective strategy in combating poverty are unacceptable. Conflict, especially between classes, seems to them unchristian, and if their interdiction of group conflict is enforced, then being Christian means accepting the notion that poverty is an individual matter to be surmounted individually.

This idea, however (Gutiérrez calls it *arribismo*, which might be translated "getting-ahead-ism"), is just as much a part of the middle-class ideology of the privileged as the need for collective action is a part of the world view of the erupting poor. This difference of opinion is an example of exactly the kind of conflict that the presence of the angry poor within the church will inevitably churn up. But to demand that poor people give up their understanding of how justice is achieved as the price they must pay to be Christian is an illegitimate requirement. As the poor who are already in the church gain some awareness of how their exploitation came about and how to end it, there will be much more class, race, and gender consciousness inside the church than the more privileged religious leaders of the past have been accustomed to.

"GOD" IN LIBERATION THEOLOGY

Ideas of God in classical Christian theology have varied widely and could be contrasted in a number of ways. One of the puzzles that has come up time and again is how one is to reconcile the love and mercy of an omnipotent deity with the suffering and injustice that persist in the world. If God is both loving and all-powerful, why are innocent children allowed to starve? Some theologians have postulated an all-powerful God who allows for suffering and injustice for reasons that —although mysterious now—will one day be clear. "Farther along," as the old song goes, "we'll understand why." Others posit a God who is not all-powerful but finite, perhaps self-limiting, perhaps moving toward omnipotence. Besides being substantively different, the various Christian doctrines of God that have appeared over the centuries have been based on different mixtures of biblical images, philosophical ideas, and the experience of the people who invent the doctrine. The sources liberation theologians use to construct their doctrine of God goes a long way to explain some of its most striking features and how it answers this classic dilemma.

Philosophically oriented theologians have often been the ones who postulate an all-powerful (omnipotent) deity. This is a quality of God that has come to be accepted in most Christian theologies: "I believe in God the Father Almighty." In recent years, however, especially during the period of the decline of the churches' temporal power, another image has appeared both in popular devotion and in sophisticated theology: the suffering rather than the all-powerful God. The Sacred Heart of Jesus, pierced with a sword and bleeding tears, became a favorite Catholic devotion during the nineteenth century. The Protestant theologians Dietrich Bonhoeffer and Jürgen Moltmann, both influenced more by biblical than by philosophical currents, wrote in the twentieth century about a God who suffers with people in the world.

The God of liberation theology, however, is neither all-powerful nor a powerless sufferer. Rather, God is portrayed as one who must contend with strong and stubborn evil. God suffers, but in confrontation, not in acquiescence. God is *el dios pobre*.

This picture of God draws both on the day-to-day experience of the erupting poor in the base communities who have to confront powerful corrupt structures, and also on the biblical portrait of God as the vindicator of the weak. However, this is not a totally new doctrine of God for Latin Americans. There are antique elements in Spanish and Latin American folk piety that undergird it. Santiago (St. James), the national saint of Spain, was once believed to return to earth to defend his people when they were in trouble. The walls of the Prado are hung with canvases showing him locked in hand-to-hand combat with the Moors. Other saints are revered as patrons who use their strength and influence to protect those who count on them. In the theology of the base communities this folk belief is transposed into that of the biblical God who sides with the weak against the mighty and defends those who have no other defender.

Liberation theologians base this image of God on the biblical revelation and on the actual experiences of the poor people with whom
they work in the slums and villages. The principle source is the
portrait of Jesus on the New Testament gospels. Those gospels portray Jesus neither as an omnipotent superman nor as a powerless
victim who accepts docilely the injustices inflicted on his people.
Rather, he is depicted as a man who entered into a fearless confrontation with the corrupt political and religious authorities of his day
and whose suffering was the consequence not of compliance but of
resistance to evil. For liberation theologians, the whole career of
Jesus, not just his death, reveals the character of God, and his crucifixion is the direct result of his risking opposition to the powers of his
day. As in its ecclesiology, the doctrine of God in liberation theology
leans very heavily on the life and teaching of Jesus Christ.

One interesting if unintentional by-product of this emphasis on
the biblical and experiential bases for the doctrine of God is that it
makes liberation theology more accessible to Protestants than some
other Catholic theologies are, since Protestant theologies are often
more biblical and experiential. Still, liberation theology continues to
be viewed with great suspicion by most Protestant theologians. Their
criticisms vary but they tend to fasten on what they regard as a
"politicizing" of the church, the loss of its transcendent dimension,
a careless confusing of the sacred with the secular. Many of these
criticisms focus not on the liberationist idea of God as such (though
there is some of that) but on what this theology prompts the church
to do, namely to become a partisan participant in earthly controversy.

We have seen that embedded in the ecclesiology that liberation
theologians have developed in their work with the base communities
one can find the elements needed in any theology. These include a
view of the nature of the contemporary world (its *logos*) and of the
nature of God *(theos)*. These theologians see the current world as
characterized by the conflict of corporate entities (classes, cultures,
races); and they see God as a participant in these conflicts on the
side of the weak. Both elements are important. Without their corporate-conflict view of the world, the members of the base communities would settle for the individualistic "get-ahead-ism" of the
dominant culture. But even if they accepted a conflictual view of the

world, they would still not dare to act were it not for their belief in a God who has a predilection for the poor. The odds against them would seem too great.

Liberation theology is not just a skillful theological rationale for whatever the base communities do. Liberation theologians do not simply write in four-syllable words what local base community members say more simply. They do not romanticize the folk theology of the poor, which in any case often contains a large dose of the dominant religious system of the society. Still, they do not dismiss the religion of the base communities as irrelevant or naïve either. They insist that just as the higher classes have the right to sort and systematize their ideas, so do poor people have the "right to think," and the results of such reflection cannot be determined or decreed in advance. Indeed, there may be points at which the "folk theology" of the base communities calls the dominant theologies into question. We will return to this issue later in our discussion of the relationship between liberation theology and various forms of traditional and folk religion.

13. But Is It Really Theology?

> Liberation theology is obliged to juxtapose the disci-
> plines that are concerned with the past as well as
> those that interpret the present in order to under-
> stand the word of God as a real message addressed to
> us in the here and now. . . . It does not allow the
> theologian to set aside lightly—as academic theology
> often does—the great problems of today . . . on the
> pretext that they belong to other fields and disci-
> plines.
>
> —Juan Luis Segundo
> *The Liberation of Theology*, 1976

Our description of liberation theology has shown that it cannot be
adequately understood as merely one more school of thought. It cannot be usefully evaluated by subjecting it to the scrutiny of the canons
of modern theology since it is precisely those canons which liberation
theology calls into question. Nonetheless, it is evident that liberation
theology does function in some ways as a theological movement.

The American Roman Catholic theologian David Tracy attempts
in his book *The Analogical Imagination* to provide an evaluative model
which can be applied to all theologies, including liberation theology.[1] Tracy suggests that any theology must deal with three different audiences. It must speak to the *churches*. It must speak to the
academy, the community of scholars in which methods, modes of
discourse, and the internal logic of a position are examined. Finally,
any theology must speak to the *public*, to those who stand outside
both church and academy.

As for "speaking to the churches," little needs to be said. Liberation theologians are severely critical both of what they call avant-gardeism, a tendency of religious leaders to derogate the opinions and abilities of ordinary people and to arrogate all leadership to themselves; and also of what they term "religious populism," the endowing of the poor with all wisdom and skill, a romantic overestimate of what impoverished and often brutalized people are actually capable of. Whatever legitimate criticisms may be directed toward it, liberation theology is a "church theology" par excellence, emerging as it does from base congregations vigorously engaged in mission, and informing the activities of these ecclesial groups on a day-to-day basis. What we need to find out, however, is whether in the two areas of the academy and the public realm liberation theology also complies with Tracy's criteria.

THE ACADEMY

When liberation theologians work with the relatively unsophisticated campesinos and *favela* dwellers of the base communities, they can use a language of faith that suffuses the cultures of the whole Latin American continent. But like other educated people, they inhabit a second world as well. They also live in the global fraternity of those who read and write and ponder abstract ideas, and this is a world whose language and assumptions are modern. When liberation theologians drive away from La Chispa and put on ties and jackets to attend professional conferences or offer lectures and seminars at universities, they need to shift gears. Granted that liberation theology is the critical expression of the faith of the basic Christian communities, how does one know whether it is accurate or authentic? Who says God favors the poor? How do we know there is a God? If there is, how does one choose between the liberation theology understanding of the *dios pobre* who is present with the poor as they struggle, and some other idea of God? Why should one choose a corporate-conflict model of the world rather than, say, the "homeostatic" one favored by many sociologists, in which a self-correcting stability, rather than conflict, is the norm?[2]

Trying to answer these questions moves the discussion a big step away from the terrain with which the liberation theologians are familiar. It moves closer to the preferred turf of the more academic North American and European theologians. Yet it is important to try to understand how the liberation theologians defend their positions. Let us look first at how they establish their model of society, since that is the issue on which social scientists are so divided, then at how they defend their idea of God.

1. The theologians of the base communities suggest that no social theory or world model is free of ideology, that churches and theologians like everyone else live and think inside history with all its influences. But unlike some social theorists, the liberation theologians do not decry this. They do not reject "ideology" as an epithet. To be successful, they say, any social movement needs the admixture of values and empirical data and interpretations that we call "ideology," so they argue that ideology is dangerous only when it is not recognized. Therefore one chooses the theory that works best, that helps poor people move toward the goal of justice by focusing their energy and organizing their thinking. These considerations lead them to prefer the corporate-conflict model.[3]

These theologians point out that whatever else one may say about the world depicted in the Bible, it is hardly homeostatic. It seethes with corporate conflict: the Israelite slaves against the Egyptians; the Babylonians against the Israelites; the Persians against the Babylonians. The prophets confront the kings; and Jesus and his followers live in constant conflict with priests, Pharisees, and Romans. Liberation theologians choose the corporate-conflict model on theological, empirical, and political grounds.[4]*

The idea that the Bible reveals exclusively "religious" truths and teaches us nothing about human life in history is not self-evident, especially if one keeps the centuries-long sweep of biblical interpretation in mind. Seeing the Bible as an exclusively "religious" authority carries "modern" and "liberal" overtones, derived from the nineteenth-century intellectual concordats. Even if one does not want to defend the quaint fundamentalist notion that the Bible re-

---

* To most academic theologians and nearly all social theorists this choosing of a world model on the basis of utility, analysis, and revelation sounds bizarre. This is just not the way it is done. Most sociologists try to minimize the ideological element in their analysis and some claim it can be eliminated almost completely. Most theologians rely on sociologists to provide models of society and do not accept the idea that the world views of the Bible should enter in.

veals the date of creation, this still does not require the liberal retreat
to the position that the Bible is valuable only for its "spiritual ideas."
Cultures influenced by the Bible have a different feeling for history
than those shaped by other religious traditions.[5] The liberation theology argument that a Christian theology's picture of the *world*, not
just its picture of God, should reflect a biblical perspective has much
to recommend it. It is analogous to the conservative Christian argument we discussed earlier—that faith must have a content. It is also
reminiscent of the point made by Fritjof Schuon that we suffer in the
modern world both from an unduly constricted view of what faith is
and from a tragic severance of faith from intelligence. Even in recent
philosophical speculation about the origin and nature of the natural
world, traditional religious views are no longer ruled out routinely. *

2. There is also a solid basis for the liberationist doctrine of God.
In February 1980, a group of Mexican theologians published a paper
entitled "Dios y El Hombre: Una Historia" (God and Man: A History). "We are using," they wrote, "a method of biblical-theological
reflection which is being worked out here in Latin America . . . a
process of reading, reflecting, searching, coming closer, such that
already we consider it irreversible." What is specifically Latin American about this method, the theologians wrote, is that it begins with
concrete history—with the here and now—and therefore it is not
"conceptual reflection" but "experiential reflection." Some, they
continued, have criticized this method for being "novel," perhaps
because it breaks out of an older, more deductive method of reflection
derived from the Greek and Latin tradition. But

> . . . it appears to us that this criticism denies and obscures the
> novelty [*novedad*] of God in history. The method of ancient Israel,

---

* The imminent historian of science Stephen Toulmin gives his book *The Return to
Cosmology* the intriguing subtitle "Postmodern Science and the Theology of Nature."[6]
Toulmin asserts that modern science's pictures of the world must be understood as having
a cosmological and even theological significance. He further argues that this means it is
not possible any longer for scientists simply to ignore religious cosmologies as unscientific.
Toulmin also believes, correctly I think, that one cannot disassociate conflicting cosmologies from the rise and fall of rival social movements. All of this suggests that the
"modern" theological attempt to turn over views of the cosmos and of history to natural
and social scientists may have been a mistake, and that furthermore the mistake was being
discovered by the secular thinkers before it came to the attention of most modern theologians.

now being reappropriated in Latin America today, was an inductive one: from a series of actions and results which are inexplicable on a human basis alone, one discovers a God who is involved in constant salvific activity . . . a God who cannot be manipulated or encased in concepts and who overflows [*desborda*] the human imagination.[7]

Also, in arguing for their understanding of God, liberation theologians see experience and the Bible as two sources in constant interaction.

Looking at the method from a North American perspective, one recognizes that Latin Americans use biblical and experiential sources in a distinctive way. They do not mean the individual "religious experience" that William James describes in his famous book *The Varieties of Religious Experience*. They do not even mean mystical insight or ecstatic ascent. They mean the experience of the presence of God in the pain, anger, joy, and hope of disinherited peoples and in the effort to confront the causes of injustice wherever possible. "Experience" is not something esoteric, but is tangible and ordinary. It is "praxis."

The distinctive feature of liberation theology's use of the Bible as a theological norm is related to its use of "experience." Liberationists are not fundamentalists in their approach to Scripture. They are willing to make use of historical-critical tools. But unlike most historical critics they do not believe that the meaning of a biblical text has been established once the exegetes agree on what it says (as liberal Protestants often do), or that its authoritative meaning is decided by the churchly magisterium (as many Catholics hold). Rather, they contend that the most reliable guide to its meaning is seen in what the text means to the poor.[8]*

Liberation theologians, working closely with the base communities, defend their positions with a judicious mixture of biblical interpretation, social analysis, and careful attention to human experience. Again, from the point of view of some North American and Euro-

---

* Ernesto Cardenal has devised an inventive method for determining this "poor interpretation." He simply tells the biblical stories to groups of peasants, most of them illiterate, and then tapes the discussion the stories elicit. He has published three volumes of this unique commentary on the New Testament under the title *The Gospel at Solentiname*.[9]

pean theologians, this is still not enough. It stops short of that form of discourse some scholars call "metatheology." Metatheology raises such questions as why either the Bible or experience should be considered a theological norm at all, and examines the nature of the arguments that could be used in such discussions.

For good reasons, liberation theology has not yet fully developed this metatheological level of thought.[10] One reason is that, as we saw earlier, liberation theology is basically "pastoral." It is meant to guide, criticize, and clarify the thinking and action of churches. It is not designed to persuade skeptics or convince intellectuals. Also, historically, liberation theology in Latin America has arisen on a continent where critical thought has focused more on the misuse of Christianity than on skepticism. The basic tenets of Christianity are a part of the cultural fabric. At a certain point theological arguments can appeal to the consensus of the Catholic culture without needing to move to yet another level of abstraction. This covert appeal to cultural consensus cannot be carried off successfully by Christian liberation theologians in Asian countries, where Christianity constitutes a small minority. However, where the appeal to cultural consensus is not possible, liberation theology has still not turned to a metatheological level but has tackled the problem by an appeal to praxis. We shall return to this pressing issue when we examine the promising relationship between liberation theology and religious pluralism.

PUBLIC THEOLOGY

We have seen in our discussion of the reemergence of political fundamentalism in the United States that its leaders want it to be a decidedly public theology, that it already exhibits an ambitious effort to exert an increasing influence on the larger body politic. Is there any comparable strategy or intent visible in the work of liberation theologians or the base communities movement? The answer is that there are at least two such strategies. Both identify the base communities themselves, not theologians, as the means by which this theology "speaks" to the public realm.

The first strategy suggests that exposure to the base communities will not only inspire and motivate people but will give them the kind of democratic participatory experience they will come to want and demand in society at large. This strategy also includes the possibility that the base communities can act politically, as Christian groups, to advance the cause of justice.

The second strategy holds that although the base communities are indispensable both as vehicles to enable Christians to be present within movements of popular protest and as the places where the mystery of the presence of Christ in the poor is confronted, they should not expect to be the main agents of social change. It will be the angry poor who will be the main vehicle for changing the world. The churches will become agents for such change only when they work with and for these people.

This question of the proper role of liberation theology and base communities in the public realm is raised in an indirect way in discussions over what is really "base" about the communities. The U.S. Catholic theologian Rosemary Ruether, for example, writes:

> Base communities imply a reversal of the hierarchical concept of the church. The church arises from the base, from the local gatherings of the people. Members of base communities meet as equals, engaged in learning from and ministering to each other. . . . This is not possible unless such groups are self-defining, not agents of control from above. [11]

Gutiérrez, however, sees it somewhat differently. The issue, he says, does not have to do with a hierarchical versus an egalitarian idea of the church. It is not a battle "between base and cupola," which would be an intraecclesiastical question, one that is not of much interest to the members of Latin American base communities. "The primary point of reference for understanding 'base,' " he says "is, strictly speaking, outside any ecclesial characteristics; it has to do with the world within which the church is present and in which it gives testimony to the love of God." [12]

Gutiérrez and the other liberation theologians recognize that the base communities are frequently more communitarian than other forms of church life, that especially in big impersonal cities like São Paulo and Monterrey, Lima and Quito, they offer a place where

displaced and rootless people support each other and find some identity. One theologian, Roberto García Ramirez, has written a
thoughtful article analyzing the base communities as "primary
groups."[13] But the liberation theologians insist emphatically this is
not the main point. Going back again to his practice of placing
ecclesiology within the theology of history, Gutiérrez suggests that
what is "base" about base communities is that they are the churches
of those people who are at the bottom of society. They are congregations of those attempting through their collective action not just
to rise individually but to change the system which perpetuates top
and bottom patterns. They are "base" because they are at the bottom
of the world, not the bottom of the church.

An intriguing question is why the Latin American theologians not
only do not put much emphasis on the egalitarian aspects of the base
communities (while Europeans often do), but even warn outsiders
against injecting this perspective. Part of it may be that many of the
leaders and organizers of the base communities are priests, and that
many bishops also vigorously support them. Another reason, however, is that many Latin Americans view the anticlericalism that
often appears in the Italian, Dutch, and American base communities
as a residue of the modern "progressive" bias of liberal ideology. In
their combination of traditional and radical elements into a "postmodern" synthesis the Latins find that neither clericalism nor anticlericalism holds much interest. In their insistence on the "worldly"
definition of the "base," the Latin Americans are projecting a decidedly "postbourgeois" worldview, one that recognizes class conflict
(rather than, say, science or education or reform) as a principal
mechanism of social change.[14]

The idea of a world in which justice must be sought collectively,
and where class conflict is accepted, will not sit well either with the
conservative religious critics of modernity or with most liberal theologians. Even those who accept the idea that the church has a mission for justice prefer conciliatory modes of operation and feel that
while individual Christians may involve themselves in partisan
causes, churches as collective bodies—and this would include base
communities—should not.

How do the liberation theologians speak to Tracy's public realm?
In one sense they are skeptical of the concept of a "public theology"

as it is now practiced. They distrust the way liberal theology has appealed to the ruling elites in attempts to persuade the dominant classes to alter this or that policy. Rather, they prefer to communicate with the people at the bottom who believe change comes not through persuading the elites but through a structural transformation brought about from underneath. Liberation theologians do not accept the usefulness of carrying on a conversation in a society whose institutional patterns of domination thwart and distort the possibility of such a discussion. Rather, they can be understood as trying to create the kind of postmodern society in which genuine public theology would become possible again.

It is evident that when one examines liberation theology in light of the revealing questions Tracy asks about any theological school or option, it can stand on its own two feet. It can engage the church, the academy, and the public realm. But somehow, after this case has been made, it seems not quite to have caught the inner essence of what liberation theology is about after all. One is reminded again of Gutiérrez' warning that what matters is not liberation theology but the base Christian communities and the promising but precarious historical process of which they are a part. What matters is the coming to awareness of millions of people who once believed the squalor they lived in was decreed by fate or willed by God but have now begun to know themselves as coworkers with God in the shaping of the future: "What matters is not theology, but liberation."

14. Christian Radicals and the Failure of Modern Theology

> There remains an experience of incomparable value.
> We have for once learned to see the great events of
> world history from below, from the perspective of the
> outcasts, the suspects, the maltreated, the powerless,
> the oppressed, the reviled—in short, from the per-
> spective of those who suffer.
> —Dietrich Bonhoeffer
> *Letters and Papers from Prison,* 1944

> When the wretched of the earth awake, their first
> challenge is not to religion but to the social . . .
> order oppressing them and to the ideology supporting
> it . . . and since religious elements are present in
> these ideologies, religion must be criticized. . . .
> Given that fact, the first question cannot be . . .
> how are we to talk about God in a world come of
> age, but how are we to tell people who are scarcely
> human that God's love makes us one family.
> —Gustavo Gutiérrez

The failure of modern theology is that it continues to supply plausible
answers to questions that fewer and fewer people are asking, and
inadvertently perpetuates the social bases of oppression. Radical
Christian theologians see people not as believers or nonbelievers but
as exploiters and exploited, a category they contend is far more biblical. Liberation theology is part of a larger social process, the "awak-

ening of the wretched of the earth." Like fundamentalism, liberation theology and the base communities must be seen as one important sector of a much larger historical movement. The legend of Francisco Juliao and the beginnings of the base communities portrays them as mixing in with popular protest movements as part of "a single stream." The moment has now come in our discussion to look at liberation theology with reference to this wider history, and to ask, as we did of the religiously conservative critique of modernity, just how credible it is and how useful it might be in the formation of a postmodern theology.

Understanding liberation theology requires a certain act of imagination, a willingness to look at familiar happenings and figures in a different light, a readiness to recognize that those who are heroes for some will be villains to others. Liberation theology is part of a larger history of protest. The difficulty North American and European theologians have in understanding it has less to do with its ideas than with the moral and historical assumptions on which the ideas are based.

A good example of the shock effect of liberation theology's view of history "from the underside" can be seen in its treatment of the standard heroes of Western emancipatory thought, such as John Stuart Mill. In *On Liberty*, published in 1859, Mill insisted that the state has no moral right to regulate individuals so long as they do no harm to others. The essay is still honored as an affirmation of individual freedom not only from the state but from the tyranny of the majority as well. What is often overlooked about the essay, however, is that Mill explicitly exempted certain groups and classes of people from his dictum. Children, for example, must be protected from themselves until they reach the age of discretion. But, he continued, so also must "barbarians," for whom "despotism is a legitimate mode of government . . . provided the end be their improvement." Is Mill voicing a nineteenth-century political equivalent of the Big Gap theory of the difference between "us" and "them," one that excuses the deprivation of that liberty he was seeking to defend? Mill's words are clear when he writes:

Liberty as a principle, has no application to any state of things anterior to the time when mankind have become capable of being improved by free and equal discussion. Until then, there is nothing for them but implicit obedience to an Akbar or a Charlemagne, if they are so fortunate as to find one.[1]

When one recalls that this text appeared the same year as Darwin's *The Origin of Species,* which for social philosophers also provided an intellectual rationale for declaring some nations and races more ad-vanced or developed than others, the point becomes apparent. From the perspective of the "barbarians," both *On Liberty* and *The Origin of Species* supplied additional weapons to the intellectual armory of domination. Paradoxically, the emancipation of Europe—or better, of some of the people of Europe—proceeded on the basis of the same ideas that contributed to the oppression of other peoples. Among those who were not benefited by these ideas are precisely those people from whom the radical critique of the modern world and its theology is now emanating.

The radical critics' attack on what they often suggest was a kind of theological sellout to the ideology of domination can hardly avoid upsetting most modern, "liberal" theologians, who have devoted whole careers to the attempt to interpret Christianity in terms of the modern world view. Some read the radicals' critique as an overstate-ment. What the radical critics sometimes appear to overlook in their assault on the alleged spinelessness of modern theology is that mod-ern theology and the bourgeois classes with which it was allied were once liberating forces. There was a time when they carried some of the same emancipatory élan the base communities and liberation theology do today. It could be argued, in fact, that "bourgeois" the-ology foreshadowed liberation theology.[2]

Ernest Renan is one of a number of theologians who can be cited as examples of how certain strains of modern liberal theology pre-figured the concerns of contemporary liberation theology. Renan's bestseller, *The Life of Jesus,* published in 1863, is the epitome of liberal biblical studies and became a favorite among bourgeois anti-clericals throughout Europe.[3] Still, despite (or because of) its modern qualities, Renan's book could almost serve as an introduction to one of the recent radical "biographies" of Jesus by Latin Americans like Leonardo Boff or Ignácio Ellacuria. Renan interpreted Jesus as a "democratic chief" who took the gospel to the poor and whom the unwashed multitudes recognized as their spokesman. The established powers, wrote Renan, have never entirely recovered from the crucifixion. "How," he asked, "can they assume infallibility over the poor when they have Gethsemane on their conscience?"[4]

The radical critics should see in Renan a forebear, not an enemy. These critics live in Latin America, where a highly traditional church and culture once sheltered the masses from some of the destructive currents of modernity, and where significant segments of that same church now support their liberation; therefore they sometimes overlook the fact that the churches of the *ancien régime* with their retinues of obedient theologians were often formidable obstacles to liberation in the Europe of a century ago. Edgar Quinet, a radical anticlerical French historian of the middle nineteenth century, realized this and saw himself as a reformer, secularizing Christianity by stripping it of its feudal encrustations and bringing it into the service of freedom. "Voltaire," he wrote, "is the destroying angel sent by God against his sinful Church. . . . He strikes, reviles and overwhelms the infidel Church, with the weapons of the Christian spirit. . . . You seek Christ in the sepulchre of the past; but Christ has left his sepulchre . . . he is alive, he is incarnate, he descends into the modern world."[5]

Christ descending into the modern world to judge the church! The theme is an appropriate one for a guerrilla poster or an Orozco mural. The spirit is hardly that of spineless compliance. What the radical critics frequently fail to see—because they are understandably focused on the calamitous impact that European modernity came to have on their part of the world—is that at a certain point it was right for theology to ally itself with the energies of the emerging bourgeoisie. It was appropriate to embrace and champion modernity. But what was theologically valid in the nineteenth century may not be today. Some of the social forces that introduced modernity played a liberating role (never fully liberating, as Mill's acceptance of despotism for "them" reveals), but they no longer always do.

Theology has no permanent philosophical place in this world. It must use idioms and ideas from its milieu. It must be ready to move on, like Quinet's Christ, out of any sepulchre, and reincarnate itself in a new environment. The radical critics forget that the cluster of institutions and ideas called "modernity" often played a liberating role in history. The values we rightly associate with the modern age —the "liberty, equality, and fraternity" of the French revolution— are all endangered today not by the dead hand of tradition but by modernity itself, and they can be salvaged only by moving beyond it. And as the radical critics of modern theology sometimes forget, in "moving on" we must carry with us many of the values the bourgeoisie and its theology shaped. We cannot allow ourselves to deny the religious and theological history of that period. If "modern theology" is now finished, its contribution to the history of human awareness should nevertheless not be derogated.

The propensity of some liberation theologians to disparage all modern theology as a gigantic error can best be avoided by remembering that it did not all happen at once. There are four crucial historical moments in the story of Christian theology's response to the bourgeois revolution with its capitalist economic pattern and its "modern" religious mentality.

The first is the moment of total opposition. Completely integrated into the intricate pyramid of medieval society, both in its organization and in its mode of theologizing, Christianity at first resisted the stirrings of the new class. It insisted that only Jews were fit for the finance business, and burned rebels against the injustices of feudalism as witches and heretics. The bourgeois revolution, especially in the most Catholic countries, became rabidly anticlerical.

During the Reformation, however, a large section of the Protestant church, especially its Calvinist wing, became the ally of the bourgeoisie. A vast amount of literature has been written about this complex alliance, which was never completely stable; but the values of the bourgeoisie and those of the Protestants frequently converged and at times became interchangeable. Christianity helped the bourgeoisie make its vital historical contribution, and the ideas of liberty, equality, human rights, and democracy became the reigning values of the day.

By the middle of the nineteenth century, the limitations as well as the promise of the bourgeois revolution had become evident. In the abortive French revolution of 1830 the new elites not only found themselves thwarting a popular uprising rather than sponsoring it, they even resorted to installing a king (the "bourgeois monarch") to prop up their unlikely alliance with the same feudal monarchists they had once despised. They needed the alliance to beat down a newly emerging class, the urban workers, who were already bidding to replace them. By now, however, theology was so well allied either to the bourgeoisie or, in the case of many Catholics, to the *ancien régime*, that no dialogue with the new class seemed possible. Predictably, just as the earlier revolutionaries had become anticlerical, many of the proletarians and their leaders (including Karl Marx) declared themselves atheists.

It was at this point that modern theology made the move that has caused such difficulty since and has aroused the ire of the radicals. Now a participant in the new alliance of old-fashioned religious believers and the scientifically oriented bourgeoisie, theology made the problem of skepticism its main challenge. However, the unbelief it set out to answer was not the angry agnosticism of the working classes, which was more anti-Church than anti-God. Rather, theology became absorbed in the task of responding to the sophisticated skepticism of the educated classes. As a result, theology's conversation partner became the dominant classes, and it lost contact with the lower ones—assuming, mistakenly, that if the elites could be won back to the faith, the plebeians would follow. Not only did social theology, already hemmed in by the concordats, become even less important, but the link between injustice and the unbelief of the poor was lost. Theology became an enterprise that proceeded within the bourgeois stratum of the modern world.

Today, in the countries where the mind-set of the triumphant eighteenth- and nineteenth-century revolutions still sets the tone— mainly in Europe and North America—most theology still operates within the "modern" world view. In much of the rest of the world, however, this "bourgeois" class and its culture, though still dominant, are threatened by another self-conscious and powerful class— the global poor—with its own world view, values, and agenda. Christianity is responding to this new class challenge just as it did before—first with total opposition and then, in some places, with openness. The Protestant Reformation and Calvinism were the historical vehicles of Christianity's alliance with the bourgeoisie. The new Third World Church—especially the grassroots Christian movements in Latin American and elsewhere, and the "liberation theology" it has spawned—is the historical embodiment of Christianity's emerging alliance with the wretched of the earth.

In evaluating the prospects for liberation theology, it would not be fair to imply that it can be viewed merely as an exotic novelty emanating from an energetic but unpredictable continent, a religious equivalent of the samba or the cha-cha-cha. Clearly, for those who work within them, the base communities and the theologies of liberation pose a challenge to the entire world church. They represent a question put to Christianity as such, the answer to which will determine the character of its future. The liberation theologians insist that through the base communities the world church is being summoned back to its essential task. Recalling Jesus' parable of the king who stages a banquet no one attends, and who therefore sends his servants to bring in the beggars and ne'er-do-wells, Gutiérrez says that the whole church, not just the base communities, should be oriented toward the "uninvited." It is these wayfarers and neglected ones who make the banquet possible.

Although he rarely mentions it, Gutiérrez' idea that the poor purify the church, that they are the subjects and not the objects of mission, also has venerable antecedents in Latin American Catholic theology as well as in Christian theology as a whole. It goes back at least to the Franciscan idea, especially popular among the friars who came to New Spain, that a corrupt and worldly church might be renewed and revitalized by drawing the Indians into its life. The Indians were seen in this theology not just as the targets of catechizing efforts but as the agents God would use to cleanse the church.[6]

The image of the poor as God's agents in purifying the church for its mission never died in Latin America. There was always a kind of religious mystique of the poor; sometimes even a certain idealization of poverty.* Despite some romanticizing, the poor were rarely portrayed as slothful or as victims of a divine disfavor as they sometimes were in Calvinist cultures. This old idea of the historic religious mission of the poor has been revived in the liberation theology of the base communities, but with a new twist. Now for the church to "become poor," to accept voluntary poverty, does not mean to enter

---

* It was this sentimental portrait that Luis Buñuel lampooned in his film *Viridiana*, which includes a scene in which uncouth beggars ruin a banquet hall.

into a fixed estate, or a fated destiny. It means to become the church
of the "erupting" poor. As Gutiérrez says:

> If the ultimate cause of . . . exploitation and alienation is selfish-
> ness, the deepest reason for voluntary poverty is love of neighbor.
> Christian poverty has meaning only as a commitment to . . . those
> who suffer misery and injustice. The commitment is to witness to
> the evil which has resulted from sin and a breach of communion.
> It is not a question of idealizing poverty, but rather of taking it on
> as it is—an evil—to protest against it and to struggle to abolish
> it.[7]

For many North Americans and Europeans the *dios pobre* emphasis
in the Latin American base communities is puzzling, especially when
Gutiérrez writes that "the church is not involved in the question of
poverty by the fact that it is present in a poor country. It is involved
primarily and fundamentally by the God of the Bible to whom it
wants to, and must, be faithful."[8] But this is hard to do in a country
where the poor are invisible. One characteristic of the modern world
is that classes and races (and age cohorts) are physically segregated
from each other. How in an American suburban parish does one
embrace this presence of Christ in the poor? How can it happen at
St. Francis Xavier in Hyannis, or Southwest Baptist Church in
Amarillo, or Grace Episcopal in Syracuse?

Some of the middle-class European base communities are facing
this issue. They point out that the word "poor" in the Bible means
without material resources, but that the significance of not having
such resources is that the poor are deprived of effective access to
justice and to full community life. Poverty means powerlessness, mar-
ginalization, and exclusion. The middle-class European base communities have made impressive efforts to become the friends and
advocates of physically and mentally disabled people, prisoners, and
migrant workers. The St. Paul base community in Rome has an
ambitious program of interpreting the needs and rights of disabled
people to the larger society. The members of a base community in
Belgium welcome mentally retarded persons into their homes not as
an act of charity but as a way of learning the kinds of patience and
love they believe only such persons can teach.

Still, there remains the danger that broadening "the poor" to include everyone can soon deprive the term of any real meaning. Millionaires can take comfort in the realization that they too may be "poor in spirit," and therefore blessed. To guard against this kind of trivialization those base communities that exist outside poor areas constantly underscore the necessity of forging links with other base communities made up of poor people and of recognizing the global and structural character of poverty.

This happened in a small and complacent Baptist congregation in an East Coast North American city. A group of refugee Haitian Baptists asked to use the church building for services in French on Sunday afternoons. The congregation agreed. Soon, however, the isolation of the original congregation was disrupted forever. The Americans could not avoid meeting the Haitians, getting to know their families, learning about conditions in their homeland. Within a few months a joint group of Americans and Haitians was formed in the church to study the history of the Caribbean, the economics and politics of Haiti, and the ethics of American immigration policy. The Americans quickly learned that in order to help their Haitian friends they would have to become politically involved, something they would not have dreamed of a few months earlier. The first step toward being a recognizable base community had been taken.

Are the base communities and the liberation theology they represent the first signs of a postmodern form of Christian religious life? I think they may well be, but there are two dangers to be avoided. One has to do with the democratic ethos of the base communities, the other with the use of the Bible.

While there are differences of opinion between the Latin American base communities and those in Europe and the United States about how important the communitarian aspect of the base communities is, it is hard to imagine a future church which does not have this participatory, equalitarian dimension. The history of democracy in the Anglo-Saxon world demonstrates how the sects and religious congregations of Cromwellian England provided the initial experience of voting and democratic governing which their members, having first learned them in the church, then carried over into the larger public world.[9] There may not be many things the base communities can learn from Protestant history but this may be one of them.

The Latin American Church has been led for centuries by men

and there are no women priests or bishops. It may be harder for Latin Americans to recognize that even in Christian communities consisting of people from the bottom of society, women can still be excluded unless the whole patriarchal principle of vertical forms of authority is subverted. True, it would be a serious mistake to organize base communities solely to confront an "intraecclesial" issue like hierarchical domination in the church. But insofar as the church is a part of the world, the persistence of such forms in the church is a political and "worldly" issue.

Since the use of the Bible as a guide to action in society is such a universal ingredient in base communities, it will continue to be central to whatever forms the current base communities evolve. Here Protestants have much to learn from Catholics. As the theologian Rosemary Ruether has observed, although Protestants were the ones who originally emphasized Bible reading (and Catholics, as I was assured as a boy, were "not even allowed to read it"), it is mostly Catholics who have rediscovered the Bible in our time.

Protestants "lost the Bible" in two ways. First, the development of the historical-critical method of analyzing the Bible actually took it out of the hands of lay people and, instead of returning it to the priests, gave it to the scholars. In effect, among Protestant liberals the hard-won right to read and interpret Scripture on one's own was forfeited to the claim of the scholars that only they were competent to establish what the Bible *really* says.

In reaction to this scholarly capture of priestly power, fundamentalism arose as a way of reclaiming the authority and accessibility of the Bible from the "modernists." Fundamentalists claimed that the Bible interpreted itself and every word was equally inspired. There was no discrimination between passages: the genealogies and "begats" could assume the same level of importance as the Sermon on the Mount. But the myth of self-interpretation allowed even eccentric numerological and quasimagical readings to run rampant without any real basis for challenging them. The literal verbal inspiration theory led some people into believing that one could simply allow the Holy Book to fall open and find out what God was saying on whatever page was uppermost. All this tended to reduce the Bible to a kind of I-Ching. It removed its liberating message from the hands of ordinary people just as much as the critical scholars had.

Catholics, however, never went through either the excesses of critical-historical dismembering of the Bible or the fundamentalist embalming of it. Catholics were not encouraged to read the Bible on their own until relatively recently. When they did begin to do so, however, they read it with a freshness that had not characterized such reading since before the Bible was either minced or frozen. This "postcritical" approach to the Bible is an essential element and must be carefully kept in the church nuclei of the new era. This means that neither the scientific exegetes nor the priestly interpreters nor the fundamentalists can be allowed to hold a monopoly on the Bible. It must be given back to the ordinary people from whom all these well-meaning authorities have removed it.

We have reached the end of our exploration of the two major religious movements that are challenging the modern religious sensibility and modern theology, its intellectual expression. We have crept into the big tent of renascent political fundamentalism, probed its curious dalliance with high-tech media gadgetry, and traced its volatile connections with the older and broader tradition of religiously inspired opposition to modernity. We have sat on the benches of poor base communities, wrestled with the *fuerza* of the gospel of liberation, and noted the place of both in the history of popular protest against the injustice and indignity of the modern world. It is now time to ask what both these movements mean for the future of Christianity and of Christian theology.

Our inquiry has demonstrated that the "modern world" can mean almost anything, as this allows it to be the convenient target of diverse and disparate groups. Consequently, those who array themselves against it may actually be striving for contradictory objectives under the same escutcheon. Traditionalists and radicals united in Iran in 1979 to depose the Shah, whom they took to be an embodiment of all they despised. But having deposed him they soon discovered they had less agreement on what to do next. The critics of modernity would also probably be at each other's throats as soon as modernity—whatever it is—left the airport with its Swiss bankbook in hand. My first task in sketching the basis for a *post*modern theology will be to clarify what I mean by "modern." I will turn to that task in the next chapter.

Likewise, there has been more than one theological dialogue with modernity. Various "dialogues" have directed themselves to its different facets. Some engaged its science, others its philosophies, others —more recently—its various psychological schools and political movements. These dialogues cannot be evaluated with a single judgment. Also, the "modern world" is not a static state but a historical process. It has gone through various phases in its roughly three hundred years. During these years "modern" ideas and institutions have played different roles. No generalization about theology's response to "modernism" can possibly be depended on.

Where do we go from the Secular City? In the following chapters it will become evident that I do not believe we can surmount "modernity" or get beyond modern theology unless we first positively appreciate both. It is not only useless to regret that something called modernization took place, it is wrong. Modernity is not just the name of some faceless phantom. It is the separate actions of thousands of women and men who, often in the name of Christ, attacked the worldly power of churches and their theological apologists.

In his clamorously anticlerical *Life of Jesus,* for which he was denied a teaching post because of church pressures on the government, Ernest Renan paints an imaginative picture of an Elijah-like figure striding down from the hills into contemporary Paris, stalking past the sentries at the Tuileries, and confronting the emperor with the news of the impending revolution.[10] Some critics believe Renan was projecting his own autobiography into his account. Perhaps he was. But his fanciful flight reminds us that "secularization," one of the most severely chastised children of modernity, is also the unappreciated offspring of the prophets, including the prophet of Nazareth, who railed against religiously sanctioned injustice with as much fervor as any anticleric. At its best, such secularization was once a sturdy strand in the history of human freedom. It was a legitimate response to the illegitimate use of the sacred for demeaning purposes. It spoke with the same voice that once cried out through heresies, witches' covens, popular agnosticism, and even, at times, atheism. If it eventually went to excess and produced its own pseudosacred devices—the goddess of Reason in Paris or the tomb of Lenin in Red Square—this means only that eternal vigilance is still the price we pay for the freedom God intends for all peoples. If freedom once required a secular critique of religion, it can also require a religious critique of the secular.

Religion may indeed be returning to the secular city. But the worst mistake we could make today would be to convince ourselves that the bad old days when the sacred could be misused are over, that the critical blade of modern theology can now be safely sheathed. The sorrowing people of Ireland and Iran, among others, are painfully aware that religion and clericalism can still be cruel and powerful devices in the hands of power-hungry men. If we are to have religion in the postmodern world—which we certainly will—then we will also need some very critical theology, and maybe even some secularization here and there, to keep it honest.

PART THREE

From the Bottom and from the Edges: Sources of a Postmodern Theology

I am enclosing the outline of a book that I have planned . . . I hope I shall be given the peace and strength to finish it. The church must come out of its stagnation. We must move out again into the open air of intellectual discussion with the world, and risk saying controversial things . . . I feel obliged to tackle these questions as one who, though a "modern theologian," is still aware of the debt he owes to liberal theology. There will not be many of the younger men in whom these two trends are combined.
    —Dietrich Bonhoeffer
    Letters and Papers from Prison, August 3, 1944

15. The Great Inversion

> There will be grinding of teeth when you see Abra-
> ham, Isaac and Jacob, and all the prophets in the
> Kingdom of God, and yourselves thrown out. From
> east and west people will come, from north and
> south, for the feast in the Kingdom of God. Yes, and
> some who are now last will be first, and some who
> are first will be last.
>
> —Luke 13:28–30

Dietrich Bonhoeffer was an amazingly prescient man. Sitting in his
Gestapo cell and aware that his days were numbered, he also knew
that the kind of theology he had grown up with would no longer do.
"I have discovered," he wrote, just a few weeks before his execution,
"that only by living fully in the world can we learn to have faith."
But not even Bonhoeffer could foresee the massive changes in the
world—and in theology—that were on the way.

Religion and theology in the dawning postmodern world are
undergoing two jarring inversions. From all directions of the compass
new peoples are arriving at the feast of the Kingdom, and many who
were last are last no longer. Whereas once theology was manufactured at the center for distribution in the provinces, the direction of
the flow is now being reversed. It is the periphery which is now
threatening, questioning, and energizing the center. And, whereas
the model once asserted that religious truth must be promulgated at
the top and then "trickle down" through layers of hierarchy to the
local level, now that vertical path has also been upended.

This capsizing of the movement of theological currents will require
some important changes in the scope and method of theology. Lis-

tening to the edges will require a much more imaginative way of dealing with religious pluralism, for it is from the margins of Christendom that the most forceful challenge of other faiths comes. It will also require that theology deal more creatively with what has been known variously as folk religion, grassroots piety, and *religión popular.*

So far, the liberation theologies have dealt effectively with the poor as outsider and as "other." They are only beginning, however, to cope with the otherness of other faiths and with the significance of folk piety for any theology which is interested in the liberation of real folk. In confronting these two challenges—of popular piety and of other religions—theology comes up against the two most powerful vehicles bearing the traditional conservative complaints against modernity.

In previous chapters I have already defined "theology" as that activity by which human beings relate their faith in God (*theos*) to the patterns of meaning that prevail in any historical period or culture (*logos*). If Christian theology is to address itself to the modern-becoming-postmodern world, then it cannot fail to be explicit about both the God pole and the world pole. It must present a persuasive picture of the postmodern *logos,* showing its characteristic sensibility or ethos and how it differs from the modern one in which most of us have grown up. It must be equally clear about *theos,* the essential gist of the Christian message, the divine truth that must be conveyed to the temporal world.

Modern theology was Christianity's answer to the modern age. It assumed a variety of expressions, from Friedrich Schleiermacher to Karl Barth, from Jacques Maritain to the Roman Catholic modernists, from Nicolai Berdyaev to Paul Tillich. In fact, some theologians would argue that the differences among these thinkers are so great, it is misleading to call them all "modern." However, these disparate modern theologians were all preoccupied with one common underlying question—how to make the Christian message credible to what they understood as the modern mind.

In this sense, Friedrich Schleiermacher is recognized as the "father of modern theology." When he wrote his *Speeches on Religion to Her Cultured Despisers*[1] in 1799, he set the agenda for an entire era. Writing the introduction to a reissue of that historic book more than a century later, the German religious scholar Rudolf Otto observed that what Schleiermacher was trying to do was "lead an age weary

with and alien to religion back to its very mainsprings; and to re-
weave religion, threatened with oblivion, into the incomparably rich
fabric of the burgeoning intellectual life of modern times." *Speeches*,
adds the historian Wilhelm Pauck, was a "turning point" in the
history of theology, since it marked "the first creative effort . . . to
interpret the Christian faith in relation to the 'modern' world view."

Theologians have differed with Schleiermacher about what the
modern world view is and how the "reweaving" should be done.
Some, like Karl Barth, rejected his method completely. Barth had
no patience with "liberal theology" and would probably have been
deeply vexed even to be thought of as "modern," a term he found
empty and useless. But the fact is that nearly all theologians since
Schleiermacher have in common an imaginary interlocutor: the
thoughtful troubled "modern" person, wracked with doubts and mis-
givings about God, "weary with and alien to religion." Even those
like Rudolf Bultmann who appealed to decision rather than intellect
still employed critical-historical methods and fashionable philosophical movements, such as existentialism, to get their point across.
Despite the variety of their approaches, their target audience was
always "the burgeoning intellectual life of modern times," the cultured despisers of the faith.

Modern theology was a remarkable intellectual achievement. It
created a wide variety of plausible answers to the question it set for
itself: how to "interpret the Christian faith in relation to the 'modern' world view." The problem now is not that the responses created
by modern theology are no longer credible. Rather, the question has
changed. Every modern theology had a *theos* pole and a *logos* pole, a
view of the nature of God and a theory of what the modern world
essentially was. However, though neoorthodoxy and neoscholasti-
cism and process theology differed from one another in defining these
poles, the differences do not look as profound, in light of the postmodern situation, as they did to those who originally argued over
them. What all these discordant schools had in common was a fervent desire to appeal to the thoughtful, educated, skeptical "modern
mind." Neither Barth, Maritain, nor Tillich wrote for the masses,
certainly not for the masses of ordinary believers. One might even
argue that they were writing for that part of themselves which knew
—from the inside—what it meant to be a skeptical "modern man."

With the coming of postmodern culture, all three ingredients of modern theology—its God pole, its world pole, and, most critically, its implied interlocutor—are thrown into question. By the time the impact of World War II had been fully absorbed, the picture of the modern world that informed modern theology began to lose its credibility. Doubts about the plausibility of that world picture multiplied as the unfolding history of modernity revealed sinister sides that had not figured in the modern theological equation. When the disclosure of what happened at Auschwitz did not lessen the modern world's capacity for mass slaughter, and the realization of what took place at Hiroshima did not evoke a shrinking back from the making of more nuclear weapons, something began to change. Growing numbers of people began to regard the modern logos not as something one tried to weave religion back into but as a world view which was itself fatally flawed. The modern mind became not the audience but the problem. The so-called crisis of modernity was upon us, and one secular philosopher declared that it could never be solved until the world came to see that the "root of the crisis is the modern project itself."[2]

This is the change that augured the end of modern theology. With its primary goal—the need to adapt religion to the modern world—now thrown into doubt, modern theology also found itself to be more a part of the problem than of the solution. Its world pole lay in shambles.

Modern theology's God pole also began to teeter. Previously theologians disagreed mainly about the details of this second component. There were many different "doctrines of God." But they all agreed that God was universal, equally approachable by all and available to all. There was little room in modern theology either for a partisan God who takes sides in historical struggles or for a God who has to be sought in radically dissimilar ways by different peoples. Now, however, this assumption of universality was questioned too.

From the periphery of the modern world and from the ghettos and *barrios* there came a strident challenge to this God pole in the form of a *theos* who takes the side of the disinherited against the powerful, and who can be known only in highly particularistic ways. All modern theologies had claimed to be, in principle, universal, commending themselves to all men and women of faith and reason. Now, however, that claim to universality was questioned. Blacks and women, poor people and non-Westerners all insisted that these allegedly all-inclusive theologies were narrow and provincial—white, male, Western, "bourgeois"—and inadequate because they seemed blithely unaware of their own nearsightedness. The God pole of modern theology swayed and finally fell in the face of what seemed to many of its practitioners to be a nearly polytheistic upsurge of partial and even idiosyncratic perspectives. Was God black or poor or red or female? Each image seemed to issue from a highly particular experiential base.

The most telling challenge to modern theology did not come from the questioning of its two poles. It came rather as a rejection of modern theology's implicit understanding of its "audience." The new generation of postmodern theologians, many of them Latin American, African, and Asian, refused to agree that their labors should be addressed primarily to the "cultured despisers" of religion. Instead, they began to forge a theology in conversation with the disinherited and the culturally dominated sectors of the society. Their interlocutors were now the "noncultured despisers," but these were not people who despised religion. They were the despisers of the modern world itself. This is what made the real difference.

Trained to concentrate on the content of theology rather than on the process of theologizing, modern theologians hardly noticed this change. Still, the transformation of interlocutors was by far the most significant dislocation. One could safely debate various ideas of God and world within the parameters modern theology was used to. But when one changes the social and institutional setting within which the whole theological enterprise proceeds, and when one alters the definition of *for whom* one constructs theology and *why*, when theologians turn from the despisers to the despised, then something fundamental has been altered. It is the game itself, not just the plays that are possible within it, that has been changed. Modern theology, with its astonishing capacity for inventiveness and creativity, might have survived a radical shift in its paradigms of God and world. It could not survive a fundamental redefinition of its purpose and agenda, with whom it was to be discussed, and by whom it was to be held accountable. But this is just the kind of challenge postmodern theologies were bringing.

We must be careful not to paint a monochrome picture of modern theology. Thinkers as wildly disparate as Dostoyevsky, Kierkegaard, Blake, and Pius IX questioned the modern theological program. Yet when we read these men today they often sound modern despite themselves, preoccupied as they were with the new age and the mistakes they believed their contemporaries were making in dealing with it. It is unclear how much help any one of them can offer in the task theology now faces, that of moving beyond the challenge of "modern times" to the construction of a theology that speaks to a world neither the modern theologians nor their critics could have foreseen.

In this final section of the book I will draw on the ideas of certain contemporary social philosophers who have thought carefully about the postmodern world into which we are now moving. After that I will go on to suggest why the type of religiousness that became characteristic of the modern world is no longer adequate. I will conclude by suggesting that two massive realities, both virtually ignored by modern theology—global religious pluralism and popular piety— must replace the "cultured despisers" of religion as the principal conversation partners of a truly postmodern theology.

16. *"The Devil Is a Modernist"*

> Modernism (from Latin *modernus* = of the present
> mode or fashion; from modus = a measure; cf. modo
> = just now), 1. Deviation from ancient and classi-
> cal manner or practice, anything recently made or
> introduced. 2. Modern character; modern method or
> way of thinking or regarding matters.
> —*International Encyclopedic Dictionary*, 1900 ed.

In his fine book on what he calls "the experience of modernity," the American writer Marshall Berman reminds us that it was Jean-Jacques Rousseau who first used the word *moderniste* in the sense that we have come to use it today.[1] Berman also points out that Rousseau is a principal source of "some of our most vital modern traditions, from nostalgic reverie to psychoanalytic self-scrutiny to participatory democracy," and that he was decidedly of two minds about the whole thing. Berman might have added that Rousseau was also confused about what the essential features of modernity or modernism were, and that this problem of definition has dogged us ever since.

My own first exposure to the word "modernism" came as a child in a Baptist church, and it could not have been clearer that the preacher who spat out the word felt no ambivalence at all. For my generation and that of my parents and grandparents, "modernism" in its religious context meant nothing less than the betrayal of the faith, the wily machinations of overeducated men intent on tearing down the truth of the Bible, denying the divinity of Christ, and casting doubts on all we had been taught was trustworthy and true.

Rousseau's symbol for modernity was the agitated street life of Paris, *le tourbillon social*, the social whirlwind. He was frightened by the whirlwind, afraid it might deprive him of any sense of who he was. Writing through the persona of Saint-Preux, the hero of his novel *The New Eloise*, he describes how he experiences the giddiness:

> I'm beginning to feel the drunkenness that this agitated, tumultuous life plunges you into. With such a multitude of objects passing before my eyes, I'm getting dizzy. Of all the things that strike me, there is none that holds my heart, yet all of them together disturb my feelings, so that I forget what I am and who I belong to.[2]

Fear, hesitation, terror of losing everything: Rousseau feels them all. Yet he plunges in.

As a boy listening to our Baptist preacher describe the menace of modernism I felt some of the same fear and trembling—and attraction. It seemed to me that if modernism won in its epochal struggle with God, Christ, and the Bible, then the cover would be removed from a bottomless pit. My young fingers gripped the edges of the pew. Surely the modernists, proud agents of all that was evil, had to be put to rout. My stomach tingled with the awful cosmic scope of the battle. "The devil," the preacher warned, "is a modernist."

Yet, like Rousseau and Saint-Preux, I also felt strangely drawn toward *le tourbillon*. The devil can be terribly intriguing. Before I even knew what modernism really was, the strident timbre of the preacher's voice, the urgency and importance he attached to it, beguiled me. Even if the modernists could be defeated would the seamless robe of truth ever be the same again? No matter what finally happens in the epic story of modernism's attack on tradition, a dilemma that will now haunt humankind forever is whether once questioned, once picked up and examined, traditional truths can ever have the same weight, even if the challenge is ultimately turned back. The real impact of modernism hangs not on whether its irreverent querying of tradition is successfully answered but on the fact that the query has been raised in the first place, and heard. The preacher is cornered. In answering the modernist he agrees to play the modernist's game; and even if he wins, he loses. The seamless robe will always have stains and patch marks.

As I grew up and went to college, seminary, and graduate school,

I continued to be fascinated by the paradox of modernism. In literature and poetry courses we studied the people our professors told us were "modernists"—Proust, Joyce, Pound, Yeats, Gertrude Stein. I read them all with the fervor of an undergraduate would-be intellectual, but I could never piece together what these "modernists" had to do with the satanic churls who were always being chased away from the pulpit of my boyhood Baptist church. I also learned about "modern" philosophy, which we were told usually began with Descartes and the turning of the mind onto the problem of its own capacity to know. In seminary we studied "modernism" as a movement represented by people like Loisy, Blondel, and Tyrrell in the Catholic Church.[3] Later on I heard much about "modernization," mainly in economics and political science courses. It had to do with industrialization, capital formation, and economic development. I also came to appreciate Picasso, Miró, Dali, and what was called "modern" art, and to enjoy "modern" jazz. But I still did not understand how they all fit together with the modernism I had first heard about so many years before in evening revival services.

"Modernism" means the attempt to come to terms—in art, poetry, religion, or anything else—with the modern world, the world supported by what I call the "five pillars" of modernity. Viewed from this angle, the "modern" world is (or was, depending on how far gone one thinks it is) constituted by 1) sovereign national states as the legally defined units of the global political system; 2) science-based technology as the "modern" world's principal source of its images of life and its possibilities; 3) bureaucratic rationalism as its major mode of organizing and administering human thought and activity; 4) the quest for profit maximization, in both capitalist and allegedly socialist countries, as its means of motivating work and distributing goods and services; and 5) the secularization and trivialization of religion and the harnessing of the spiritual for patently profane purposes, as its most characteristic attitude toward the holy.

These are the five pillars, once proud, now leaning, of modernity. Together they support an imposing edifice of art and music, literature and theology. These cultural creations in turn refine, inform, and embellish the supporting pillars. Modern theology also finds its place in this whole complex. It rests on the modern separation of church and state, which is supposed to function as the underlying institutional basis for the segregating of religion from political and economic power. At its own level, it interacts with art and philosophy and the other cultural artifacts as one discrete "field" among others.

Pictured in this way, however, "modernity" seems abstract and external. Rousseau knew it was not: "All of them together disturb my feelings, so that I forget what I am." How can we examine modernity and gain some hold on why it is coming unstuck, not as something going on outside us but as a subjective reality as well?

In some ways a major commercial airport is modernity incarnate. What better place is there to ponder this epochal Spenglerian thought than the waiting room of one of the modern world's immense and barren airline terminals? Here all the brilliant achievements and perverse flaws that have made the modern world what it is are joined and welded and on display. The sovereign nation state is here, as invisible voices announce departures to the great capitals of the globe —Cairo, London, Jakarta, Lagos—in modulated affectless tones. If we are on an international flight we clutch our passports and visas, paper reminders that however much we would like to be citizens of the modern world, it is a national government that decides whether we leave and where we can enter.

Science and technology gleam here. Numbers, the favored language of *scientia* in our relentlessly quantified era, claim an equal stature with words. It is flight four thirteen, leaving at two twenty from gate thirty-two on corridor three. *Techne* is here too, though the shattering roar of the great jet engines is muffled by the carefully engineered insulation in the walls. The sky, the rain, the wind are tamed, held at bay by weatherproof windowpanes. Everywhere the machine shimmers: the sleek, shiny planes; the ingenious devices for moving thousands of people along endless corridors, from one level to another, in and out of planes; the quietly mysterious computer screens that summon up one's name and flight plan out of a vast electronic cerebrum. Science does not need to flaunt itself at an airport. It pervades everything.

Here also System, Standard Procedure, Rational Method, and Regular Mode of Operation rule. The smiles of the uniformed attendants behind the counters, scrupulously marked for appropriate function, serve to smooth the transaction without inviting intimacy. Television screens carry an endless blinking parade of arrivals and departures carefully arranged for rapid recognition. Newsstands, gift counters, coffee shops, and washrooms are placed as though some prescient deity knew exactly when and where they would be needed. The spaces between people are defined entirely by function. Who is going where, on what airline, at what time? When we meet our fellow voyagers depends on what stage of the thoughtfully segmented boarding process we are in. Conversation, if any, is pleasant and shallow. Everyone shares the feeling that this experience should be made as temporary as possible.

And money talks, discreetly. Here at the Big Airport the whole world is literally within our reach. In the space of a few hours we can be on any continent, savor snow or desert, sample chapatis or tacos or pasta, view mosques or pavilions or temples. It is a prospect that would have made Magellan or Marco Polo or even Ali Baba giddy. We have only to pay; preferably not with currency notes but with the little plastic pearl of great price that allows us to plug into a universal treasury of merit and enjoy momentary satisfaction at the cost of some vague future day of reckoning. Nor does capitalism, communism, or socialism matter much here. Whether the money is charged as rubles or pesos or dollars or francs is irrelevant. It is money, any money, that makes these magic carpets fly.

And religion? Where is God? At Logan airport in Boston there is a niche thoughtfully set aside for the divine. Squeezed into a side corridor, not far from where lost luggage can be sought, the footsore traveler can say a prayer to Our Lady of the Airways. The chapel is modern, almost chic, trying its best not to look too anachronistic in its improbable setting. There is a priest assigned to Our Lady of the Airways. Masses occur, occasionally funerals, sometimes even weddings. Unkind rumor has it that being assigned there is a kind of mild punishment imposed on a cleric who has come to the Chancery's attention once too often. Surely no Ricci or DeNobile bearing the gospel almost single-handed to China or India, no Adoniram Judson wading ashore in pagan Burma ever faced as unpromising a field as someone who is sent to make God's ways known here in the Big Airport, the modern world in miniature.

As we sit here waiting, somehow both impressed and intimidated by what is around us, we also know in our innards why this world has cracked. We discover that despite the ordered, soft-pedaled ambience of the waiting area, we occasionally have the impulse, like Dostoyevsky's man from the underground, to smash it all up, or at least to overturn one ashtray. But we also know we do not need to. As we look around we realize that despite its subtle suggestion of permanence this terminal is already decomposing, that its quiet assurances of competence and efficiency cannot deliver what it promises.

We know that here before us the five pillars of modernity are being eaten from the inside. National sovereignty? There is something in this technology itself and in the electronic networks that link these counters to their look-alikes in Calcutta and Bangkok that is already flashing the obituary of nation states. It is the one thing on which the bankers who make a withdrawal from Zurich and a deposit in Caracas with the same telex signal, and the guerrillas who slip back and forth across the borders of Lebanon, El Salvador, and Namibia agree. The only real question is what kind of world community will replace the collapsing system we now have; and will it develop quickly enough to prevent the dying nation states from trampling everyone to death in their final throes and twitches?

We also know that science-based technology, whatever its future in a postmodern world, can never again make claim to the prestige and power it has enjoyed in ours. Why is our flight delayed? "Mechanical failure." One's mind, schooled by previous experiences not to dwell on such things, hardly pauses on the question of what would have happened if the failure had come to light at forty thousand feet, or just at liftoff. Yet crashes and mishaps do occur, attributed almost always now to human, not mechanical, failure. But that is the issue. It is humans who must steer the great technological system. Humans fall asleep, are overtaken by moods, nurture grudges, lose their train of thought. Humans kill and torture and control each other more efficiently with every advance in technology. What, amid all the talk about appropriate scale and limits to growth and the built-in restrictions of the scientific paradigm, will be the place of science in the postmodern era?

We also know as we sit on our plastic bench and wait for Someone Else to tell us when and if our flight will fly, that we have been neutered. Like those seated around us, smoking, sleeping, reading the newspaper for the fourth time, we have no capacity at all to affect our situation. We have no cohesion with our fellow passengers, and even if we did, the only way we could alter our circumstance, escape from our absolute dependence on those who rule this little piece of the world, would be to leave. True, in an airport this syndrome may reach its extreme limit. But the "administrative mode," the allegedly rational system by which patterns of domination and control are made plausible, is turning out to be the feature of the modern world that enrages people more than anything else.

Sometimes the *demos* responds to the blank stare of management. Forced by an administrative snafu to wait in a London airport for days a few years back, a jumble of American students formed a cooperative. The coop helped them share food and money, settled disputes, negotiated with the airlines, and even contrived an equitable formula for deciding who would go on the first available flights. It was a game gesture, and it symbolizes in miniature what millions of people in many parts of the modern world have begun to do: they have started creating small, democratically ordered counterinstitutions to help them alter or dismantle the "official" behemoths that have become the predominant mode of governance in all societies in the modern world.

Most of the people in the world today are, by anyone's standards, poor. Nearly half are hungry every day. These people do not appear in airports very often, so we rarely see them there, a reminder of the clever way modern cities insulate the opulent from the impoverished. Still, there are reminders. At every large airport in the world now we line up docilely for a security check. Bored attendants poke through briefcases and X-ray our luggage. Buzzers signal suspicious metallic objects. Why do we put up with all this? Because, despite the untroubled appearance the airport strives to convey, we live in a world at war with itself, where some people feel desperate enough to enter a flight deck, weapon in hand, and change everyone's best-laid travel plans.

Very, very few of the world's poor people are terrorists, and most hijackers are not poor. Yet the security check barrier, with its nonchalant inspectors and yawning-but-armed guard, tells us something the Big Airport would rather we did not know. Behind its polyurethaned surface there is struggle, conflict, and death in the modern world, and most of it occurs when ordinary people, poor but in other respects not unlike the young people who formed the *ad hoc* Heathrow coop, try everything they can to obtain their rights as human beings—and then turn reluctantly to metallic objects. The institutional violence of imposed hunger and poverty and the counterviolence of rebellion and insurgency have become interlocking hallmarks of our era. When one combines a scene in which nation states armed with annihilation weapons can no longer maintain peace; in which technology has long since exceeded its safeguards against human error and malice; in which administrative tyranny intrudes ever deeper into what is left of human intimacy; in which the bottom line ultimately determines who will live and who will die—then it becomes clear that either the modern age is over or it will be the last age of all.

And what about religion? What place has it had in the modern world, and what might it contribute to a new age? We will consider this question in the next chapter. But before we do let us return for a moment to Our Lady of the Airways, perhaps in a more appreciative mood. Granted, the chapel seems consummately quaint and irrelevant. But at least it has a cross on the altar, the symbol of God's limitless love and of a man who once placed himself among the superfluous and wretched people of his day and was not afraid to face down the impersonal pyramids of power. It has a picture of Mary who once sang a song about the filling of the hungry, the casting down of the mighty, and the severe judgment God metes out to the rich. Could it be that without intending to, the airport of modernity has allowed a place in its apparatus for the only possible energy that can save it from its own contradictions and help bring forth something healthy from its death spasm? Maybe Our Lady of the Airways can help us in our quest for a Christianity that deals with the devil of modernism by constructing a world which that Old Tempter may still cause trouble but in some other guise.

The modern world was the world of sovereign nation states, most of which appeared in their current united form only in the past two hundred years. It was the age of science-based technology which, though its roots reach back to the Renaissance, attained its zenith only during roughly the same period. It was also the epoch of rational bureaucracy and, more recently, the administrative invasion of previously tradition-oriented human groupings and activities, a development which is closely linked to the fourth: the spectacular spread of the capitalist mode of production and marketing into every corner of the globe. Finally, it was not the era of no religion but of trivialized and tamed religion. Those who ruled it, though they first attempted to get rid of religion altogether, eventually settled for using it as an instrument for secular purposes, mainly the maintenance of personal virtue and public order.

If one sees these pillars carrying the culture of the modern world, then one can delineate at least the negative profile of the postmodern one. First of all it will not be built on the unlimited sovereignty of individual nation states. Both the nature of modern weaponry and the technical organization of the global society make that option impossible. Any world that tries to perpetuate this pattern will end inevitably in radioactive cinders. The decline of the nation state does not mean, however, that patriotism will have no place in a postmodern world. The examples of Poland and Nicaragua both show that patriotism need not be fused to right-wing ideology, as it has since the late nineteenth century. What remains at issue, then, is what shape the postmodern global system will take and what place will be found in it for love of homeland.

The postmodern world will also be one in which the exaggerated claims made for science and technology will be modulated. We already see an impressive element of self-criticism in recent scientific thought, a growing unwillingness to claim that science is either the best or the only mode of knowing. The advent of nuclear weapons and the recognition of the finitude and precariousness of the planet have also given some scientists pause. It is no longer obvious that *if* one can do something then one *should*. However, the answers to questions about the proper role of science and the appropriate place of technology are still unknown.

The growth of counterinstitutions, including free and alternative schools, solidarity and support groups, self-directed therapy groups like Alcoholics Anonymous and even schizophrenics anonymous, musicians' coops, and base communities in the churches, points to a period in which top-down administrative procedures will no longer be the predominant form for ordering life. The signs of this change are everywhere. Similarly, the lurching movement of the "capitalist" countries toward more and more centralized planning and the complementary drift of the Communist nations toward market economics will continue.

The big question now is not whether there will be planning, but who will plan, and for whose benefit? So far it appears that those who already hold the political and economic power have no intention of willingly sharing it with those who would plan things differently. This is one reason why we shove our suitcases through X-ray machines at airports. There is little chance that the conflict around this issue will abate, and just as little certainty about what kind of economic system will dawn after the twilight of capitalism.

Finally, I think the signs all suggest that religion will play a considerably more important role in the postmodern than it has in the "secularized" modern world. How it will do so is the question I turn to now.

17. The Gelding of God and the Birth of Modern Religion

> Religion by its nature is a metaphysical poem married to faith. In this way it is effective and popular; for, except for a tiny elite, the pure idea is but an empty word, and truth, to be felt, must put on a body. There must be rite, legend, ceremony.
> —Hippolyte Taine
> *L'Ancien Régime*, 1876 [1]

Living in the bustling port of Rotterdam in 1517, the great Christian humanist Erasmus wrote that he discerned the "near approach of a golden age," in which "the three chief blessings of humanity are about to be restored to her." These three blessings were true Christian piety, learning, and "the public and lasting concord of Christendom." Some learning did flourish, and a renewal of Christian piety occurred—though most of it was hardly of the kind the irenic Erasmus appreciated. The concord of Christendom, however, did not appear. Erasmus did not know it in 1517, but the next century and a quarter would witness some of the most dreadful intra-Christian discord of an already strife-torn history.

It is perilous to attempt to peer into the future, even a close-at-hand one. Efforts to foresee the shape of religion in the postmodern world are no exception to this rule. But there is another tactic that can be used. A particularly reflective zoologist once remarked that in the age when the great lizards—the tyrannosaurus and diplodocus—dominated the steamy, fern-covered earth, even a very careful observer might not have noted the tiny warm-blooded mammals that scampered around the feet of the giant dinosaurs. Yet given the hypertrophy of the big reptiles, their failure to evolve, and their ultimately self-destructive bulk and awkwardness, it was these tiny marsupials who held the key to the future. In any transitional age it is wise to watch for the adroit, swift-moving creatures who seem at first so weak and vulnerable, trying mainly to avoid being squashed or devoured by the overgrown behemoths around them. Very often it is the titans whose days are numbered and the field mice who inherit the jungle.

The historian Arnold Toynbee made his share of questionable generalizations and false judgments during his lifetime. He also made some acute observations about the history of religions that have a certain kinship to the theory of the megalosaurs and the mammals. He held that as any world civilization reaches senility a creative "internal proletariat" appears. This germ cell, usually inspired by a religious vision, becomes a fetus that grows within the larger body politic but is sufficiently independent of it to survive. Eventually it provides the spiritual core of the succeeding civilization. Without accepting Toynbee's thesis in all its detail, one could at least agree that it traces a plausible overview of the history of the West, leading to the emergence of our present global metropolis. It suggests further that to gain some insight on what to expect next, we concentrate not on the brontosauri but on the small, more agile marmots we might otherwise overlook.

As Toynbee himself believed, the minuscule Christian congregations that were springing up in Ephesus, Rome, Corinth, and Alexandria, though they can hardly have been viewed as much more than pests by their contemporaries, were nonetheless the tiny progenitors of a new civilization. They carried a responsibility far beyond anything their size or power hinted at. Not even the most prescient of their contemporaries could have predicted the importance future historians would attach to them.

The conversion of the Emperor Constantine radically altered the status of Christianity. Theologians will probably always argue about whether the conversion, which occurred in the fourth century after Christ, provided early Christianity with a historic opportunity or corrupted it almost before it had begun. What is clearer is that at the same time the modern age is ending, the millennium and a half some

have called "the age of Constantine," in which "Christendom" provided the *ethos* of Western civilization, is also coming to a close.
These simultaneous endings mean that Christianity now finds itself
in a situation more like its pre-Constantinian one. And this suggests
we probably have more to learn from those who were disquieted by
the Constantinian deal than from those who found it comfortable.

The discomfort started immediately. As the era of Constantine
began, and before the "eternal empire" sank into a memory of what
had been, handfuls of men and women who hated the agreement the
church had made—to become the privileged religion in return for
supplying the imperial ideology—retreated to the desert. There,
crouched in caves and huts, they took on the laborious task that must
always occur during the *Untergang* of an empire, when the legacy of
one historical period is sifted and selectively absorbed again by the
next.

Whether Constantine did Christianity a favor or not must be discussed with great care. I do not subscribe to the interpretation advanced by those Christians who say that Constantine politicized and
thus corrupted an essentially spiritual and nonpolitical Gospel. Jesus
was executed as a threat to the Roman imperium and Christianity
was a political factor from its earliest days. But I cannot accept,
either, a benign judgment on the "Constantinian compromise."
Christianity was forced by the conversion of the emperor and subsequent events to play a civilization-building role it was not equipped
to play. Consequently, what we know as the "Christian civilization"
of the medieval period was actually more Roman and Hellenistic
than Christian. The church took over the "diocese," a Roman invention, as its jurisdictional unit, and the classical natural-law theory as
the basis of its ethics. Its theology became as much neoplatonic as
biblical. The pope sat in Rome "like the ghost of the vanished emperor." Still, Constantinianism was neither the unmitigated disaster
some Christians claim nor the beginning of the golden age of Chris-
tiandom some medievalists still celebrate. It did not succeed in translating the unique message of Christianity into a civilization. The
miscarriage was not that Christianity became political, but that it did
so in the wrong way.

This is what the early cenobites and monastics sensed. It is why
they retreated to the desert. Most of them believed that the church's

assumption of imperial power was a mistake. They were not all opposed to Christianity's playing a culture-forming role. Still, they realized that it would take time to draw on the resources of the past
and of their own experience to assemble the psychological, cultural,
and social elements of a world that was really new. It was this task
they took on, even when they did not fully realize it. No fetus knows
it carries the future of the species. There are some important similarities between the pre- and post-Constantinian eras. Both represent
Christianity without Christendom. Therefore it is valuable to return
for a moment to that earlier time in order to get our bearings for
moving ahead.

Erik Erikson, that intrepid explorer of the stages of individual lives,
once remarked that the anguish a civilization suffers as it moves from
one era to the next is not unlike that of a person negotiating a new
stage of the life cycle, from adolescence to young adulthood, say, or
from middle to late adulthood. Just as the passage beyond a personal
phase of life always brings back memories of previous ones, a culture
must also look back as it goes forward. This may explain why the
scholars of the Renaissance felt the attraction of the Greeks, and the
Protestant reformers returned to St. Paul and St. Augustine. Memory
of the past can provide an emancipating energy in the present. As
the modern period approaches its decline, blacks are fascinated with
African roots, women scholars search for a prepatriarchal era, and
colonialized people try to reclaim Machu Picchu.

This gathering of strength for the next move, what Freud called
"regression in service of the ego," cannot be hurried. The coming
age may take a long time in its prenatal phase. A new epoch requires
at least three elements before it can breathe on its own: 1) a characteristic *personal style*, a mode of individual being that is, despite the
obvious continuities of life, somehow significantly different from
what has gone before; 2) an *integrating cultural system*—stories and
rites, symbols and values—that tells its collective history and anchors
its morals; 3) an *organizational pattern*, a societal scaffolding that will
support the institutional frame, without which no civilization can
live. If we look at the time of the formation of Christendom, the
legendary life stories of three saints illustrate these three ingredients
(which were also at the same time the levels at which the long
gestation process took place).

The first is *St. Anthony*, whose lurid temptations have seduced generations of artists. He is the exemplar of the inner quest, the knight errant of a new personal identity. Fearlessly descending into the lowest locked chambers of his own and his culture's psyche, he met with unspeakable horrors. His nocturnal wrestling matches with his demons, both the loathsome and the voluptuous ones, can be seen today as a kind of courageous psychoanalysis-without-analyst, an exploration of a region where ogres and incubi lurk, in order to wrest from the terror the new style of selfhood every succeeding era requires.

At the level of symbol and religious metaphor stands *St. Jerome*. He translated sacred texts that encoded the culture's primal spiritual legacy. But translation always involves more than words. Real translators must grasp the gist of two different cultural wholes, which is just what St. Jerome did. Like St. Anthony he linked the past with the future.

Thus the search for what we would now call a counterculture in the Christian empire began. But it went on almost entirely among expatriate fugitives and isolated groups until a third figure, *St. Benedict*, appeared. His life task was to provide a workable organizational pattern. Only with this contribution did the monastic quest become the monastic movement. St. Benedict never actually founded a monastery, and his *Rule* did not initiate anything. It provided a wise and practical polity. The fact that it is still used all over the world today testifies to its uncanny sensibility to the pitfalls human beings always face when they try to live a common vision (and sleep under the same roof).

What St. Benedict never anticipated as he drew up his *Rule* was that the movement he was helping to shape from a gaggle of stubborn recluses, introspective dreamers, social rebels, and fanatics was the seedbed of the next phase of Western civilization. His desert riffraff were the mammals among the dinosaurs.

In 1964 Pope Paul VI proclaimed St. Benedict the patron saint of all Europe. The designation is apt. As the *pax Romana* first teetered and then folded, the monasteries began to play a new role. Schooled by the disciples St. Anthony and others had created, and nurtured by the texts St. Jerome and others had translated, they ceased being places of retreat from the chaos, and became the energizing sources of the new culture of medieval Europe.

The refugees found themselves in the center. In the formerly pagan backlands of northern Europe, a Benedictine monastery, usually with a school and a library, with advanced knowledge of agricultural methods, and with a style of personal life that balanced prayer and work and guarded both solitude and community, often became the model for all to see and emulate. As previously illiterate Huns and Goths began the imposing task of creating a written language, a history and a national epic, the learned monks were there to write—in many cases even to determine—this new kind of group memory. The stories of the monks and the missions, of St. Patrick and Sts. Cyril and Methodius and the rest, were bound into the national epics.

I have mentioned the earliest years of the monastic movement not because I advocate its restoration but because I believe we already have its functional parallel in the world today. At a time when the modern age is teetering, we have the equivalent of the clusters of outsiders, in the same kind of anarchic but energetic state in which St. Benedict found their predecessors. Today we have an assortment of people in communities of Christians who either because they chose to, or more often because they were pushed there, have lived outside the power center of modern society and its theological mind-set. These disparate collections of the despised and rejected, the forgotten and the ignored—of rednecks and blacks, women and poor people, of Asians, Africans, and Latin Americans—hardly constitute a cohesive community today, let alone a new counterculture. Yet they are engaged in a variety of ways in doing the work of Anthony, Jerome, and Benedict. They are creating a new and vigorous sense of what it means to be a human person. They are constructing a theology by translating the biblical sources and their own experiences into a new key. They are building a new pattern of corporate life through the Christian base community movement. Once again, on the edges and not at the centers of religious and political power, an energetic source of renewal is appearing, one that might do for a waning modernity what the monastic movement and its later descendants, the heretics and schismatics, the Waldensians and radical Franciscans, the Diggers and Anabaptists—did for previous failing eras.

The architects of the modern secular experiment knew it was failing, and they knew it when it had scarcely begun. After their parents had tried to abolish religion, the second and third generations of the bourgeoisie reinstated it with almost unseemly haste, before the bodies of their agnostic grandparents were cold in their unblessed graves. As a result, we do have religion in the modern world, but the important thing about that religion is not whether it is Catholic or Protestant. The thing to notice about modern religion in all its varieties is that it is *modern* religion. Both the function it serves and the meaning it has for people are mediated by the shape of the modern world. What makes modern religion modern?

In 1876, as the United States celebrated its first centennial, the French historian Hippolyte Taine published his *L'Ancien Régime*. Taine had begun his career as a devout anticleric and a fervent believer in the Enlightenment. Busts of Voltaire and Rousseau presided over his study. As he grew older, however, and witnessed the bloodletting of the Paris Commune of 1870, he began to change his mind on the subject of religion and its relation to society. What he said in 1876 sums up perfectly what many of the nineteenth-century revolutionaries came to believe about this subject (and many conservatives believe today):

> Religion by its nature is a metaphysical poem married to faith. In this way, it is effective and popular; for, except for a tiny elite, the pure idea is but an empty word, and truth, to be felt, must put on a body. There must be rite, legend, ceremony, if it is to talk to the people, women, children, the simple, every man engaged in daily labour, to the human mind itself in which ideas willy-nilly express themselves in pictures. Through visible form it can throw its great weight upon the conscience, be a counterweight to natural egotism, cool the mad impulse to animal passion, guide the will to self-sacrifice and devotion, direct men to give themselves wholly to the service of truth or of others, make ascetics and martyrs, sisters of charity and missionaries. In every society religion is a precious and natural organ. Men need it to think of the infinite and live well; if it suddenly failed, they would feel a great sad void in their soul and would hurt each other the more. You would try in vain to snatch it from them. Hands which attempted it would touch no more than the envelope; it will grow again like flesh after a bloody operation. Its roots are too deep to be pulled up.[2]

This is an extraordinary paragraph. Except for the lyrical style it could easily have been written by a contemporary American neocon-servative such as Daniel Bell. In his influential *The Coming of the Post-Industrial Society*, Bell writes, "The lack of a rooted moral belief system is the cultural contradiction of society, the deepest challenge to its survival."[3] "The real problem of modernity," Bell wrote in 1976, "is the problem of belief. To use an unfashionable term, it is a spiritual crisis . . . a situation which brings us back to nihilism."[4] Taine would have agreed.

Like Bell and many other American neoconservatives, Taine came to believe that the widening gyre was getting entirely too wide. Excesses of dissatisfaction and self-indulgence were undermining the foundations of society, religion—*some* religion—was needed to "be a counterweight to natural egotism, cool the mad impulse to animal passion . . ." Like nearly all disenchanted revolutionaries, Taine came to believe that people need religion.

What had happened between Tom Paine and Hippolyte Taine, between the Bastille and the Commune, was that, as the history of the modern world unfolded, some religious sanction for its rulers' right to rule became more necessary than anyone had first expected. The bourgeoisie did not need religion to convince themselves they had that right. They had Reason on their side, and in addition they had been victorious in the bloody contest with the *ancien régime*. Nor did they need the spiritual arm to persuade the defeated legions of monarchy and feudalism to stay out of their way: there were just not enough of them to matter. But they did need religion, church, and theology after all: to persuade the people who had been left out of the deal not to rock the boat. A new kind of bourgeois mentality arose. The old fire-breathing agnostics and atheists disappeared as they discovered that, true or not, religion was useful, perhaps essen-tial. Radical anticlericalism declined, Masonic orders became social clubs, and the pope was allowed to name bishops again. As this happened the clericalists also softened their voices. Together, the new directors of the modern world came to believe, if not in the substance of religion, then in its function.

Taine had really not initiated the cagey bourgeois return to reli-gion. The more perceptive of the old agnostics had begun to come to some of the same conclusions at least two decades earlier. In Novem-

ber 1848 a Parisian priest, the Abbé Maillard, wrote to the Bishop of
Autun,

> As for what is now called *la classe bourgeoise,* so hostile to the
> church before February, I do not really think it has changed its
> mind, but the memory of the archbishop's devotion has made an
> impression; and then it is afraid. . . . A month ago I was with
> several industrialists and proprietors, each more concerned than
> the others to discredit the systems of Proudhon, Cabet . . . , but
> none of them much concerned (I knew them) with God and the
> Gospel. There was a discussion on socialism and communism, and,
> inevitably, communism and socialism were soon borne down by an
> avalanche of serious or humorous arguments. The right of property
> remained sole master of the field, and was proclaimed to universal
> applause sacred, fundamental, inviolable.[5]

As the conversation continued, the businessmen pressed the priest
for his own views. Finally he suggested that there was no strictly
secular basis for private property and that only belief in a God who
condemns theft and rewards the virtuous in a future life provided a
secure basis. The letter continues:

> "So according to you," asked with a preoccupied air, a big industri-
> alist, owning a factory worth more than a million, "without religion
> property is no longer a right and Proudhon is right?" "That's it."
> . . . Since that time two of the company (including the industri-
> alist) have come to find me, and have started discussions on reli-
> gion, from which I expect, with God's grace, the best results. That
> is how things are with the bourgeoisie: it will help us as a counter-
> weight to doctrines that it fears, and as a kind of spiritual police,
> called to obtain respect for the laws which benefit it. But that is
> the limit of its esteem and confidence in us.[6]

For theology even this limited esteem arrived not a moment too
soon. Having come within an inch of losing influence altogether (for
who needs a specialist on heaven and the soul when neither one
exists?), theology was now back at the old bench, justifying the ways
of God to men.

The rulers of the modern world had learned a lesson and learned it very quickly. They found out that no regime rules either by reason alone or by brute force. Every governing caste in history tries to create at least acquiescence, and if possible even affection, in those it governs. The symbolic culture of the society usually provides the vehicle for the winning of people's hearts and minds, and religion is usually its main content. The modern world turned out to be no exception. Its obvious inequities cried out for some theogony, some plausible explanation of why a world its leaders pronounced to be so emancipatory seemed so cruel to others.

But in taking on the onerous task of making the new world religiously plausible when it must have seemed—especially to Taine's women and laboring men and Mill's barbarians—to be terribly harsh, theology carried a severe handicap. It had already been divested of its authority to speak about those areas, like the mines and mills, which made people miserable. The rulers who had deported theologians from these precincts were reluctant to have them return lest they begin saying things about usury or the just price again.

The solution to this problem which theology hit on provides an essential key for understanding why it has now run its course. It "projected" its own cramped situation into a statement about God and the world. Now not only was theology incompetent and uninterested in politics, science, technology, and the rest, so was God. These fields, the faithful were assured, were autonomous realms with their own built-in self-guiding mechanisms. If managed competently by experts skilled in such matters, they would eventually serve the good of the commonweal. One had only to be patient, work hard, not meddle in the things one knew nothing about, and—above all —not tear up paving stones. Having been squeezed into a corner by the modern world, theology made a virtue of necessity and wrote its own reduced status into the being of the divine.

Now God, maker of heaven and earth, became the deity of religion, approached through what came to be called "religious experiences." Modern religion was born. A faith which had once proclaimed a Lord who lifted up and cast down emperors, who condemned extortion and profit gouging, was now reduced to being concerned exclusively with the inner spirit or at most with frictions between individuals. God did not question the institutional structures of ruling and money-making.

What happened to God in the hands of Abbé Maillard's bourgeoisie makes Nietzsche's account of the murder of God sound like an act of kindness in comparison. At least in Nietzsche's famous story there are blood and cruelty—and a corpse: "God is dead for you have killed him!" Here, however, there is no passion, only prudence. God is not murdered but neutered. "What have you done to God?" the madman would have to say to the entrepreneurs and their accomplices. "You have caged him, tamed him, domesticated him, and the priests have pliantly lent their aid. The roaring bull has become a listless ox. You have gelded God!"

There were still the old questions. Why did some people seem to live so well and others so badly, despite the experts and the self-guiding mechanisms? Theology accepted, almost without question, the current bourgeois solution: since the only real sin was ignorance, salvation came from schooling. Through education, the pedagogues taught, one could rise in a new ascent of Mt. Carmel and eventually become one of those at the top, especially if book learning was salted with honesty, perseverance, and cheerfulness. True, for dark-skinned people and the other natives, the road might be a bit longer since they, alas, were so unfortunate as to lack both schools and the right religion, but the road—in principle, was open to all.

Here was the hope. Some races and nations were now ahead of others, admittedly; but this was due largely to their hard work and frugality. The others might eventually catch up. It was wrong to consign them to eternal inferiority. This became the period of the greatest missionary activity and only those who would deny the ultimate equality of all persons (a good Enlightenment and modern doctrine) would refuse to share the gospel, schools, and the parliamentary system with the lesser breeds.

The problem with this theological solution to the riddle of how to make the modern world seem legitimate to the millions of people who felt it from the underside is that their own tired backs told them it was not true. The reason few of the excluded peoples of the brave new world ever accepted the modern theological concordat is not that they were unable to follow the argument. The reason was that it did not ring true. It did not correspond to what their daily lives revealed.

They rejected it in different ways. Some clung to premodern religious practices and beliefs. Others, especially the urban workers of

Europe, where the older forms were less accessible, became atheists or, more likely, functional agnostics. Africans often accepted the new religion but retained many of the beliefs they had before. In many of the mission fields converts did what the Latin Americans had done centuries earlier—they hid the idols behind the altars. The black churches of the United States have never accepted modern liberal theology. Even when a liberal-trained preacher like Martin Luther King, Jr., appeared, he could be heard by black people only because he still spoke the language of Zion. Women, more tightly integrated into modern society than other "minorities" because of their position in families, nonetheless continued to spark and lead many of the revolts against it. Anne Hutchinson, Mary Baker Eddy, Madame Blavatsky found ways to circumvent the modern theological consensus, sometimes successfully but often at great cost to themselves. It should not be surprising that as the modern world enters its final phase, these otherwise disparate groups have now begun to discover each other across the barriers that have separated them. They were not consulted in arranging the concordat. They feel no loyalty to it now.

This sketch of the role religion eventually came to play in the later phase of the modern era raises some disturbing questions. Will the postmodern era need religion? Does every civilization need it? Bonhoeffer wrote that the world was entering a time of "no religion at all," and that Christianity must shed the "outer garb of religion." He thought the future task of theology was to develop a "religionless interpretation of the Gospel." But the questions persist. The history of the modern world hardly answers them since those who initially sought to build a society on reason panicked as soon as the *hoi polloi* who had apparently been watching at the Bastille began to bash down some gates on their own. The rulers of the modern world wanted religion back in the world from which they had sought to banish it so God could undergird law and order. But they got more than they bargained for. Once set in motion, a religious revival cannot be controlled. The disciplines of the spiritual life cannot be commended only to other people. Religious symbols, despite the diagnoses of old-fashioned "vulgar" Marxists, develop a momentum of their own. Religion for the bourgeoisie became not just a means to keep the populace controlled but also the way they controlled themselves, a good and necessary thing not only for "them" but also for "us." It kept everybody's animal instincts at bay.

Nothing if not consistent, the rulers of modernity were willing to play by the rules they had invented. The early image of the bourgeois as swashbuckling and iconoclastic, willing to run risks and try anything once, now gave way to that of the cautious clerk carbuncular with his rolled umbrella. The pirate had become a patsy, and religion had made the difference. No wonder that by the time the young neurologist on the Bergstrasse began peering into the unconscious recesses of his patients' minds, religion had become almost totally identified with the censoring superego. Freud seems to have considered the possibility that religion might also be linked even more closely with the id or the ego. But he never went very far with the idea any more than Marx pursued his belief that religion could at times be much more than a sanction for the ruling classes. Neither seriously considered the possibility that what they saw around them was not Christianity in its original form but the peculiar expression of religion characteristic of the bourgeois era, playing the role the rulers of that era assigned it both in the society and in themselves.

It is just this willingness to see oneself as part of the crisis, to discern the *nihil* within as well as the anarchy around, that distinguishes the authentically spiritual conservative from the often cynical "neo." No genuinely religious person, even one who finds his diagnoses and prescriptions mistaken, can doubt the fundamental Christian spirituality of T. S. Eliot. His quest for personal and social salvation led him to ever deeper levels of faith. At the same time, it is understandable that seriously religious people often become enraged at what they view as the neoconservatives' tendency to see religion as fulfilling what one of their critics, Peter Steinfels, calls an "essentially negative" function: "it contained and diffused fanaticism, violence, cruelty, frenzy, and mass emotion inherent in the human condition. . . . Religion is always linked with restraint—or at most the temporary release that makes restraint possible."[7]

Yet behind what began as a somewhat cynical reimportation of the sacred to keep the folks in line and then became the faith of an era, there lurks the dim recognition of a genuine truth. After all, even Taine said that religion was needed because of "the human mind itself in which ideas willy-nilly express themselves in pictures." Taine here seems to be going beyond Hegel's idea that religion is the philosophy of the masses. He is making it more universal. The picturing, symbolizing, world-view-making faculty of human beings—what James Fowler calls the capacity for "faith-ing"—appears to interact with an individual's moral reasoning at every stage of human growth.[8] People tend to make moral choices on the basis of what are often vague, precognitive images of what the world is like and how they fit into it.[9] These images are most frequently housed by the culture in those systems of symbols and meanings to which anthropologists give the name "religion." In this sense, morality does emerge from "faith," and not just among the masses but in everyone.

Much more research is needed in the new discipline of comparative faith development studies. However, if the early evidence holds up, Bonhoeffer was wrong in foreseeing a fully "postreligious" era. Human societies will always have some "religion." The task of a postmodern theology, therefore, is not to work out a "religionless" interpretation of Christianity but to recover the real purpose of Christianity from its modern debasement into a conscious means of personal self-discipline and of social control. It is to begin exploring the full implications of Pablo Richard's statement that "for those who suffer its injustice, the reconciliation between religion and the modern world is a sacralization of oppression."

This task starts when one sees that those who hauled religion back into the secularizing world of nineteenth-century Europe did the right thing, if for the wrong reasons. They knew that "no one lives by bread alone." But instead of turning to "the Word which proceeds from the mouth of God"—which is how that verse continues—they introduced a word that was so circumscribed in function and so diluted in content that it could only serve the shallow purpose for which it was intended—to keep the natives in their place, and to cool everybody's mad impulses. The makers of the modern world saw what my old teacher Talcott Parsons once said Emile Durkheim taught him—that it is not enough to say religion is a social phenomenon. The truth is, society is a religious phenomenon. And this means that theology in the modern-becoming-postmodern world will have to deal with religion.

18. The Resurrection of Life

In the sixth century, Saint Benedict abandoned the worldly city and took refuge in the mountains so as to be able to find a favorable environment in which to seek God and live the Gospel. This led him to create a community of men who lived the same life as "the poor of the earth." Today, perhaps, St. Benedict would abandon the countryside and the mountains, now covered with gracious and comfortable villas. Perhaps he would abandon all those places where the rich and powerful have chosen to live and would go live among the dependent and exploited masses of the city in search of the "right place" to reread the Gospel.

> —Giovanni Battista Franzoni
> (St. Paul Christian Community, Rome)[1]

Our emerging postmodern period will be a religious one. This is not necessarily good news at all. Religion is always a mixed blessing, a source of good and of evil. It produces the sublime and the perverse: Torquemada and St. Francis, hospitals and inquisitions, *The Cloud of Unknowing* and *The Protocols of the Elders of Zion*. But since we are going to have religion in the postmodern era, Bonhoeffer's pursuit of "nonreligious Christianity" cannot be theology's purpose today. Still, this definitely does not mean that theology should restrict itself, as modern liberal theology sometimes did, to dealing with "religious experience" or the inner content of the faith or the primitive *kerygma*, while ignoring the all-important question of the roles religion actually plays in society. Before we move on to consider what resources we will need to undertake this postmodern theological task, we have one more important lesson to learn from our predecessors. It has to do with which religion or religions we will encounter in the postmodern world.

Auguste Comte is known as the founder of positivism. This word has now come to mean many things. For him it meant simply that the exclusive way to truth lay through scientific experiment. He hoped passionately that science could establish ethics but his careful investigation of the history of ethics led him to the unwelcome con-clusion that people are not moved to morality by cold empirical data. They need something warmer. Comte called it "affection," and through further historical studies he came to believe that religion was the only source powerful enough both to inspire and to discipline the affections.

But here Comte hit a snag. As a scientist he felt he could not believe in the miracles and the absurdities of religion. Further, he was afraid that as scientific knowledge spread, no one else would be able to either. Thus the dilemma: morality had to be supported by religion, but it could not be the only religion Comte knew, Chris-tianity.

Comte refused to retreat from the unnerving logic of his own reasoning; the only thing left to do was to invent a new religion, one that everybody—including the most scientifically trained—could be-lieve in. For Comte it would have to be a religion in which humanity would be the object of devotion, not God.

Today no one except a few specialists has ever heard of Comte's "new" religion—complete with mass, saints' days, and all the rest. But the old religion, the one he thought would disappear, is still very much alive and includes among its adherents many people even Comte would have accepted as scientifically sophisticated. The les-son of the heroic and also tragicomic story of Auguste Comte is that he was right to recognize that morality and religion are intertwined inextricably. He correctly sensed that the "affections" play a decisive part in the ethical life of the race. He knew as Taine did that "the human mind itself," and not just women and savages, thinks with pictures. He was mistaken, though courageous, to try to invent a new religion.[2]

Like any other world, the postmodern world will need religion.

Will it need a new one? Since religions, as Comte and many others have demonstrated, cannot be invented, the question must assume a somewhat different form. Is it possible that a new religious vision will appear, one that will help move us out of the dying and death-obsessed modern age and into the next?

One cannot merely pass over the possibility. New religions have appeared in the past, and Christianity is one of them. In fact, as religions go, it is one of the more recent ones. Some seers once looked to communism or socialism as the faiths of the future. Few do today. Some have tried to invent a comprehensive world faith like Bahai by assembling various elements of existing ones, a kind of spiritual Esperanto. Both Bahai and Esperanto are alive and well, but they can hardly be said to have swept the world before them. Some feminists have tried to revive or create a contemporary cult of the goddess, but so far their efforts have appealed to only a small number of women.

Given the lack of evidence that any new religion is waiting in the wings to enliven the postmodern era, the next logical question is what spiritual resources, if any, are appearing which might provide the basis for the new world we need and want? We are back to the dinosaurs and the field mice.

I do not mean to imply that Christianity will provide all the religious resources for the postmodern world. I do believe, however, that Christianity can and will make a decisive contribution to this new global civilization, and will do it in a manner completely different from the way it contributed during the modern age. Only a radically transformed and "demodernized" Christianity can possibly make such a contribution. Is a postmodern or "demodernized" Christianity possible?

At first glance, the prospect does not appear promising. Most of the institutions of Christianity and most of its doctrinal and ethical formulations are so encased in the dying modern world that it is hard to see how they could possibly either move us or serve us in a post-modern future. But there are some theologians who, although they have given up on modern religion including its Christian variant, have not given up on a Christianity released from its current captivity. Pablo Richard suggests that the only way to recuperate what he calls the "liberating core" of Christianity from its alliance with the modern world is to look at it from the perspective of those who are Christian but in some sense not "modern." We must rethink the Gospel from the viewpoint of those who have been excluded from or trampled by the modern world. They constitute the "absolute other" of this world, he says, and since they have not fully internalized the modern world/liberal theology synthesis, they stand in the only possible position to transform or subvert it.[3]

For Richard the modern world's "absolute other" is the poor. I would add some of the "others" on Taine's and Mill's list—women, "barbarians," the "simple working people." All these have internalized modern Christianity in some measure. It is the dominant current religious ideology, and no one who lives in the world can avoid it entirely. But these "others" have not absorbed it completely and have frequently even relied on their own interpretations of parts of it as alternative sources of meaning and identity. Some have even drawn on Christianity as a point of leverage for subversion and rebellion. These "other faces of Christ," embodied both in religious communities and in theological reflection, because they have resisted being utilized to make modernity credible, supply the only secure launching pads for moving beyond it. It is these interpretations alone that can provide the Christian contribution to the religious core of a truly postmodern world.

The main stimulus for the renewal of Christianity will come from the bottom and from the edge, from those sectors of the Christian world that are on the margins of the modern/liberal consensus. It is coming from those places where Christians are poor, especially Latin America; from areas where they live as small minorities surrounded by non-Christian cultures as they do in Asia; from the churches that live under political despotisms as they do in the Communist world and in parts of South and Central America; from the American churches of blacks and poor whites; from those women who are agonizing together over what it means to be faithful and female in a church that has perpetuated patriarchy for two millennia. These are disparate peoples; but what they have in common is that they were all dealt in and dealt out, included and excluded from modernity and its religious aura. Their forced removal to its sidelines (or better, its basements, kitchens, slums, and colonies) is what now enables them to offer a version of Christianity that is liberating because it has not been squeezed through the concordat or distorted by the straitened function the modern world has assigned religion and theology.

Pablo Richard's formula for evolving a postmodern theology provides just the structural basis that is needed. A viable postmodern theology will be created neither by those who have completely withdrawn from the modern world nor by those who have affirmed it unconditionally. It will come from those who have lived within it but have never been fully part of it, like the women in Adrienne Rich's poem who, though they dived into the wreck, have not found their names inscribed within it. It will be created by those who, like black American Christians, have refused to accept the slavemaster's gospel but have also refused to jettison the Gospel altogether. As Marshall Berman points out in his *All That Is Solid Melts into Air,*[4] the nineteenth-century modernist always saw both the peril and the promise of the modern spirit. Only in the twentieth century has the all-or-nothing attitude that either canonizes or anathematizes it appeared. What is needed, however, is not some measured middle ground, some mellowed balance of what has been good and what bad in modern liberal theology, but a theology forged by those who have been both inspired and abused, both touched and trampled on by the religion of the modern age.

Modern theology was fascinated with the mind. It concentrated on ideas and was especially interested in the question of good and evil. Postmodern theology will concentrate on the body, on the nature of human community, and on the question of life and death.

This is not just a prediction. When one examines the emerging theologies of the various excluded Christian communities, the Resurrection or something clearly akin to it is central to each. The Latin Americans have been emphasizing an "antifetishistic theology of life" against what they view as a culture of lifeless commodities and gray death. Asians talk of the presence of a life-giving spirit of God in their Hindu and Buddhist neighbors. Blacks decry the lack of "soul" in a blanched world. Women speak frequently of the need to restore the human body with all its senses fully alive to a Christianity that has become arid and cerebral. Poor white church people do not theorize about it much; but what always strikes middle-class visitors about lower-class Pentecostalism, for example, is its embodied energy, its dancing and shouting and ecstatic utterances.

The religious foundation for a new world civilization does not have to be invented. It is already present. The mice are scampering among the mammoths. The puny congregations in Corinth and Rome and Ephesus thrived in the niches and interstices of an empire that was cracking apart. One tiny cluster of the saints apparently even met "in the household of Caesar." Later the monasteries and still later the conventicles of the Radical Reformation became the spawning grounds of the next phase of history. Today the rudiments of a post-modern civilization are sprouting on the edges and in the crevices.

The three ingredients needed before any civilizational era can reach its take-off point, a *style of personal existence,* a *theological vision,* and a *corporate form,* are all coming from the militant outcasts of modernity.

1. At the level of *personal life style,* we can see the appearance of a form of "worldly spirituality," of "engaged mysticism" that is replacing the monastic and pietistic modes inherited from the medieval and modern periods. The title of a recent book on spiritual direction, *Inviting the Mystic, Supporting the Prophet,*[5] reveals the focus of the new postmodern spirituality. Unlike that of St. Anthony, this new spirituality is nurtured not by a single-minded withdrawal from the world but by a rhythm of advance and retreat, of wading into the pain and conflict of the secular realm, and repairing regularly into the sustenance of solitude and of a supporting community. A biography of St. Anthony says of him, "Nearly twenty years he spent . . . pursuing the ascetic life by himself, not venturing out and only occasionally being seen by anyone." Eventually his friends became concerned about him and tore down the stout door he had closed between himself and the outside. Then, the biographer continues, "Anthony came forth as though from some shrine, having been led into divine mysteries and inspired by God."[6]

Postmodern spirituality begins with the premise that periods of solitude are essential but that one need not meditate in a cell for twenty years to find God. God is present in the confusion and dislocation of the world. One encounters God not by turning one's back on that world but by plunging into it with the faith that the divine-human encounter occurs in the midst of the encounter of human with human, especially in the struggle to create signs of the coming of God's reign of peace and justice. Jon Sobrino, writing from the tortured land of El Salvador, says:

> The novelty of the new lifestyle is spelled out programmatically in the Sermon on the Mount. . . . The kernel is the assertion that love, service and truth constitute the only kind of power capable of anticipating the kingdom. Seen in this light, the command to love one's enemies expresses the complete radicalness of Jesus' demand . . . love of one's enemy is what verifies one's conversion, for the enemy is the most extreme and acute embodiment of other people.[7]

It must be emphasized that we are not talking here about a novel theoretical spirituality being elaborated by a new breed of theologians, but a form of discipline that is emerging in daily human living. Theologians like Sobrino would be the first to admit that what they are doing is not commending or creating a style of spirituality but clarifying and commenting on one that is appearing in their midst.

It is appearing among those communities, congregations, cultures, and peoples who have been willing to hold fast to the Christian message while refusing the dominant modern interpretation of what that Gospel says. Should it be any surprise therefore that the exemplary "saints" of the postmodern world include a black preacher (Martin Luther King, Jr.), a woman (Dorothy Day), and a Latin American (Oscar Arnulfo Romero)? These were all persons of profound faith who instead of looking for a cave, or accepting the institutional insulation that separates most of us from the agony of the world, immersed themselves in that world. They did so, however, not just as "activists" or "change agents" but as followers of Jesus who were willing to run the risks of discipleship.

2. At the *theological* level, the new religious vision can be found in the spirited conversations going on within and among the communities of Christians we have called "the others." Using the term loosely, the theologies percolating from these communities are what we mean by "liberation theology." But there is no unified "school of thought." There is no single theology. What all these theologies do have in common is a determination to break loose from the dominant

schools of theology hatched in the universities of Europe and the United States, encoded almost entirely by white males, and designed to respond to what are viewed as the religious needs of educated, "thinking" (read: doubting, questioning) readers.

What the liberation theologies have in common is their desire to reappraise Christianity and other religious traditions as well from the perspective of those who have been banished historically both from theological reflection and from the formulation of religious symbols. Despite differences, all the liberation theologies wish to effect what the Latin Americans call a *ruptura*, a radical disjunction from the methods, imagery, and agenda of the currently dominant theologies. This is not an effort to get away from Christian theology as such, but from those parts of it that have hurt them. Consequently, women, blacks, and Asians differ on exactly which features of this theological heritage they want to be liberated from; this is what produces the creative conflict among them.

There are those who believe these various theological tendencies not only have little relationship to each other but are moving in sharply different directions and are, ultimately, irreconcilable. Take for example the Asian liberation theology one now finds in the Christian churches of countries with predominantly Hindu or Buddhist religious traditions.[8] Some of the theologians who involve themselves in this work claim that Western liberation theologies, notably the black American and Latin American types, are too narrowly and uncritically Christian, too "Western," maybe even imperialistic. They fault the Latins especially for showing no interest in the challenge of religious pluralism. The Latins on the other hand complain that worrying about religious pluralism can lead to a kind of mindless tolerance and provide a respectable excuse for failing to confront the religious undergirding of unjust societies.

Women have accused blacks and Latin Americans of being blind to sexism, not only in the dominant theologies they criticize but also within their own. Blacks have criticized feminist theologians, most of whom are white and from middle-class educated backgrounds, of overlooking racism.

Despite all these frictions, I do not believe these various liberation theologies are necessarily antagonistic. Rather, they are particularistic. They do not pretend to be universally applicable but to articulate very specific settings. This suggests that the theology of the postmodern world will not be as coherent and systematically unified as modern theologies sought to be. They will be able to tolerate a higher level of jaggedness and lack of cohesion. There is a good reason for this. People who have lived within oppressed and dominated sectors of any society know that systems and symbols that emphasize universality and inclusiveness very often end up shortchanging diversity and particularity. Whatever their pretensions to evenhandedness and being all-encompassing, in the gritty dust of the real world unitive systems of thought usually become ideologies of domination. The effort of modern theology to be all things to all people everywhere may itself be one of the qualities of its modernity that should not survive into a postmodern world in which particularity will flourish. Likewise, narrative may now replace modern theology's near-obsession with systematizing and internal coherence, both of which tend to drain the color from religious expressions. Postmodern theology will thrive on stories.

3. At the level of *corporate form,* the resources for a postmodern Christianity also need not be invented but are pushing up through the cracking pavement of modernity. These new structures of Christian social existence take on as many shapes as liberation theology; but they all share the characteristics we have seen in the so-called base communities. Like liberation theology, the base community movement has come into being in the past two decades, starting among the impoverished and uprooted Christians of Latin America's rural villages and urban *favelas.* The movement has grown spectacularly, and has now reached Europe, Asia, and North America. It is made up of hundreds of thousands of local groups focused on Bible study and political action, and often critical of ideas, organizational patterns and liturgical practices of the more established sectors of the church.[9]

No religious movement in history has ever gone very far on ideas alone. Religions, unlike philosophies, are always embedded in rituals and symbolic practices, in songs and stories. Only when its ideas are coupled with such corporate realities—arising from them and influencing them—does a religious movement become significant. The Christian base communities of the Third World and their analogs in other places are providing that vehicle today. We have already visited La Chispa and examined the base communities movement. Here I want only to recall two features that underline the importance of these communities as the future form of corporate Christian reality.

The first is that like the various liberation theologies, the social shapes of postmodern Christianity also differ among themselves because they challenge different distortions in modern liberal Christianity. Women naturally tend to press for changes in polity that will permit them to exercise equal responsibility and leadership in the churches. They often support the ordination of women and the rewriting of hymns and prayers in a more inclusive language that does not use masculine words for everyone and does not always refer to the deity as "He." Black churches preserve and nurture the characteristic Afro-American qualities of worship and preaching that are often derogated in predominantly white congregations. South American base communities attack the traditional political alliance between the hierarchy and the oligarchy. European grassroots groups work for lay participation in a setting where churches have been extremely clergy-dominated. Thus all are pressing for the practical equivalent of the theological *ruptura* sought by liberation theology on the intellectual level.

Second, just as the Resurrection of Christ and of the human body is coming to supply a focal motif in the theology of postmodern Christianity, so the resurrection of the "mystical body," the rebirth of corporate community, is becoming the principal organizational quality of the new cells. In the modern period, Christian churches became a conglomerate of individuals. Congregations turned into collections of discrete persons (or at best households) who created a church through a kind of social contract—an idea with a distinctly modern pedigree. In the emergent base communities, however, the bonds are at once more particular and more holistic. Women discover sisterhood. Blacks affirm a kinship with others whose skin color has made their history what it is. The poor discover a closeness to others who share their disinheritance. The word "solidarity," with roots in the labor movement, has been used at times to describe this discovery of a deep bonding that the early Christians talked of as being "members one of another." In classical Christian theology this extraordinary tie was understood not as the result of mere natural consanguinity but as something made possible by the gifts of the

Spirit and the presence in the assembly of the One who had risen from the grave. The theologies of the postmodern Christian movements celebrate life against death. Their organizational styles stress community against individualism, organic instead of mechanistic modes of living together. Their spiritual disciplines emphasize coming forth from cell and cloister into the surging stream of life. Wherever one looks it is the message of Easter, the one that enlivened the early church, which seems to be the central proclamation of the postmodern churches.

19. Toward a Postmodern Theology

> What are the ideas with which those who have re-
> sisted capitalist modernization for centuries have
> identified? . . . Such movements drew their strength
> mainly from the potential of traditional ideas, from
> religious ideas.
>
> —Jurgen Habermas

For centuries theology's principal sparring partner has been philosophy. Augustine argued with the neoplatonists, Aquinas carried on a
lifelong conversation with Aristotle. Nineteenth-century theologians
conversed with the philosophical idealists and twentieth-century
theologians with the existentialists. As the end of the road for modern theology comes into view, however, it is becoming evident that
both theology and philosophy are desperately in need of new partners. For theology, the world religions and the traditions of popular
piety are now becoming key dialogue partners. Philosophy may come
to the same decision, since philosophers like theologians seem to be
increasingly aware that, "we are living in the closing of an epoch and
the project of modernity . . . has played itself out."[1]

Like theologians, philosophers thrash about for which way to go
now. One strategy, advanced by what some critics call the "antihumanists," is to declare that all of modernity has been an unmitigated
disaster from the beginning. The devil is indeed a modernist. Better
still, the modern is the devil. "The crisis of modernity cannot be
resolved through the fulfillment of the modern project," says Joel
Whitebrook in summarizing this view, "because that project itself is
the root of the crisis."[2]

In his book *The Twilight of Subjectivity*, Fred Dallmayr characterizes this position as follows:

> . . . the malaise of modern, contemporary life can be traced, either directly or indirectly, to its anthropocentric and subjectivist thrust, or its focus on the thinking subject; according to some, the malaise has already reached a crisis stage with the result that the "end" or "death of man" is imminent (if not an accomplished fact). . . . The remedy consists in a radical shift of attention, aimed at dislocating or "decentering" man in favor of overarching structures of systematic relations.[3]

For this school of thought, then, represented at its intellectual apex by the late German philosopher Martin Heidegger, the way back is the only way ahead. We must start by admitting not only that modernity is finished but that it should be.

For a second group of thinkers the modern age was not a total fiasco but a mixed bag, half devil, half angel of light. It included some elements that were liberating and others that were stifling. It was a battle between tendencies, with the Enlightenment representing, by and large, the bad guys and the Romantic movement the white hats. This perspective on the modern world emphasizes that whatever its failings it conceived powerful images of what a better world might be, elevated the ideal of liberty, and created the possibility of the individual person as a moral agent.

One of the main objections this second group has to the first school is that the "decentering of the subject" which the hardline antimodernists advocate could result in disaster. It could end up not just decentering the person but losing the person altogether. For this second school, the modern age has accomplished much, even though it is now in crisis. Its writers and poets never forgot that human beings are not pure intelligence but that they also have yearnings and desires that cannot be ignored—something Enlightenment thinkers tended to overlook. It may be this romantic recognition of the "reasons of the heart" that caused such thinkers as Franz Rosenzweig, Martin Buber, and Ernst Bloch to be highly sympathetic to religion. They distrusted many features of the modern world but also saw in it an opportunity to fulfill some of the promise of faith and of human emancipation.

The third position, represented today most vigorously by Jurgen Habermas, holds that although modernity is in real trouble, the way ahead is the way ahead: we must continue on the course set by this vast and ambitious "modern project."[4] For Habermas, there is nothing essentially wrong with the underlying idea of modernity; it is just that other powerful forces, capitalist consumerism in particular, have despoiled and distorted it. Habermas is particularly concerned that what now passes for "reason" in the modern world is not what the original celebrants of reason had in mind at all. Reason has become "how to," what Habermas calls "instrumental reason"; so we need to restore the original modern idea of a kind of reason—he calls it "practical reason"—which asks not just "how?" but also "why?" and which involves itself in morals and values. Neither angel nor devil, the modern world is more like a confused traveler who has lost his way and needs direction.

Habermas is also convinced that although the modern world is mortally threatened by the suffocating omnipresence of the "administrative mode," still it is the moral ideals and legal sanctions of the same modern age which allow for the appearance of the very countermovements that could liberate us from its distortions. He bases his theory on something which is akin to the old notions of "natural law." He calls it a theory of "communicative praxis."

What Habermas means is that the inner key to human nature and the norm of any society must begin with the fact that people talk to each other. They consult, converse, argue, hint, demand, request, negotiate—all in language. Habermas holds that where people are free to converse and then to carry out the decisions they arrive at, and where the social structures allow for and encourage such talk, community and justice will flourish. Where talk is banned as it is in totalitarian societies, or made useless and irrelevant, as it is in "administered" ones, freedom languishes. People can talk freely only when they meet each other as equals, when there is no unspoken threat against speaking freely. The built-in logic of human communication is that the people's right to form and nurture the places and occasions where this talk goes on not only must not be limited but must be renewed and deepened constantly. For Habermas, "in the beginning was the word," and although the word is not God (he is not a believer), it does become the norm by which all else is judged.

Habermas' theory is reminiscent of the work of John Rawls of Harvard, who holds that in the grammar and logic of moral discourse itself, one can discern built-in norms, something St. Paul might have identified as "the law which even the heathens have written on their hearts." Like Rawls's theory, that of Habermas creates an opening for theological questions that many other theories do not. Basically, Habermas' position on modernity retains a chastened confidence that it was and is a worthy "project" and that human beings possess the built-in capacity to carry it through.

When one looks at these three positions—the antimodernist, the ambivalent modernist, and the "critical modernist" position of Habermas from a theological perspective, which most commends itself? Which promises to be most helpful to Christianity in making its contribution to a postmodern world?

Many religious critics of modernity—Christian, Moslem, Hindu, and Buddhist—fall into the first camp. They see the entire "modern project" as a grotesque error that cannot be repaired but must simply be undone. This may be why so many contemporary religious thinkers find a resonance in Heidegger (although he too, like Habermas, insisted he was an atheist).

However, their rejection of modernity is too sweeping, too singular, too devoid of nuance. The devil may be a modernist, but the entire modern world is not of the devil. I am skeptical also of the "anti-Enlightenment" tendencies of the ambivalent modernist group. The history of Nazism has convinced me that too much fascination with the dark forces and inchoate feelings of a *Volk*, when not disciplined by unfettered critical thought and even by "reason," can prepare the way for calamity. I distrust the idea of "thinking with your blood." I welcome the prominent place given to utopianism in this second stream, but utopia must include a place for exposing destructive myths and unmasking fraudulent feelings.

Habermas' idea that the moral and legal gains of modernity are genuine and must not be lost, that they help provide an essential opening through which we may be able to muster the resources to move on to the postmodern, is valid. I also agree with Habermas' concentration on human communication in community. But, perhaps on the basis of a more theological view of human nature, I do not share his confidence that reasonable conversation alone, removed from a moral and religious tradition, can accomplish what he hopes for. People need larger ethical and symbolic frames of reference in which to converse; these grander settings have to be communicated through scriptures, stories, rituals, and traditions.

I accept, wholeheartedly, Habermas' belief that reason must be saved from its reduction to merely instrumental functions. But instead of just reclaiming "practical reason," what needs to be added to the restoration is what Fritjof Schuon calls "contemplative intelligence," the ingredient that philosophers of old were not ashamed to call "wisdom." This would involve the reconstitution of the segmented mind of modernity, so that not just morals but also meanings would be recognized as objects appropriate to human intelligence.

Like all ethical thinkers who criticize society, Habermas must eventually disclose where he finds the moral norms he brings to bear. Ordinarily, he says, they come from the implicit values present in human communication. But in an interview in Berlin in 1981, asked what real advantage he thought his theory of communicative praxis had over previous critical theories of society, Habermas stated that the gain in a communicative praxis theory is that "the normative contents of a humane social life can be introduced in an unsuspicious way . . . without having to secretly smuggle them in by way of a philosophy of history."[5] Previous theories had enabled one to speak only of "agents . . . acts, consequences," and so on, the vocabulary of most philosophical ethics today. But with a communicative praxis theory, it now becomes possible "also to speak of the characteristics of the life-worlds in which these agents . . . move."

When we look further for what Habermas means by these "life-worlds," we suddenly find ourselves in a territory that is familiar to theologians. Habermas says:

What are the ideas with which those who have resisted capitalist modernization for centuries have identified?
    Well into the 19th century it was not so much with the ideals of bourgeois emancipatory movements and certainly not with the ideas of socialism. Instead, such movements drew strength mainly from the potential of traditional ideas, from religious ideas, from

religiously founded natural law, etc. I don't mean just the Peasant Wars, but rather this extends far into the artisans' movement of the 19th century. These movements are driven by direct provocations of feelings of injustice as well as the need for spontaneity and expression.[6]

Habermas may not realize that many of the traditional and religious ideas people once drew on to resist "capitalist modernization" (and other aspects of modernization as well) are still alive. For millions of people, religious ideas have never ceased being the sources from which they draw their strength and inspiration. One need only mention Poland and El Salvador to see what this means today.

Habermas goes on in his interview to point out how the same traditional life-worlds placed severe limits on the political effectiveness of these movements. But that only heightens the importance of understanding how traditional religious movements are escaping from these limitations today. It could even be argued that the most effective resistance against the destructive elements of modernity—administrative misrule and bottom-line hunger—is coming "certainly not with the ideas of socialism" but from religiously motivated "life-worlds." It would make the gods smile if Habermas' hope that the "project of modernity be carried through" came true only because modernity's despised and rejected outcasts made it possible.

This trick of the gods could well be the case. The postmodern Christian theology, emerging already from the edges and from the bottom, will need to come to terms with two quite formidable realities, global religious pluralism and popular piety or *"religión popular."* The "lived worlds" of which Habermas speaks do not live in the minds of social theorists. They live in the stories and customs of particular peoples all over the world. And these symbolic structures of the lived worlds are almost always preserved and developed in religion, both in the "high" religions discussed in textbooks and in the common folk piety that often goes unnoticed. I will now leave the philosophers and move on to the conversation Christian theology must take up with the other world faiths and with popular piety, asking of each what it can teach us about the liberation of humankind from the faltering "project of modernity."

20. The Ancient Runes Speak—
Postmodern Theology and the World Faiths

> In a period when Western society is no longer felt to
> be the world but just a small, often very pretentious
> constituent of a larger whole . . . which, further-
> more, smarts under the painful impact of Western
> aspirations and practices, the Christian claim that
> "in no one else is there redemption" meets with loud
> protest. "Christian imperialism" is a constant and
> accusing cry.
>   —Edward Schillebeeck
>   *Jesus, An Experiment in Christology*[1]

The postmodern world is a religiously pluralistic one. But both renascent political fundamentalism and grassroots liberation theology are
distinctly Christian movements. Both draw their main strength from
continents that are predominantly Christian in their religious and
cultural traditions. Furthermore, both fundamentalism and liberation
theology tend to be Christ-centered theologies. Fundamentalism op-
poses what its spokesmen call the wishy-washy Fatherhood-of-God
thinking of liberalism. Liberation theology emphasizes Jesus Christ
against excessive saint veneration and religious fatalism. As they
grow and spread to other areas of the world, however, both movements are finding it necessary to cope with global spiritual heterogeneity. The question whether either will be able to deal satisfactorily
with this unavoidable fact of contemporary life remains to be answered. It will provide one of the main tests of their capacity to break
out of their regional confines and exert their influence more widely.

There can be no doubt about the religiously heterogeneous quality of the dawning postmodern world. Not only do we live on a spiritually multiplex globe, but nearly every continent, nation, and city is itself increasingly pluralistic. As a result of nineteenth-century Christian missionary activity, worldwide migration patterns, and the spread of Asian religious practices in the West, previous "spheres of influence" arrangements no longer work. It will not do to think of Christianity for the West, Buddhism for Southeast Asia, Islam for the Middle East, and so forth. Everyone is now everywhere. There are native-born Presbyterians in Cambodia; third-generation Buddhists in the United States; and Hindu temples in the Caribbean. Ghetto religions—those that rely on an element of isolation to survive—are dying out. Hare Krishnas chant in St. Peter's Square in Rome; Christianity is reappearing in China; and young Indian untouchables calling themselves "panthers" recently began converting to Buddhism to escape the Hindu caste system. Religions now coexist and interact whether or not theologians or mullahs or bishops approve.

Religious pluralism is an irreducible fact. But in facing up to it, both fundamentalism and liberation theology will have to overcome formidable obstacles. Fundamentalism has been the branch of Christianity least sympathetic to other religious traditions. Fundamentalists have generally viewed Buddhists and Moslems as idolators, pagans, or infidels. Liberation theology, insofar as it springs from a Latin American background, is limited by the relative religious uniformity of its home continent. Unlike Africans or Asians, South American Christians have not had to deal over the centuries with the vigorous presence of "rival" religions, since indigenous Indians and enslaved Africans were restricted to the margins of society and in any case often accepted Christianity as their own. Neither fundamentalism nor liberation theology seems particularly well suited to deal with religious pluralism, and until quite recently neither one had done much to overcome this limitation.

In modern academic theological circles, however, the picture is quite different. In the past decade religious pluralism has emerged as the most debated question of all. Page through the titles of the articles published in the most influential journals of theological and religious studies for the past ten years. Glance at the catalogs of books on religion rolled out by the presses. Look at the course offerings in seminaries and college religion departments. Sometimes one gets the impression that religious pluralism is the only thing worth talking about. Nor is it merely something tacked on or restricted as it once was to "comparative religion" courses. It is changing nearly every field of religious study. Instead of emphasizing the uniqueness of the ancient Hebrew faith, Old Testament scholars search for parallels with the Canaanites. Once viewed as peripheral, the gods of the Syrians and the Babylonians are now studied sympathetically. New Testament students compare the Pauline epistles and the synoptic gospels with Gnostic scrolls and Buddhist or Hindu texts. Students of ethics have become fascinated with the moral exemplars and law codes of other religious traditions. Philosophers of religion ransack Western and Asian texts for universal values. Scholars investigate the comparative psychology of religion, the comparative phenomenology of religion, and comparative spiritual practices.[2]

But one can compare and contrast religions only up to a point. The people who study religion are not ciphers. They are faced with the same questions of life and death and right and wrong with which the various religions deal. They cannot avoid the question of truth forever. Economists who investigate rival theories of savings and inflation must decide how to invest their own money. Students of comparative religion eventually have to decide how they are going to live their lives and make their decisions. They have to ask what faith, if any, will guide their ultimate choices. This unavoidable need to choose has pushed the academic study of religion toward a frank acknowledgment that no one can study religion merely descriptively. This in turn makes the modern myths of neutrality and objectivity increasingly implausible.

Neither fundamentalists nor liberation theologians have ever thought that the study of other religions could be neutral. Both see something terribly important at stake, the salvation of souls from hell or the liberation of captives from oppression.

Ironically, the momentum of current academic studies in religious pluralism is pushing it toward an approach which is similar to more praxis-oriented theologies. The crisis is a genuine one, and although it is seriously doubtful that fundamentalists will make a significant contribution to its resolution, liberation theologies could.

"LET THE ANCIENT RUNES SPEAK"

Modern theologians are beginning to realize that they have
reached a certain crossroads in the study of world religions. In the
spring of 1982, after spending a number of years examining the confusing welter of literature that has appeared on this topic during the
past decade, a scholar named Carl Raschke attempted to make some
sense out of the babble. Raschke realized that the question of the
diverse claims to truth made by the different traditions would finally
have to be faced.[3]

Raschke lists four ways students of religion deal with the "truth
question." The first is the careful and sympathetic study of the various expressions of faith by a method that tries not just to observe
but to feel its way into their singular and concrete reality. This
method assumes that one should listen without preconception, since
what people actually believe is often not what the theologians say
they should. The various faiths are studied without making any judgments about their validity or truth.

This first approach requires a certain mixture of attention, caring,
and suspension of judgment. It is equally applicable whether one is
sitting in a serpent-handling church in West Virginia, swaying with
the devotees in a Krishna temple in Vrindavan, listening to the
chanting of Tibetan monks, or pondering an opaque scriptural text.
It is not the cool, objective detachment of analytical observation.
What is required by this method is a trained capacity for entering in,
listening to, and watching without evaluating. It is a method most
American undergraduates take to almost instinctively.

The trouble with this listening and feeling approach is that, before
long, anyone investigating faith confronts issues of life and death. It
is one thing to appreciate at some depth why thirteen-year-old Iranian boys walk into an Iraqi minefield secure that if they are blown
to bits they will be rewarded by Allah with eternal life. But religious
faith by its very nature has to do with the things one will live and die
for; so the question "Is it true?" inevitably arises.

The second route Raschke registers is also familiar to me since it
has come to be associated with my colleague Professor Wilfred Cantwell Smith, former director of the Center for the Study of World

Religion at Harvard.[4] Wilfred Smith's highly original contribution is often capsulized with the phrase "one doesn't study 'religions,' one studies people." Even the word "religion" he says is itself a misleading abstraction. For Smith, what one should study is "faith." And faith can be found only in humans and in the traces they leave in rite, scripture, and custom. For Smith, faith is that great confidence and joy which alone enables human beings to feel at home in the universe. It is what permits them to find meaning both in the world and in their own lives. Furthermore, this confidence must be sufficiently deep so that—unlike a belief or opinion or idea—it remains stable no matter what happens at the level of immediate events.

This approach too falls short of providing any way to confront the question of truth. Wilfred Smith wants the method to be more than descriptive. He believes that when religious men and women discard abstractions like Buddhism and Christianity and deal honestly with themselves and each other as creatures of faith, a certain "convergence" is bound to occur. They sense a common source of confidence. Smith has never succeeded in showing how such a convergence happens. Expecting this convergence may itself be a matter of faith, something which, along with Professor Smith, one can hold to and hope for, but cannot demonstrate to "those of little faith."

The third approach, according to Raschke, is exemplified by those scholars who contend that behind the infinite particularities of the various expressions of faith there lies a single primordial tradition.[5] This primordial tradition is not readily visible, but it is there. It is the underlying stratum of which the separate "religions" of the world are so many surface stalagmites, and it can be uncovered by the careful geologist of faith. Religious thinkers in this school view Christianity and the other traditions as variants of something larger and more comprehensive—God's inclusive revelation to all creatures, or the universal human capacity for religiousness.

This unity-behind-the-diversity position is very widely held, among both scholars and lay people. One clear expression of it is that of Professor John Macquarrie of Oxford University. Taking a philosophical approach, Macquarrie sees the riddle of religious pluralism as analogous to the age-old debate about "the one and the many," an argument that goes back at least to the ancient Greeks. "God," for

Macquarrie, is the name of the ultimate unity beyond all seeming contradictions and differences. He writes,

> These religions will be living side by side on earth in the foreseeable future. They must seek to draw more closely together and demonstrate by common life and action their fundamental commitment to the One, however that One may be named in each religion. . . . No single faith has yet attained to the understanding of the fullness of the One. . . . Therefore each faith must be respectful and ready to learn from the spiritual insights of others.[6]

Raschke describes this correctly as a "Hindu solution" to the question of pluralism. It claims, in effect, that the variegation in religious traditions is only a secondary quality, that underneath, all the separate rivers and rivulets of faith draw on a single mighty reservoir. All the gods are avatars of the divine reality.

Again, as we saw with Wilfred Smith's confidence in the "convergence" of persons of faith, this third position may be true; but it is not demonstrably true. Like Smith's hope, this vision of an unseen unity also requires a considerable leap of faith. In this case, however, the leap is into a faith that would be much more acceptable to an educated modern Hindu whose tradition already posits a single divine source with a million faces than it would to most Moslems or Orthodox Jews. It would appeal to the mystical strains in the world's religions (Sufism, Esoteric Buddhism, Gnostic Christianity) but not to their more orthodox branches. All of this does not mean this approach is not true. It only means that it postulates a certain answer (a "Hindu" one) before the other alternatives are carefully investigated.

Finally, Raschke discusses a fourth method of dealing with pluralism, one advocated by the Indian Catholic Raimundo Panikkar. It is a form of dialogue among persons of different faiths, but it is not the kind of dialogue that focuses on the differences and/or similarities among religious traditions. What Panikkar advocates is a dialogue that draws partners into the "unspoken center" they share.[7]

For Panikkar, a priest and mystic whose father was a Hindu and whose mother was a Spanish Roman Catholic, most dialogues between religious persons go astray when the participants begin

advocating, comparing, defending, conceding—like diplomats negotiating a treaty. What Panikkar yearns for is more respect for si-
lence, more shared awe and ecstasy. One neither hides the
differences nor trumpets the similarities but allows both to be what
they are. One waits and listens. The procedure is a nonviolent one,
reminiscent of Gandhi's *ahimsa*.

Clearly, all the methods Raschke mentions for confronting the
dilemma of religious pluralism have their strengths. But when one
adds them all up, the question of truth is still missing. Raschke
recognizes this. He suggests that it is time for both the study of
religion and the dialogue among religious persons to be taken out of
the sphere of description and comparison. Those engaged in the
activity must recognize that there is another dimension, that the
reality to which their words and silences point must also become a
part of the process itself. Dialogue must cease to be secondary reflection about religion and become itself a religious quest. When this
happens he believes dialogue will also become an occasion for further
revelation, a new disclosure of the divine.

Raschke thinks that the course he is advocating will carry us "beyond theology." He even suggests coining a new word, "dialogy," to
make the change clear. True, the path he suggests will take us beyond
modern theology, and modern religious studies as well, but must it
take us beyond theology as such? For Raschke the answer is yes,
because for him theology inevitably entails what he calls "circum-
scribing the divine as an object of reflection," whereas dialogy "cuts
through all standard representations" in order to "let the ancient
runes speak." Raschke is afraid theologies are already too jelled, too
fixed; and that therefore even a crosscultural theology will remain at
the level of mingling and sorting existing traditional connotations:
nothing new can happen. Dialogy would bring these beliefs into
"interpretive tension" and "relax their iconic rigor" so that one became aware of multiple layers of meaning.

By "dialogy" does Raschke mean something close to what I am
calling "postmodern theology"? He might not agree that he does, but
this may be because of his conception of theology as a static way
of thinking, one whose boundaries are already firmly nailed down.
But what if theology were not as graven in stone as he thinks it
must be?

The German theologian Eberhard Jungel's *The Doctrine of the Trinity: God's Being Is Becoming*[8] is a highly serious treatise in which one will look in vain for any mention of "ancient runes" or relaxing "iconic rigor." Its author reminds us that in the classical biblical tradition, God is not a fixed entity, a static ideal, or the mere embodiment of eternal principles. Rather, God is a "Becoming." This means that people of faith must be ever alert to new, unexpected, and unprecedented perceptions of God, not just because they learn to see what was always there, but because God "becomes"; new qualities of God emerge.

Jungel may be providing the metaphysical basis for Raschke's "dialogy"; and Raschke may be suggesting one method by which these new qualities of God might be discerned. Still, both of them would profit from the richly imaginative thinking about God that is now coming from the edges and from the bottom. The Chinese Christian theologian C. S. Song, writing in what a Japanese colleague calls a "post-First-World Age" vein, gently suggests that God suffers and feels the pain of human beings.[9] From El Salvador, Jon Sobrino shows that a God who loves actually and not just figuratively must be wounded and hurt just as the people in whom God dwells are hurt.[10] Isabel Carter Heyward, a daring feminist theologian, suggests that God is not only changing and becoming, but that God's entering into real give-and-take with human beings means that human beings actually contribute to the redemption of God.[11]

In the final analysis it does not matter if the postmodern theologies now arising are called "theology" or "dialogy" or something else. What is important is that Christians meet their fellow human beings of the other great religious traditions not in a detached or aggressive way, but with a willingness to listen together to what the ancient runes say. It is important that this mutual listening take place not in some demarcated religious sphere but in the day-to-day combat and compromise of real life. The inner logic of the strictly academic approach to religious pluralism is leading it out of the academy and into the grimy world, in which both fundamentalism and liberation theology are also trying to cope with the same cacophony.

PAGANS, LIBERALS, AND OTHER INFIDELS

Jerry Falwell, with his usual disarming candor, is talking about how he as a fundamentalist can work for certain moral and political objectives alongside people he believes are going to hell. "I can do so," he says, "as a private citizen," not as the minister of Thomas Road Baptist Church. He is careful, he says, when speaking to Mormons, Catholics, and Jews, not to offend them or to "witness" to them, not even on the Old Time Gospel Hour. "Fortunately, fundamentalists like me have been growing up in the past twenty years," he says. "We have been finding we can fellowship only with truth, but we can have friendship in many other affinities." Friendship but no fellowship, political coalition but not compromise on doctrine: it is a delicate balancing act but he seems to manage.

For liberation theology, the basis for the interreligious alliance is the struggle of the poor. For Falwell, however, this is exactly the kind of cause that must be strenuously avoided to keep the coalition together on the essentials. "People ask," he says,

> What about the poor? We could never bring the issue of the poor into Moral Majority because the argument would be, Who is going to decide what we teach those people? Mormons? Catholics? No, we won't get into that. As private persons and ministers, we make a commitment if we feel convicted. But for Moral Majority, no! If we go in there, create jobs, raise funds, and get involved with the local pastors, the problem is, which pastors? If we say the Mormon pastors, the fundamentalists are gone. If we say the Catholic pastors, the Jews are gone, and so forth. We just have to stay away from helping the poor. [12]

Mormons and Catholics? To most Protestants, cooperating with these groups might not seem to constitute crossing a major ecumenical hurdle, and would hardly qualify as a case of dealing with religious pluralism. But for fundamentalists the differences between Catholics ("who believe in works righteousness") or Mormons ("who have another Bible") and Buddhists or Hindus is inconsequential. There are no degrees of truth. There is no reason why the same moral and political considerations that lead Falwell to cooperate with Jews and Mormons should prevent him from working with any religious group in the world. "We are even willing to work with the feminists," he says, using an example which for him is probably more of a borderline case than Sikhs or Shintoists, "and we do—on pornography."

Yet when pressed, Falwell admits that there is a theological base which undergirds this moral/political alliance. It is not just built on pragmatism. The theological foundation is expressed in Proverbs 14, which he interprets as meaning "Living by God's principles promotes a nation to greatness; violating God's principles brings a nation to shame." He believes that in the past God has always honored the United States because its citizens have honored God's principles. This, he says "has nothing to do with whether people go to heaven or hell. It is a personal relationship to Christ that determines that." But America must remain free if its churches are to be able to evangelize the world, and it will stay free only if God's principles are honored. Moral Majority is serving the gospel indirectly—by creating and preserving freedom.

We have seen that the basic Christian communities have a theology of history just as the fundamentalists do. Both movements see the church operating in a larger setting in which God works through corporate entities—the nation for fundamentalists, the global poor for the liberationists. But it would be misleading to push the comparison very far, for the similarities are incidental rather than substantive, and the differences are enormous.

Most Latin American liberation theologians ignore the issues of religious pluralism. The Hispanic Catholic tradition is pervasive on their continent and they have been relatively blind (until recently) to indigenous and African religions in South America. But liberation theologians and grassroots communities in other parts of the world, especially in Asia, have begun to tackle the issue and it is to them we now turn.

The liberationist approach to religious pluralism comes from politically committed Christians in those sections of the world where pluralism is not merely an intellectual question but also a political one and a fact of everyday life. It has started among Christians who have come into close contact with revolutionary movements in regions where issues of injustice and class confrontation are interwoven with those of caste, religion, and communal loyalties.

Tissa Balasuriya is a Roman Catholic priest from Sri Lanka, the country Westerners used to call Ceylon. As an Asian he lives in a part of the world where Christian churches exist as tiny minorities. He also lives in a region which has felt the full impact of European colonial control and the erosive power of Western business enterprises, both emanating from allegedly Christian continents.

As an Asian Christian, Balasuriya says he welcomes liberation theology, especially in its Latin American form, as a long-needed break from the dominant role played by European and North American theologians. For many years these theologians have provided the agenda for theologians everywhere. However, the Western thinkers who developed them were usually unaware of how much the Western context in which they lived, that of capitalist affluence, tinctured what they wrote. As a Sri Lankan Christian who is committed to the ongoing attempt by those who suffered from the colonial heritage to begin again, Balasuriya also welcomes liberation theology as a contribution to the actual liberation process.

As a politically active Asian Christian, Balasuriya also has some criticisms of Latin American liberation theology. He has voiced them frequently as the theological interaction between Asia and Latin America has been stepped up in recent years.[13] The Latin Americans' concentration on the relatively recent history of capitalist expansion as the historical form of social sin leads them, he believes, to overlook the longer history of white European expansion, a process driven by more factors than economic ones. He believes this oversight explains the failure of Latin American theologians to express much concern about the monstrous destruction of the Maya, Aztec, and Inca civilizations that were flourishing before the arrival of the Spanish. He also asks why nearly all Latin American theologians (like the secular ruling circles within Latin America) are lighter skinned and of European origin, while the poorest people are of Indian or black African descent. Balasuriya believes there is a religious, cultural, and racial blind spot in Latin American liberation theology, and this is a point on which he is supported especially by some North American black theologians.

Is there somewhere within Christianity itself, not just in its modern form, a defective gene that propels it into periodic outbursts of ruthless expansion, of crusades, pogroms, and conquests, at the expense of other people's cultures? If not, is there a quirk that makes Christianity susceptible to being used by expansionist or dominating secular movements? Why has it been possible for the so-called Great Commission ("Go ye into all the world and preach the Gospel") to be exploited time and again by imperial forces bent on conquest and rapine rather than on love or service? Does this proclivity stem from the church's early entanglement with the Greek idea of *paideia*, the responsibility of the Hellenes to "civilize" barbarians? This would make the flaw more a malformation resulting from an infantile trauma than a genetic one: serious but not fatal. Was the "religionizing" of the message of Jesus itself an error which for millennia has unnecessarily divided Christians from people whose lives have been shaped by what the modern world calls "religions" (a concept itself invented —as we have just seen in Wilfred Smith's work—by the Christian West)? Without denying that it has allowed itself to be flagrantly misused by a money-obsessed system that contradicts its inner essence, the hard question remaining is whether there is something in Christianity as a "religion" that makes it susceptible to this perversion. If there is such a defective gene or quirk, then Balasuriya is right: the scale and scope of the theological changes needed are much larger than those that most liberation theologians presently envisage. Only a serious dialogue between Christians and people from religious traditions that have not exhibited this expansionist obsession, at least not as egregiously, will enable us to answer these questions.

Balasuriya believes Latin American liberation theology would be greatly strengthened if it took more seriously not only the religious experience of its own indigenous populations but also the experience of the world religions. He knows the narrow focus of Latin American theology is in large measure simply the result of a history which spread Catholic Christianity across an entire continent. "But," he says,

in many other parts of the world the struggle for human liberation has to take place within the context of pluralistic societies. Hence the action-reflection groups and even the "grassroots communities" would be not only of Christians but also of believers of other religions such as Hinduism, Buddhism, Islam, Confucianism, etc. The "revision of life" then would have to be based on a much wider inspiration drawn from different traditions including a deeper understanding of the human person, of the world and of the Absolute. This would involve a wider form of ecumenism than is generally met in Latin American theological reflection.[14]

This "wider ecumenism," Balasuriya believes, would have far-reaching implications for mission and evangelization. It is important to recognize that for this Asian Christian it would not mean a watering down of the Gospel so as to make it more acceptable to Buddhists or Hindus. Rather, he sees an Asian liberation theology celebrating a "Cosmic Christ" who is present in all cultures and religions as well as being the (more "Western") Lord of History.[15] Thus Asian liberation theology has begun to address the vexing issue of religious pluralism, the same question that exercises the academy so much. But again, one should not be misled by superficial similarities. There is a vast difference between the academic and the liberationist approach to religious pluralism.

THE POSTMODERN CHRIST: A CONVERGENCE OF THEOLOGIES?

The "liberation method" is political from the outset. It rejects the notion that there can be any neutral theology or any detached understanding of who Jesus was and is. This means that significant thinking about Jesus can go on only among people who are seriously following Jesus—that is, trying to make Jesus' life purpose their own. The purpose of Jesus' life was the coming of the kingdom of justice and peace, of which he was himself the chief exemplar. Hence the struggle for the reign of divine justice provides the only appropriate context within which any meaningful discussion about Jesus can go on.

Balasuriya and his liberationist colleagues have a point. Arguments about the significance of Jesus ("Christology") have always been political as well as theological. The various titles and interpretations of

Jesus—Messiah, Son of Man, the Pantocrator of the Hagia Sophia, the bleeding Man of Sorrow—were not invented in seminars but came out of a contentious and conflict-ridden human history. At the scene of the crucifixion itself a dispute broke out among the priests and the Roman officials about what should be written on the sign above the Cross. The argument continues today. The centuries-long battle over how to answer the question "Who do you say I am?" is in part a debate between those who want to control the meaning of Jesus because they recognize his political significance all too well. We can understand and evaluate these different images—such as the "historical Jesus" or the "Cosmic Christ"—only as we recognize the politics of Christology and only as we participate in that same history.

This point about the ongoing political history of Christology is also crucial in contending with religious and cultural pluralism. The struggle for the coming of the kingdom provides the context for the "wider ecumenism" Balasuriya calls for. As he sees it, this context includes people who are not Christians. The argument about who Jesus was is also about who he is. It is inseparable from the question of what the reign of God means, and how and where it is appearing today. These discussions did not stop with the Gospels, the Apostle's Creed, the "classical Christologies," or more recent reformations. The important point is not only that the discussion goes on but that it proceeds among participants and within history, not above it.

For liberation theology the principal objective of christological thought is not to make sure this or that formulation is conceptually aligned with one of the orthodox confessions. It is to determine how a given formulation actually contributes to the coming of the king-dom, and this is a question to which people other than Christians can contribute. Words mean different things at different times and in different settings. The same christological title that once clarified the meaning of Jesus and signaled the coming of the New Era can now distort his original meaning. Therefore theologians must always ask how, by whom, and for what purposes various christological images are used. The most difficult continuing critical task of Chris-tology is to prevent the misuse of ideas about Jesus to thwart his purpose, stifle his emancipatory message, and control the people among whom he was and is opening God's reign.

What I have sketched here is not an answer to Balasuriya's question about a "Cosmic Christ." It is a description of how liberation theologians would go about addressing such a question. It not only asks the ancient runes to speak again, it asks them to speak in such a way that they are heard by the outsiders and the brokenhearted as a word of hope and freedom.

FUNDAMENTALISTS AND LIBERATIONISTS: THE PERSONAL SAVIOUR AND THE COSMIC CHRIST

The favorite christological formula of American fundamentalists, one they share with almost all varieties of evangelicals, is "Jesus Christ as personal Saviour." When I was a child, accepting Jesus as "my personal Saviour" was the exclusive way in which one's relationship to Christ could be expressed. There is something odd about the authority this formula has achieved in fundamentalism since the phrase itself does not appear anywhere in the Bible; still, it is often used as a test for who is in and who is out ("for me or against me") by a number of conservative Christians.

The phrase has a history. It arose during the heyday of pietism and revivalism as a weapon protesting the bland, impersonal, and "official" Christianity of the time. At a popular level it expressed the same urgency Kierkegaard felt to attack the smug "civil religion" of Christendom and to insist on a faith that required a genuine personal decision. Although the pietistic project was eventually engulfed by romantic individualism, still one can only applaud its original intention and what its highly personal language meant then.

Today, the language about a "personal Saviour" often conveys a different meaning. Ironically, pietism, often combined with fundamentalism as a type of Christianity emphasizing individual religious feelings, has itself swollen up into the established "civil religion" of whole regions and areas of the United States. A perverted form of Kierkegaard's existential inwardness has become the predominant public theology, a support to the status quo and a pious bulwark against the wrenching changes in public life that God's Kingdom would require. For many comfortable Christians, *"personal* Saviour" has become a code. It perpetuates the privatized modern reduction of Christianity to the subjective realm. It serves to devalue the historic political dimension of faith.

The import of the "personal Savior" formula hangs on the class status and racial coloration of those who use it, and what it actually means to them. For affluent Christians this confession almost always functions as an impediment to a mature faith. It is a way of confining Christianity to the private realm. Many poor Christians, black and white, however, use the phrase to assert a social identity and dignity as persons of worth, as people whom God loves and cares for despite the cruelty and lovelessness of the cash-value world around them. The phrase says "I am somebody important" to a world that is constantly telling them they are worthless. This may be why it has appealed to rednecks and blacks alike. It gives a sense of solidarity with sisters and brothers whom consumer culture tears apart and sets against each other. Thus as a formulation that bestows confidence and human worth on a people who are deprived of these by the world itself, the "personal Saviour" language, as it is used among the poor, can be a valid confession.

This description of a particular image of Jesus in the American context illustrates in some measure how the discussion about Jesus Christ and his significance must proceed in an area characterized by both religious pluralism and class strife. The question of who Jesus Christ is and how the reign of God can be interpreted in a religiously plural world is a political as well as religious question. It can be answered only by women and men who see the gospel not as one religious tradition among others—to be compared, defended, synthesized—but as a call addressed primarily to all the rejected and outcast peoples of the world, whatever their cultural or religious tradition.

Perhaps we can clarify how liberation theology can contribute to the great debate about religious pluralism by going back for a moment to the different routes Carl Raschke describes. Liberation theology uses all of them but in every instance it does so by placing the religious dimension in its larger political and cultural setting. Liberation theologians like Balasuriya are, in some ways, "phenomenologists." They do try to "bracket" peremptory judgments about Buddhists or Hindus. They do try to enter their worlds with empathy. But the mode of their entry is guided by the Kingdom idea; they do so as Jesus did, by taking the side of the lowest castes, the outsiders, the poor and the ritually impure.

As in the second stance Raschke mentions, liberationists are also more concerned with people than with "religions." However, they are most concerned with particular people, the hurt and the helpless, the despised classes.

Like the scholars of the third approach who look for a hidden transcendental unity in all particular faith expressions, the liberationists also envision a world in which unjust divisions and racial and class hatred will be abolished. But for the liberationist this unseen reality lies ahead, not beneath or behind. It is eschatological, not primal. It requires faithful love and service, not esoteric insight.

Finally, along with Panikkar liberation theologians reject the idea that one can gain any value by merely reflecting on and comparing theological formulations. New insight comes only through reflective action.

For the majority of the world's Christians, most of whom are poor or colored and many of whom live among men and women of different faiths, the liberation approach to religious pluralism is already a great liberation.

It is a relief not to have to enter into theological debate with every Moslem or Sikh or Buddhist before deciding whether to cooperate in the combat against social evil and in the celebration of the promise of life. In story after story and teaching after teaching Jesus insists that God gives the Kingdom to the poor because they have nowhere else to turn, and not because of their doctrinal orthodoxy or moral purity. He teaches that God extends the reign to anyone who is willing to accompany the poor in their efforts to claim that Kingdom against those who withhold it from them.

In the light of this "Kingdom-centered" view of Christology, the whole meaning of the discussion among people from different religious traditions shifts. The purpose of the conversation is different. Interfaith dialogue becomes neither an end in itself nor a strictly religious quest but a step in anticipation of God's justice. It becomes praxis. Similarities and differences which once seemed important fade away as the real differences—between those whose sacred stories are used to perpetuate domination and those whose religion strengthens them for the fight against such domination—emerge more clearly.

For Christians, the theological basis for this shift in the nature of the interfaith dialogue is not so hard to find. When the disciples reported to Jesus that they had discovered individuals they did not even know freeing people from demons and asked him if they should not do something about it, Jesus quickly assured them that it was what these people were doing and not how they were interpreting it that was important: "He who is not against me is for me." At another time Jesus insisted that verbal definitions of who is "for or against" the coming of the Kingdom are secondary at best. He praised the brother who obeyed his father's command—even when he said he would not—rather than the brother whose obedience was a matter of words. Later Jesus warned his followers that not everyone who says "Lord, Lord" receives grace, but only those who do God's will. Pagans, Samaritans, prostitutes, and publicans inherit the Kingdom. The orthodox priests and temple rulers trail along later.

In the face of these clear warnings from Jesus himself it seems difficult to justify that form of interreligious dialogue in which the poor are systematically excluded. The favored format for such dialogues today is one in which representatives of the various religious traditions of the world—usually scholars or ecclesiastical leaders whose positions make them more attuned to confessional than to class differences—meet and converse about what unites or separates them. But it is the hard reality of social conflict, not the exchange of ideas, that creates unity or foments division. Christians who have participated with Hindus and humanists and others in actual conflict against the powers that be "do theology" in a different way. They do it as part of an emerging worldwide community made up of the despised and rejected of the modern world and their allies. In this new community, as in those tiny first-century congregations of ex-slaves and day workers in Colossae and Ephesus where they had also begun to hear the same good news, the most intransigent of religious, traditional, and cultural barriers no longer have the power to divide.

21. Carnival Faith—People's Religion and Postmodern Theology

> . . . the festival is one of the privileged scenes where one may observe the popular resistance to normative injunctions as well as the restructuring, through cultural models, of the behavior of the majority.
> —Roger Chartier [1]

For most people in the world religion is not something one thinks about very much. It flows through mealtime graces, holiday usages, wedding and funeral practices, aphorisms, food and dietary habits, child-rearing advice, and a general neighborhood atmosphere. Although people whose religion is "popular" in this sense may attend church, even be devout churchgoers, they experience the church as a piece of a larger whole including many more facets that convey and reinforce faith. "People's religion" is like the furniture in a familiar room. It is "the way things are done." It is part of the scene. In one sense it *is* the scene, the stage setting within which everything else finds its proper place.

People's religion is not elite or clerical religion or the religion of cultivated intellectuals. It is a resource for postmodern theology precisely because it is not any of these things. As the faith of those groups which have been least integrated into the premises of modern society, people's religion retains a living contact with those premodern intuitions and images which must become part of a postmodern world vision. People's religion also has a history of resisting and subverting the reign of modernity which will also be a useful resource in moving beyond it.

Premodern people's religion will not become postmodern faith automatically. The postmodern enterprise requires a conscious and critical reappropriation of selected elements of the premodern, and this is clearly a critical theological task.

Modern theology is not ready to take it up. Part of the reason is that modern theology arose as a repudiation of folk piety and popular religion. The central task of modern theology as its practitioners envisaged it was the purification of religious belief and practice from the dross elements that seemed to make it an anachronism and an anomaly in the modern world. For much of modern theology, people's religion was the enemy, the obstacle that prevented thoughtful people from accepting the faith. The sooner it was reformed or abolished the better. This history of antagonism makes it hard for the modern theological enterprise to recognize and draw on people's religion as a key resource in the building of a postmodern theology.

There is another reason why modern academic theology is unlikely to be able to utilize people's religion to move out of its present quagmire. This reason has more to do with the social organization of the theological enterprise than with its intellectual history.

As a creature of the modernization process, which arrived with the smokestacks of industrial capitalism, modern theology reflects the exaggerated division of labor that characterizes that system. Like any other modern corporate enterprise, and like other academic fields—such as medicine or law—theology has become increasingly specialized, requiring ever more advanced training. Biblical scholars, students of comparative religion, ethicists, and philosophical theologians find it difficult to communicate with each other, let alone with lay people. Once in a while a highly respected academic theologian like Hans Kung manages to speak to the people in the pews, but that is the exception. The editors of theological journals complain that the average article they publish, which may have taken many months to write, is read by only a few dozen people at most. There are scores of journals in each of the subfields of theology and no one can keep abreast of what is written in even a fraction of them. Ultraspecialization and information overload within the field of theological scholarship has created a world in which there is little time left for the world of everyday religion even if the interest were there. Catholics, who have historically taken a more generous attitude to-

ward traditional religiosity than Protestants, have paid more attention. Evangelical and fundamentalist Protestants, who until quite
recently felt excluded from the academic theological establishment,
have not become quite as specialized as liberal Protestants have, and
have sometimes kept more closely in touch with what was happening
among the homefolks. Yet what we have today is two separate uni-
verses, that of the academic theological enterprise and that of the
world of ongoing, everyday religious beliefs and practices. They
touch each other only by accident.

The deep rift that separates the world of academic theology from
the world of people's religion does not pertain in liberation theology.
Historically, liberation theology did not begin as an effort to purge
popular belief or to make it more credible to cultural elites. It began
as an effort to clarify and strengthen the attempts popular movements
were making to resist the cultural and religious domination of such
elites. The attitude of liberation theologians toward people's religion
has been a very different one from that of modern theology.

The sociological basis for the lack of such a rift is easy to explain.
Coming as they do from those areas of the world where capitalist
modes of social organization have not yet entrenched themselves,
liberation theologians do not observe the jealously guarded frontiers
of specialization that fragment the European and North American
theological business. Lines between disciplines in Third World countries are not as fixed. Enrique Dussel begins his *The History of the
Church in Latin America* with these words: "This is a study centering
on a limited area between the *philosophy of culture and history*, but is
basically *theology*." [2] Liberation theologians mix theology, social analysis, economics, cultural history, and other approaches that in the
Western academic world have been fenced off into mutually exclusive disciplines. This also makes them more able to incorporate into
their work the insights of those students who have never lost interest
in *religión popular.*

The other sociological factor which makes liberation theology
more open to people's religion is that it grows out of the experience
of the basic Christian communities, groups which came into being to
resist the modern world of the global market. This gives the base
communities an important element of similarity with those expressions of nonelite religion whose very existence testifies to their not

having been drawn completely into the vortex of modernity. The poor farmers in the base community at La Chispa who are trying to organize a union to fight the expropriation of their pastures by an export food cartel have something in common with the Dutch and Sicilian Christians who group to oppose the installation of nuclear missiles near their villages, and with the Upper Amazon tribe that tries to prevent highways and oil wells from invading sacred terrain. It is not some abstract whipping boy called "modern society" that is their common foe. Both are lashing back at that conglomeration of profit enlargement, technological momentum, and pulverizing individualism which modern society in its present senility has become.[3]

In their earliest stages some liberation theologies tended to be just as critical of people's religion as modern academic theology is. Most liberation theologians were trained in Europe and drank deeply at the wells of modern critical thought. Those influenced by modernist elements in Marx, like Juan Luis Segundo, S.J., of Uruguay, tended to disvalue *religión popular* as an opiate of the masses or as a diversion from the real work at hand. This condescending attitude is changing rapidly, and few Latin Americans nowadays exhibit the same hauteur toward popular piety that they picked up in their student days at Louvain or Freiburg. For some, relearning was a painful process. It required shedding some of the values most dear to modern academic theology. It required a rediscovery of the smell of Latin America and of the inner meaning of the rites and customs of the poor. One Brazilian theologian calls it "detoxification," and claims that no Latin American who has been trained in Europe can begin to do significant work until this process has been completed.

The changing attitude of liberation theologians toward one familiar devotion illustrates this laborious readjustment. In 1969 I attended a consultation in Mexico City sponsored by the Roman Catholic bishops of Latin America. Juan Luis Segundo was also there, but it was at a time when his rigorous European training (one of the characteristics that make him so accessible to American and European readers) still prevented him from seeing any value in the religious practices of ordinary people. On one of our free afternoons I asked Segundo if he would like to accompany me on a visit to the shrine of Our Lady of Guadalupe, the most popular religious pilgrimage site in Mexico. Not only did he decline the invitation rather bluntly, he also told me he was surprised and disappointed that I would knowingly patronize a cult he believed was confusing and mystifying millions of hapless people. My visit to the shrine helped make me aware that a careful appreciation of popular piety must constitute the heart of a postmodern Christian theology.

The story of Our Lady of Guadalupe can be told simply. A few years after the Spanish conquest of Mexico a poor Indian convert named Juan Diego reported to Bishop Zumárraga that the Virgin had appeared to him in Tepeyac, a place once sacred to the outlawed Aztec fertility goddess Tonantzin. The bishop refused to believe him. Juan Diego persisted and the figure appeared to him again. Eventually, to help him make his case to the skeptical Zumárraga, she miraculously filled Juan Diego's serape with roses. When he took the serape full of roses to the bishop's residence, a beautiful picture of the Lady had been imprinted on it.

Devotion to the tawny woman of the miraculous serape spread quickly, especially among the Indians, for she herself was a *morena* with black hair, unlike the fair-skinned Virgin the Spanish had brought along. For decades the clergy fought the new devotion. Eventually the Guadalupe triumphed. Two hundred years after the original appearance, the pope declared her to be an apparition of the Virgin Mother of God and proclaimed her the Patroness of Mexico. Today devotion to Nuestra Señora de Guadalupe, familiarly known as "La Vida," is the leading devotion all over the country and among millions of Latinos in the United States.

When I arrived at the celebrated Basilica of Guadalupe in Tepeyac, a crowded section at the edge of Mexico City, it was the hues and the din that first hit me. Mexican Indians in peacock-green and shiny gold headdresses danced and pounded drums in the vast courtyard. Groups of pilgrims sang. Taxis honked. Babies wailed. Somewhere beyond the crowd that enveloped me, a marching band with cymbals and slightly flat trumpets blared and banged a Sousa march. At the center of the courtyard the mood was different. There the throngs had cleared a kind of path leading to the door of the church. Along the aisle came pilgrims, singly and in groups, some crawling on their knees for the last five hundred yards of what for many had been an arduous journey of anywhere from five to five hundred miles. Over the gateway to the court flapped a hand-written sign that said "Taxi Drivers of Monterrey—Annual Pilgrimage to Our Lady."

As I entered the church itself I amost stepped on a young mother with three children who was frying tortillas over an open brazier next to a chipped pew and a broken kneeling bench. Pilgrims of all ages crowded the inside aisles, nearly all of them obviously poor. They filed to the front and reverently deposited a gift, usually flowers, at the altar rail, crossed themselves in the elaborate three-times-over fashion the Latin Americans learned from the Spanish, then got up and chatted with their friends. Those who had crawled the last portion were congratulated by their companions.

It was then that I saw him, the young man who made me wish my Jesuit colleague had come along. He was no more than nineteen, a handsome dark-skinned *muchacho* with straight black hair and a mustache that looked as though, given time to lengthen, it would resemble Emiliano Zapata's or Pancho Villa's. He wore tight black slacks and sandals without socks. His T-shirt had a picture of Ché Guevara and the words "Viva Ché" on the front and a clenched red fist on the back. He was kneeling at the altar crossing himself over and over again. Finally he stopped, remained kneeling in prayer for a few minutes, then touched his forehead, kissed his fingertips, crossed himself again, rose and sauntered out of the church smiling and glancing up at the smoke-darkened paintings on the walls. As he squeezed by me I noticed he wore a tiny silver medallion of the Guadalupe around his neck.

Opiate of the masses? I wished Segundo could have been present because that young Mexican with his clenched-fist "Viva Ché" shirt and his Virgin medal seemed to be symbolically way ahead of the theologians. He knew something intuitively about the creative synthesis of rituals and myths, about the role of popular devotion in political liberation, something that most intellectuals were only beginning to uncover. He represented to me the vigor of *religión popular*, a source of energy and inspiration which Christians committed to justice too often overlook or disdain.

One of the most prominent features of Latin American liberation theology now is its appreciation of the revolutionary potential of *religión popular*. In the fall of 1981, the 450th anniversary of the original apparition of the Virgin of Guadalupe, one of the most widely respected liberation theology journals, *Servir*, devoted two double issues to the papers delivered at a commemorative conference dealing with the devotion and the significance of *guadalupismo* for liberation today. In preparation for the conference, scholars did a good deal of research. What they discovered came as something of a shock. Not only was devotion to the Dark Virgin alive and well, but to the surprise of an earlier generation of liberation theologians, this same Lady had become a focal personage in many of the grassroots communities that provided the foundations of liberation movements.[4]

The Guadalupe has been a rebel for a long time. When Father Miguel Hidalgo, the Mexican priest who led the first phase of the fight for independence from Spain, set out for the capital from his parish in Dolores in 1810, the banner his shabby Indian and mestizo insurgents carried bore the image of the Virgin of Guadalupe. Some battles were won, but Hidalgo was soon defeated. He had to flee and was defrocked and executed. Still, his *"Grito de Dolores"* continues to be celebrated on September 16 as the real beginning of Mexican independence. Some historians believe Hidalgo's idea of an independence to be won by the poorest and the racially excluded elements of the society, all united under the emblem of the Guadalupe, terrified the upper strata, and that they discreetly arranged a form of independence from Spain that kept their own power intact.

A hundred years later, when the angry campesinos of Emiliano Zapata again marched on Mexico City, many of them carried pictures of the Virgin of Guadalupe in the bands of their sombreros. She was still the ally of the poor against entrenched clerical and political privilege. Half a century later her banner led the long procession of farm workers, organized by César Chavez from the grape orchards of Delano to Sacramento, another capital city.

But the contest over who can claim the Guadalupe continues. A year after my first visit to the smoky old basilica, the church and the government of Mexico reached an agreement to erect a new palace for the fabled serape. A North American fund-raising agency was enlisted which solicited millions of pesos, many of them by selling burial crypts priced so that the ones near the altar went for more money. Within a couple of years, a sweeping new contemporary structure arose adjacent to the old one. Inside, a motorized treadway moved pilgrims past the sacred image on the serape. Uniformed guards quietly discouraged any cooking on the polished floors. Rows of thronelike satin chairs, enough to seat the entire hierarchy of

Mexico, were placed between the Virgin's image and the main body of the church. Ironically, once again the bishops placed themselves between the unlettered peons who came to visit and the Guadalupe herself, just as Bishop Zumárraga had four hundred years before.

On the day the new basilica was dedicated, the rich, the famous, and the powerful flocked from embassies, corporate penthouses, and diocesan headquarters and jammed inside. It rained, one of those cold rains that can make Mexico City, perched on a high plateau, seem like an inhospitable city in the English midlands. Hundreds of thousands of poor people, unable to buy tickets for the grand opening, knelt outside in the puddles and prayed.

A few years after the new basilica had gone into business, Father Arnaldo Zentena, S.J., gathered some of his parishioners from the base community he helps to serve in the vast slum on the edge of Mexico City known as Netzahualcoyotl. By telling stories and then drawing people out, a method made famous by Father Ernesto Cardenal in the village of Solentiname, Nicaragua,[5] Zentena told these slum dwellers the traditional account of the appearance of the Guadalupe and asked them to comment from their own experience.

The conversations he reports suggest a liberating ingredient in the stories that many theologians had missed. The people of "Netza,"— José, Carmen, Chelo, Mary, and Rosita—pointed out that the Virgin could easily have appeared directly to the bishop, but instead she chose to appear to a poor Indian, perhaps so the bishop would have to listen at last to a *pobre*, a *más pequeño*. Even today, they said, people do not want to listen to poor people or even look at them. "Just try," one of the women said, "to get waited on at a *tienda* if you're poor and there are nicely dressed people there. They always wait on them first." Some compared the chilly reception Juan Diego received from the bishops to the deaf ear they encounter when people from their base communities try to speak to those in power.

To that part of the story which tells of the Virgin's command to Juan Diego to build a house of prayer, the people of Netza complained that the Guadalupe's house was now being sold to rich people for burial vaults, and that they would not be surprised if the Señora now appeared to another Juan Diego to tell him this is *not* what she wanted. The attempt to fence off the energies of the Dark Virgin had not been wholly successful.

Despite the continuous attempts of religious and political elites to control it, popular religion persists as a source of inspiration for the poor. Liberation theologians now recognize this and spend much time not just listening to the political complaints of poor people but trying to understand the inner significance of their religion. How can such popular piety provide a resource for postmodern theology as well?

At the scholarly level the principal focus for the study of popular religion can be seen in the attention now given to fête and fiesta.[6] Indeed, there has been an avalanche of interest in this subject, and it is worth asking why all the curiosity about the history of festivals has arisen in recent years. Could it be an expression, nostalgic perhaps, of a growing disillusionment with modernity? As our ailing age frantically cranks up productivity to ever higher levels and destroys traditional communities wherever it spreads its paving, are modern people becoming increasingly curious about what price has actually been exacted for its alleged benefits?

There is some evidence of this, and there is surely no shortage of nostalgia elsewhere, for example in the commercial "folklorization" of traditional urban religious festivals. Along with big-band music, torn copies of Action Comic Books, and quaint tubular telephones, religious nostalgia is a highly marketable commodity today. In recent years the traditional saints' celebrations (St. Anthony, the Madonna of the Cave, and others) of Boston's Italian North End have been moved from the days they appear on the Roman Catholic calendar to weekends in the summer when visiting tourists will find it more convenient to watch the procession, buy rides on miniature airplanes for the kiddies, and dine on veal scaloppine and Chianti. The rearrangement, which church officials did not oppose, also helps draw visitors from the newly renovated Quincy Market area into the orbit of North End shops and restaurants. But the old-timers in the black suits and tieless white shirts shake their heads. They say it is only a matter of time until the saints' days disappear completely. Something is missing.

All over the industrial world, as the story of the North End repeats itself and once lively festivals decline or become commercialized, historians and cultural analysts become intrigued with them. The scholarly attention does not arrest the decline. The flight of Miner-va's owl never prevents the sun from setting. It is also doubtful whether the festivals of yore, because they are what we miss most, are what people then felt to be most important about their times.

The festival was an expression of something deeper. We cannot import the festivals of our forebearers into a late-modern culture inimical to what they stand for. St. Anthony does not like his "day" changed any more than the Guadalupe liked being relocated into her ritzy new palace. Sacred time and space simply cannot be tailored to meet the needs of tourists and entrepreneurs.

For theologians interested in popular religion and customs, exam-ining the carnival is imperative. During the fiesta, values and beliefs that are mostly implicit become explicit. People tell the stories that ground their customs and folkways. Also, the tensions always present in a community assert themselves. Riots break out; people kill each other more often during holidays than on normal work days. The festival represents a point where popular culture and dominant cul-ture, premodern and modern, come into open conflict. Cultural elites, including religious elites, almost always view festivals as dan-gerous. Carnivals generate an energy that cannot be turned off. They loose passions that cannot easily be called back. Consequently the history of festivals in the modern world is the history of attempts to ban and control them, and of ordinary people fighting to keep their festivals from being abolished, altered, or turned into tourist attrac-tions.[7]

People's religion is one of the key resources for a postmodern the-ology. What does this mean for fundamentalism? Based in the lower classes of the population, and without the training in modern critical theology to be detoxified from, it might at first appear that fundamen-talism would be more open to the possibilities of popular religion. In one sense it is itself a form of people's religion, or at least it was before the TV takeover. The problem is that fundamentalism has so absolutized its own insular definition of what true religion is that it has rendered itself nearly incapable of appreciating other expressions of the same primal reality. Constrained by a narrow view of what is and what is not acceptable worship, and guided by a severely puritan-ical suspicion of revelry of any kind, conservative Protestant Christians take a dim view of both quasireligious and excessively festal activity.

I did not grow up in one of the premodern French villages that Roger Chartier, one of the principal historians of fêtes, writes about. I came from a small Pennsylvania town dominated by a steel tubing factory. Still, when Chartier writes that "the festival is one of the privileged scenes where one may observe the popular resistance to normative injunctions as well as the restructuring, through cultural models, of the behavior of the majority,"[8] I know just what he means. In Quaker-Baptist-Methodist Malvern, Pennsylvania, we had no saints' days, but we did have the annual Fire Company Fair, and no one who grew up there will ever forget it. It was a two-week carnival that generally combined gambling wheels and refreshment stands provided by the local volunteer firemen and the women's auxiliary with a Ferris wheel and side-show attractions supplied by a traveling road company. This all went on in town where gambling was technically illegal and there was none—at least in the open— the other fifty weeks of the year. During the Fire Company Fair, however, the whole town entered vigorously into a state the anthropologist Victor Turner calls "liminality." Normal rules and social identities temporarily melted. Church deacons magically reappeared as dealers and croupiers at the blackjack table and the big-six wheel. Time and again local preachers tried to stop this open defiance of law and propriety, but they never succeeded. Once when a particularly outraged Nazarene fundamentalist minister, a new man in town, managed to secure a court order closing the gambling booths, the fire company merely changed sponsors for the evening, turning the fair over to the local American Legion post, to which many of the firemen also belonged. When the reluctant police arrived with the court order in hand there was not a "fire company fair" to be found. It was now a "Legion fair" and the gendarmes left in relief, thankful they did not have to arrest their fishing buddies. The fair went on, a reminder to everyone that there is a stubborn, dark underside even in a severely upright and well-lit small town. Fundamentalism's inability to deal creatively with this other side suggests one more reason why, despite its antimodernist rhetoric, it may be more wedded to the anxious rationalism of the modern world than first appears.

The dark underside of Malvern also came out symbolically at Halloween. The biggest parade of the year took place then. It was

originally instituted by the town fathers to provide something constructive for the kids to do and thereby to cut down on the number
of garbage cans turned over and windows soaped. For weeks in advance preparation for the parade kept everyone occupied. Sunday
school classes, Legion posts, Girl Scout troops all designed and assembled thematic floats like "God Bless America" or "The Spirit of
Temperance" or "Ghosts and Goblins." A committee of distinguished town elders judged the entries as they passed by the reviewing
stand, and handed out prizes. The freshly polished scarlet engines of
the volunteer fire company always took part, noisily creeping past in
their lowest gears. The American Legion honor guard invariably led
off. The Halloween parade was a splendid example of how civic
virtue tries to keep the lid on the bawdier shades that are abroad that
night.

But the spirit of misrule cannot be easily contained. While the
handful of town police were directing traffic around the parade, the
youthful marauders who did not belong to scout troops or Sunday
school classes had a heyday with the unguarded garbage cans and
windows. There were always more drunks in the streets. The atmosphere seemed lax, almost licentious. The attempt of political and
religious elites to impose hegemony over unruly popular culture never
works completely. Liminality will find a way.

Then, too, there was the "Wild Man of Borneo." The Wild Man
appeared in the Halloween parade without fail. He was incarcerated
in a wheeled cage pulled by a car, his naked arms, chest and face
covered with cocoa makeup. His lips were enlarged with rouge and
he wore a massive stringy black wig. Inside the cage he leaped and
bellowed and clawed at the bars while his two attendants in white
coats and leather peaked hats warned the crowd to stand back. But
every few minutes the Wild Man would escape. Then, pursued by his
hapless guards, one carrying a large net, he would plunge into the
crowd to try to kiss one of the ladies. Squeals and pandemonium
arose until his attendants retrieved the Wild Man and returned him
to his cage. Then things would quiet down until his next escape a
few minutes later. The women who had been kissed complained but
rarely wiped off the brown smudge until the revelry was over. They
wanted people to see that they and not someone else had been the
object of the Wild Man's unleashed ardor.

It was my Uncle Arthur who usually played the Wild Man. He

can scarcely have known what a powerfully primal myth he was acting out, but it was all there: the dangerous savage who looks like us but not quite; the constant but futile attempts to keep him and his untamed libido caged; the orderly procession interrupted by corybantic assaults on the crowds; sobriety shattered by frenzy; the ceaseless contest between structure and antistructure, white coats and blackness.

For years I thought the Wild Man of Borneo was mainly a local custom. But "the intrusion and immolation of the wild man" was a feature of French fêtes hundreds of years ago. The Wild Man was not immolated in Pennsylvania, but he was there.

Any postmodern theology will have to deal with the underside, not just psychologically as the Jungian analysts do, but politically as well. It will have to recognize that the gambling wheels and the Wild Man of Borneo represent dimensions of the human which the modern world system has not abolished, and has had to subdue by increasingly draconian political means. In our time the dark peoples of unknown lands have emerged again from their cages, this time not just to titillate the crowds and then return, but to insist on having a share in forging the social world and the symbolic and religious culture of the future. This is a fact of life in the postmodern world with which neither modern theology nor fundamentalism will be able to cope. Only the liberation theologies, coming themselves from the dark Borneos of the modern world, stand any chance of doing so.

Festivals, says Chartier, have always been looked upon by the dominant cultures as a "major obstacle to the assertion of their religious, ethical and political hegemony." They have always been the bloody ditch where the worst infighting between popular and elite cultures went on. At the carnival the premodern and the postmodern join forces to fight against the pervasive uniformity and injustice of modernity.

Diego Irarrazával, a coworker with Gustavo Gutiérrez and an alert student of the liberating potential of folk piety, gives an example of this phenomenon from the recent history of his continent.[9] He says that the two most pervasive elements in the folk religion of Nicaragua are celebration and pilgrimage. He goes on to show how both contributed first to the people's ability to withstand some of the impact of modernization, and eventually to their ability to overthrow the Somoza dictatorship.

Since the colonial period the *patronal,* or patron saint's fiesta, has been the main religious celebration in Nicaragua. Irarrazával believes these fiestas slowed down the modernization process, which was being forced on the less powerful classes by the elites. They did so by subverting two major ingredients in the ideology of modernization, namely rationalism (which was often accompanied by atheism, agnosticism, or anticlericalism), and the privatizing of life which leads to individualism. By celebrating a saint who represents the people before God, a *patrón,* the fiesta nurtures the people's faith against agnosticism. By ritually affirming the group solidarity of the village or town, it slows down fragmentive individualism. The fiesta resists the elite ideology by which the dominant classes seek to extend their control.

Pilgrimages instill the belief that people need not remain mired in any situation. They can "move with God." Pilgrimages are movements, but ruling groups want people either to remain quiescent—to stay where they are—or to go where they are sent. Therefore, any kind of uncontrolled movement can be dangerous. Processions can become protest marches. Pilgrimages can become incursions or even uprisings.

Irarrazával gives the example of the *fiesta patronal* of the city of Managua, which began only toward the end of the nineteenth century, later than most such traditions. It is a holiday devoted to "Santo Dominguito," or "Mingo," as he is affectionately referred to in the vernacular. Mingo is the saint of the poor people of the surrounding countryside. On his day they throng into the city carrying his images, dancing and singing. For a day the streets belong to Mingo—and to his people. The next day Mingo's people return to their mountain villages, or at least they are supposed to.

By 1961, however, the Fiesta of Santo Dominguito was getting out of hand. Archbishop Gonzáles tried to regulate the activities, which he thought were becoming unduly raucous and prolonged; and a few years later the fiesta was prohibited by General Somoza's National Guard. The officials complained of drunkenness and other excesses, but Irarrazával believes the real reason they banned the fiesta was that they were afraid of what might happen with thousands of peasants, most of them unhappy with the government, dancing and parading through the streets under the auspices of their *Patrón*. For the people, says Irarrazával, faith was a celebration, while "for the authorities what was important was order."

The authorities in Managua had reason to be concerned. In 1881 there had been a serious uprising of country people against the expansion of coffee production, which was resulting in takeovers of small farms and land held in common to create large profitable plantations. The government, headed then by President Zavala, accused the Jesuits of fomenting the rebellion and decreed their expulsion from the country. Scholars differ on just how much the priests actually had to do with encouraging the uprising, but they agree that the leaders were Christian peasants. It is understandable that eighty years later the National Guard should have become nervous about devotees of Santo Dominguito dancing through the streets of Managua.

The latest Nicaraguan revolution is one in which Christians participated from the outset, and after the defeat of Somoza they celebrated the victory in symbols that echoed these old religious traditions. Irarrazával quotes a prayer used in a mass celebrated in a poor suburb of Managua to mark the guerrilla victory:

> We praise you, Father, for that today more than ever before, you have made yourself present in our history, and we give you thanks that the captives have been freed. . . . For this we want to celebrate this paschal day, this day of resurrection of your people.[10]

Once again in this prayer we discover the two most pervasive themes in the emerging postmodern piety—liberation and resurrection, the freeing of captives and the restoring of life and flesh, linked here to the popular religious events of festival and pilgrimage. Maybe the traditional and the radical protests against modernity, popular religion, and popular protest are not as disparate as they might first appear. Their confluence is a resource no postmodern theology can get along without.

FEMINIST THEOLOGY AND POPULAR RELIGION

Perhaps the most promising resource for a postmodern theology is the religious imagination of those people who in nearly every culture and almost all modern religious traditions have been deprived of full participation in the weaving of myths and the writing of theologies: women. At first glance, current feminist theology does not appear to have much connection with folk piety. It is mostly the product of highly trained women working mainly in elite settings. But insofar as feminist theology is built on disciplined reflection about the actual life experiences of all women, focusing especially on those aspects of women's lives which are not wholly drawn into and defined by the modern (male) system of meanings, it touches a rich vein of post-modern possibility.

As with other sources this contribution will most likely come not from all women religious thinkers but from those who, despite pressures to conform or leave, have chosen instead to remain within the community of faith and to fight against the male monopoly on the creation and formulation of religious symbols.

Feminist theology is only at its beginning stages, but it has already made an enormous impact in nearly every field of theology. Feminist biblical scholars show how male bias and inadvertence have distorted our translations of the Bible, lending them a sexist tone that was often not there in the original. Feminist historians have systematically uncovered the distorted male readings of church history and popular spirituality. Beverly Harrison has demonstrated how masculine formulations have clouded the language of ethics, and Rosemary Ruether has done the same for the language about God.[11] The quantity and quality of theological writing by feminist scholars increases every year. It represents a solid step beyond the patriarchal tone of modern theology and is an indispensable reservoir for postmodern theology.

But there is a problem with most feminist theology: somehow it still seems more modern than postmodern. It has yet to enter into a full rediscovery of the potential of folk piety. It still bears the marks of its critical, academic milieu, and has not yet been nourished by the liberating potential of people's religion. The parallel to the liberationist rediscovery of the fiesta, the pilgrimage, and the Guadalupe still lies in the future.

It is not hard to understand why many feminist theologians are reluctant to deal with popular piety. For eons women have been the victims of religious symbols and practices created to control and direct them. Women rightly see that many popular religious devotions are sexist, and the improbable model of a virgin-mother is one many of them feel they can no longer accept. Still, other groups who have also been held down by manipulated symbols have not allowed this to prevent them from using them in their own way and drawing on their enormous energy. This has been true among Latin Americans, Asian Christians, and, most visibly of all, in the black churches where some of the same images and texts that were deftly manipulated by whites to keep blacks in line became the sources that inspired their protests. Could women do the same?

When one ponders this question it is hard not to consider the many popular images of Mary. Indeed, in recent years some feminists who began by rejecting popular mariology as a male-devised means of social control have begun to see certain virgin goddesses as positive symbols of women who, like Amazons, do not need to rely on men.[12] What a cosmic paradox it might turn out to be if Mary, perhaps the most male-manipulated Christian symbol of them all, turned out to be a key ingredient in the liberation of women and in the formulation of a postmodern and postsexist theology.

This is not an impossibility. Take Our Lady of Guadalupe again as an example, not as she is defined by the hierarchy, but as she actually functions among people. This symbol which comes "from the bottom" might have potential for a nonsexist, postmodern theology. The Guadalupe represents the persistence of a female image of the divine in a culture—our own—that has been dominated for nearly two millennia by a religion stemming from a tribal war god, a male Messiah, and an official religious organization created and managed almost exclusively by men. She is a "goddess" who stands on her own with no men around her. She is never pictured with St. Joseph, or even with Jesus. She stands on the moon, a celestial queen, wrapped in a mantle of stars.

We must be extraordinarily careful not to accept without qualification the present official churchly definition of the Guadalupe as one of the many apparitions of Mary Immaculate, wearing the characteristic blue shawl of the "Immaculata." This clerical categorizing must be understood as part of the religious elite's endless campaign to capture control of vagrant and possibly explosive popular religious outbursts. Putting Guadalupe/Tonantzin in a blue shawl is the symbolic equivalent of caging the Wild Man of Borneo. But the story of

Juan Diego's problems with Bishop Zumárraga and the fierce priestly opposition to *guadalupismo* in its early years reminds us that the energies she generates and represents can escape from their carefully constructed domestication as they did with Hidalgo and Zapata.

The constant efforts of the clerical elites to purify *guadalupismo* have never wholly succeeded. In a village not many miles from Mexico City, the local priest told me once with some consternation that when he organizes the annual pilgrimage to the Guadalupe Shrine many of his parishioners refer to it as "going to visit Tonantzin." Whenever he hears them say that he corrects them and points out that they are going to visit the *Virgin*, and they nod and smile. But they know better.

In another village, in Chiapas, in the far south of Mexico, a Tzeltal Indian who was showing me the village church, one visited only occasionally by a priest, proudly pointed out not only a statue of Our Lady of Guadalupe but also, standing right next to her in the unlikely form of a seventeenth-century Spanish *caballero*, her husband, our *Lord* of Guadalupe. When I told him that I had been under the impression that Our Lady was a virgin he smiled at me slyly and told me that although some people in Mexico City or even in nearby San Bartolomé might think that, here in their village they knew the real story. Popular piety never stays where the priests put it.

In a male-dominated religious system like Christianity, in which women have been systematically deprived of leadership, the tug of war between clerical power and popular religious imagination is in part a battle between male and female visions of reality. Women have always made up a much larger proportion of the witches and heretics than their numbers would suggest. This perennial contest between the clerical and the popular, the male and the female visions of the cosmos, has also become a clash between modern and postmodern perspectives.

Religious symbols contain within themselves whole complex world views in a compact, highly concentrated form. Any powerful religious rite or image conveys a vast store of information, especially information about what time and space are like. Although this information may not be immediately available to the unsophisticated believer on the conceptual level, nonetheless it powerfully shapes the religious person's view of the nature of reality. It is precisely this capacity for conveying so much "information" so economically that gives religious symbols their immense potency.

Postmodern religion will require a skillful reappropriation of premodern religious styles by a newly self-conscious and critical mode of awareness. It will also require the fusing of certain aspects of the premodern sensibility with some of the hard-won features of modernity. The impasse male clerical elites face in undertaking this task is that they have been so engulfed by the "modern" way of thinking and feeling they have lost nearly all capacity for experiencing alternative modes of space/time reality. Only those persons and groups who have not been so fully integrated into this pervasive modern space/time sensibility are in any position to take up the task of formulating alternatives. This is where women come in.

The French philosopher Julia Kristeva, one of the most acute contemporary observers of female experience, argues that when women allow themselves to think about their own intuitive feel for time, rather than accepting the linear, departure-and-arrival time sense of the modern (male-organized) world, what they discover is something much older. Because menstruation cycles link them more closely to natural cycles than men, women hold a key to the past that men do not have. Their intuition, Kristeva says, "retains *repetition* and *eternity* from among the multiple modalities of time known through the history of civilizations."[13] Kristeva believes this exclusively female vantage point enables women to touch these two forms of time consciousness that men, as nonmenstruating creatures, can discern only with much greater difficulty. The first, the cyclic time of gestation and rhythmic reoccurrence, is a "premodern" form of time that coincides with the phases of the moon, the rising and setting of the sun, the passing of the seasons, and other expressions of cosmic time. She believes that sensing this link between the personal and the cosmic can lead to what she calls *"jouissance,"* a term we might try to express in English by combining "joy," "ecstasy," and perhaps "serenity."

Since the realization of this "cosmic connection" can produce *jouissance,* it can also open the way to a second sense of time which Kristeva calls "eternity." This is the infinite, unbounded, and all-encompassing time the mystics try, always unsuccessfully, to describe.

If Kristeva is correct, then women have a kind of privileged access to these other faces of time. If reclaiming these senses of time along with the sequential, arrow-flight time of the Western mind will be essential in any postmodern religious vision, then the experience of women will be an indispensable part of that vision.

There are many dangers here. As a woman and a feminist, Kristeva is fully aware of the strategies the men who shape religious imagery over the years have used to gain control of the social meaning of these and other female experiences. Menstruation, for example, has continued to be called "the curse." Still, she contends that women's intuitive and emotional experiences of time are still available, albeit symbolized in demeaning terms, and can be drawn upon. True, they grow out of the biological capacity of women to be mothers, and drawing attention to them risks pushing women into the male-created role in which being a woman is equated exclusively with being a mother. When proclaimed by a culture which then demotes mothering to a second-rate task, it can easily lead to yet another theft from women, including those who cannot or do not choose to bear children, of their full human dignity. Kristeva believes this risk has to be run unless women are to accept the leveling logic of modern industrial society which sees any differences between the sexes as inconsequential, a position some feminists once accepted without being aware of its sources in a mode of thinking that is very male indeed.[14]

Guadalupismo is much more than a widespread devotional cult. It preserves and incarnates an awareness of the cosmos, and of mystical time. It does so, not in a theological system but in a religious movement practiced by millions of people, not eons ago but today, not halfway around the world but in a neighboring country and indeed in hundreds of barrios in the United States itself.

Is this religious sensibility still open to the millions of disaffected moderns who, rightly sensing that our present cultural momentum is propelling us toward death and not toward life, are looking for a new vision but for many reasons either cannot see the ones under their noses or else regard them as superstition? I believe so, and evidence of this is preserved in those Orthodox and Roman Catholic doctrines that symbolically explain the temporary, but only temporary, disappearance of the goddess. In Greek and Russian Orthodox thought, the teaching is known as the "Dormition." It signifies the falling asleep (*dormitio*) of the Virgin Mary and is celebrated as a major feast on August 15. In the Roman Catholic Church, the doctrine of the Assumption, teaching that Mary was taken into heaven without experiencing death, makes the same point. Both suggest that whatever the goddess signified nonetheless *is not dead.* She is temporarily resident in another space, but it remains clear, if unspoken, that sleepers eventually awake and heaven and earth are reunited. Meanwhile, from her temporary celestial exile, Mary makes frequent incursions back to the earth, appearing in unlikely places, delivering unauthorized messages, and keeping squadrons of theologians busy channeling, purifying, and trivializing the explosive energies she exudes.

Whether she appears as cosmic queen, as Amazon, or in any other mythic guise, the dangerous feminine element which male power has tried to eliminate from the modern world is poised and ready to return. No valid postmodern theology can ignore it.

It is also possible that the return to the postmodern world of that which Our Lady of Guadalupe represents will greatly assist Christian theology in its dealing with the challenge discussed in the previous chapter, that of global religious pluralism.

I have argued that the religious basis for a postmodern civilization need not be invented but is already aborning. Evidence suggests that this emerging religious/symbolic order will combine features of the *dios pobre* of the liberationists at the theological level with the equalitarian structures now being generated by the explosive growth of base communities. With both of these I also foresee a renewed appreciation of the ritual dimension in human life. In one sense, the Guadalupe already combines all three of these elements. A dark-skinned *mestiza,* she personifies the anger and persistent dignity of people of color everywhere. A woman, she embodies the never-completely-dominated *jouissance* of the second sex. A poor person, she inspires the hopes of all those who believe that God is preferentially present in the lives of the disinherited. An echo of a pre-Christian goddess, she reminds us of the larger and older family of faiths of which ours is a part. A victim of clerical manipulation, she recalls the destructive role churches have often played in perpetuating injustice and in robbing the dispossessed of their most valuable symbols of identity and hope. It is hard to imagine a more potent symbol for that *fuerza* from the edges and from the bottom which must ultimately create both the theology and the religion of the postmodern world. The miracle is that this energy need not be concocted. Like the reign of God that Jesus announced, and like Our Lady of Guadalupe herself, it is already in our midst.

22. A New Reformation?

In reflecting on the various theologies of liberation and the different kinds of base communities from which they are issuing, I have frequently used the analogy of the Reformation of the sixteenth century. Once again in our time the currents that are promising to renew and reform Christianity are cropping up on the "margin," coming from what is often viewed as the periphery of cultural and intellectual life.

The Catholic theologians of his time eventually recognized Luther as a formidable opponent. But in the early years of his preaching they brushed him aside as a provincial upstart. They not only dismissed his theology as a squabble among the monks but looked upon him and his colleagues as "marginals," living in a hinterland comparable today to the boondocks of Latin America, Asia, and the ghettos and *favelas*. Yet religious renewal hardly ever begins in the capital. The Hebrew prophets trooped in from the sycamore forests to challenge the temple and the palace. Jesus grew up in a remote and suspect region of Palestine. Once again the question is being asked, "Can any good thing come from Nazareth?" and the answer is the same. It seems that genuine change must always begin on the edge.

Also, like the Reformation of the sixteenth century, the current reformation is not just an idea whose time has come. It is a theology intertwined with a series of social upheavals and political changes. Recalling the nasty debates over the sale of indulgences and the popish milking of the credulous, this one also involves money and power. Also like its predecessor, which had its share of mad hatters and kooks, the current reformation is subject to misuse and cooptation. It will inevitably attract its quota of charlatans, fanatics, opportunists, and easy riders. Yet just as our study of the secular dimensions of the sixteenth-century Reformation does not make it any less a religious movement, neither do suggestions that the current reformation is "only political" or is too wrapped up in earthly concerns sound convincing.

Finally, the sixteenth-century Reformation was sparked religiously by the rediscovery and proclamation of a biblical truth that had for years been neglected or underplayed. This came with Luther's seizing on St. Paul's *sola fide*, the joyous declaration that grace is God's own gift, something that could not and need not be earned. To a population strangled by religious duties and ecclesiastical obligations this came as a welcome message. Retrieved by Luther from the back shelf, the old news that "the just shall live by faith" became new news and swept through much of Europe like a cleansing wind.

Today's reformation is sparked by an equally powerful biblical idea, also lost for years but recently rediscovered. The idea is that of Resurrection: God alive in the world, life defeating death. But in liberation theology, especially in its Latin American version, the idea carries a more specific edge. It is that the special locus of God's presence is the poor and that therefore the poor have a singular and privileged role to play in the divine intention for human history. The poor are those through whom God chooses to mediate the coming of the divine reign. If anything this idea of the *dios pobre* is even more central to the Bible and is repeated more frequently than the idea of justification by faith. Yet, for the reasons we have discussed, it was lost sight of and denied during much of modern history and in nearly all modern theology. But, like the *sola fide* of the sixteenth century, the idea of *dios pobre* has always been there. Smoldering, it has now been fanned into flames and become the central religious idea of the new reformation.[1]

Still, comparisons with the earlier Reformation can be misleading. The main difference between the two is that since the current reformation is by its nature a grassroots movement it will not produce such larger-than-life heroes as Luther or Calvin. For all its eventual popular support and the local discontent that helped energize it, the sixteenth-century Reformation was led from above by determined and strong-willed men. When ordinary people did begin to assume some leadership, as they did among some of the Anabaptists and other sectors of the Reformation's radical wing, the elite leaders quickly tried to bring them to heel, and they usually succeeded. This is especially evident in those instances where lay people threatened the clerical control of the movement; or where miners and peasants applied the preaching about the equality of believers under God to the economic and political as well as to the spiritual spheres, and appeared at the manor house brandishing shovels and pitchforks. Whenever this happened, as it did in parts of Germany and in the Tessin sections of what are now southern Switzerland and northern Italy, the Protestant reformers persecuted the "left wing" as severely as the Catholics tried to repress them. Most of these radical groups were uprooted and scattered. Others withdrew or became socially quiescent. But the impulse never died completely. Indeed, it could be argued that many of the ideas now appearing in the base communities and in the liberation theologies were anticipated by these religious pioneers nearly five centuries ago.

There is one final comparison that suggests itself between the Reformation of the sixteenth century and the present one. One of the most telling results of the sixteenth-century Reformation was the change it wrought in the Roman Catholic Church, on the established religion and the reigning theology.[2] Scholars have filled shelves with arguments about whether the impact was, on balance, more beneficial or more detrimental. Did the Reformation frighten the Catholic Church into the rigidity and paranoia of the Council of Trent? Did it put a club in the hands of the church's reactionaries, one they gleefully used to clobber incipient internal reform sentiments before they could get on their feet? Or did it, if only indirectly, stimulate a form of renewal inside the Catholic Church, such as the mysticism of the Carmelites and the missions of the Jesuits, that might not have happened otherwise?

Questions of "what might have happened otherwise" are always dubious candidates for historical reflection. What we do know is that the Catholic Church that emerged from the era of the sixteenth-century Reformation did not act like a routed remnant. Changed it surely was, but it was also a robust and inventive religious community. If its theological development was retarded by the post-Tridentine (after the Council of Trent) atmosphere, still these were also centuries of astonishing growth in the number and variety of religious orders with their richly distinctive styles of spirituality and common life. Recent history always forces us to read past history through different lenses. Since the pontificate of John XXIII it has become more helpful to read the history of the sixteenth-century Reformation not as an event which split the church in two but as a painful period of renewal within the one Christian family.

Is a parallel with today possible? I think it is. The new reformation sweeping across the backlands and out of the pantries and alleys of Christendom carries a validity of its own. It must not be judged exclusively on how well it does in challenging or influencing the established churchly patterns and the dominant theological ideas of the day. Like its predecessor, this reformation needs a *ruptura,* part of which it creates by its own momentum, part of which is inflicted on it by the modern equivalent of bulls of excommunication and raw papal power.

Western "mainline" Christianity, both Catholic and Protestant, organized into roughly two hundred denominations, is the current equivalent of the Catholic Church at the beginning of the sixteenth century. If one objects that the Renaissance popes of that period, busy collecting Titians and dallying with their mistresses, bear little resemblance to today's church executives and curial administrators, it need only be pointed out that both groups faithfully reflect their respective Zeitgeists. The popes and their entourages were churchy editions of the vintage wines and baroque refinements of the Renaissance *uomo universale.* Today's ecclesiastical bureaucrats look and sound very much like the corporate board men with whom they peruse their newspapers on commuter trains. If a bit more Renaissance worldliness lingers in Rome, and a semblance of country-and-western flamboyance colors the Nashville headquarters of the Southern Baptist Convention, one can be relatively sure it is mostly on the surface. Structures of dominant ecclesiastical organization, like the personal life styles they elicit, are rarely innovative. In an imperial period they are imperial; in a feudal age they are feudal; and in our time they are bureaucratic. Only at the frayed edges and in unsupervised quarters do new modes of organization and new individual life patterns appear.

If denominational Christianity is the "Catholic" church of our modern Christendom, then what I have called "modern theology" provides the core of its system of religious ideas. Again my use of the term "modern" to categorize such a spectrum of theologies will be

questioned by those who are accustomed to using the term to designate only some of the many schools of religious thought that have
appeared in the modern centuries. I use "modern" to call attention
to the otherwise overlooked common qualities of the various liberal,
neoorthodox, neoscholastic, and evangelical theologies that students
of this period study. Differ as they may, all of them either seek some
modus vivendi with the dominant thought forms of modernity or else
attack the manner in which other schools have undertaken this task.
What is different about liberation theology is not, in the first instance
at least, the content of its ideas but its view of the role and purpose
theology should play in the world. I call those theologies "modern"
which, regardless of the content of the concepts they use, largely
agree on what theology should be doing: addressing itself to the
modern world of ideas, and thus to those persons whose business it is
to deal with such ideas. Liberation theology, on the other hand (and
again, in a baffling variety of voices), is more concerned with the
social sources and political uses of ideas. Its purpose is not to convince as much as to unmask, its intent somewhat more polemical
than apologetic, its goal more social than individual.

My point here, in drawing this comparison with the sixteenth
century, is that since it is unlikely that either denominational Christianity or modern theology will disappear completely, any more than
the Roman church and Catholic theology did after 1550, the question of what impact the new reformation and its theology will have
on the currently established church and theology cannot be avoided.
It is not an easy question. Indeed, the two theologies seem now as
irreconcilable as Catholic and Reform theology did to their most
zealous advocates four hundred years ago. To the liberationist, the
modern "liberal" insistence on analyzing and evaluating religious
ideas with little reference to their social origins or political significance reveals a blind faith in a kind of disembodied reason, the
hangover of an innocent Enlightenment prejudice. To modern establishment theologians, the liberationists' insistence on interrogating
the social sources and weighing the political valence of religious ideas
and practices smacks of reductionism and antiintellectualism. Theologians from the two camps have a hard time talking with each other
since they seem to be speaking at cross-purposes.

Things will change. The new reformation is young, noisy, and assertive. The established theologians, like the curial loyalists of the sixteenth century, continue to hope the whole thing will soon die out. But nothing stays the same. Already liberation theologians are modulating their voices and modern theologians are resigning themselves to the recognition that this is not just another flash in the pan.

Whatever happens, however they develop, I believe liberation theology and the base communities are here to stay. They are the germ cells of the next era of our culture, Toynbee's internal minority, bearing our common future. Unlike Auguste Comte, we need not break our heads to construct them. Rather, gratefully recalling the *sola fide* of a previous age, we can accept them and welcome them as the gifts of grace they are.

In the two decades since *The Secular City* was published I have gained the reputation in some circles of being a "liberal" theologian. I have never been satisfied with the label. Born and reared in a conservative Baptist milieu, I have never really abandoned that tradition. In recent years I have found myself increasingly drawn to Latin American liberation theology and have lived and taught in South America on numerous occasions. These two disparate streams of Christian faith do not seem contradictory to me, but in fact seem to confirm each other in ways I had not expected. I can feel at home in both.

As I have examined North American fundamentalism and Latin American liberation theology I have come to believe that the former has little to offer to a postmodern theology while the latter is enormously promising. Still, the liberation theologies are not export items. Eventually we North American Christians will have to develop our own liberation theology and our own base communities. When we do, however, I believe they will emerge more readily from the evangelical-conservative than from the liberal wing of American Christianity. We need a liberation theology that will draw on the folk piety of Baptists, Methodists, and the rest. We need it both to save our own valued religious tradition from being engulfed and deformed by the fundamentalists and also to absorb the liberation currents into a form of popular religion that is characteristically North American.

Perhaps I have come to appreciate my own Baptist tradition as well as the liberation theologies more in recent years because I too have been "detoxified." As this has happened I have come to believe that the great era of modern theology, of which what is loosely called "liberal" theology (in which I got my academic training) was the most characteristic expression, is drawing to a close, just as the modern era itself is ending. However, there is something different about my attitude toward this passing, and those who will still find me something of a "liberal" may not be entirely wrong. Unlike some of its conservative and radical critics, I do not believe modern theology was either a mistake or a betrayal. For me it arouses neither nostalgia nor disdain. It does elicit appreciation and admiration. It was a splendid and often inspired enterprise, a brilliant chapter in Christian history. I believe the postmodern world will require a different theology, and I have tried to suggest where that theology must come from and what it will be. But I believe that such a theology cannot be successfully formulated unless the modern liberal legacy is appropriated and incorporated. Only a theology that has taken the modern age seriously will be able to take seriously what is coming next. No one can move beyond the secular city who has not first passed through it.

NOTES

Introduction

1. Sabino Samele Acquaviva, *The Decline of the Sacred in Industrial Society* (New York: Harper and Row, 1979), p. 201.

2. Richard F. Fenn, "A New Sociology of Religion," *Journal for the Scientific Study of Religion* II, 1 (March 1972), 17.

3. See Dietrich Bonhoeffer, *Letters and Papers from Prison* (rev. ed.; New York: Macmillan, 1967).

4. Henry Scott Stokes, "Korea's Church Militant," *New York Times Magazine*, November 28, 1982, p. 67.

5. For descriptions of the role of the Church in Poland and in East Germany see: Syzmon Chodak, "People and the Church Versus the State: The Case of the Roman Catholic Church in Poland," in *Occasional Papers on Religion in Eastern Europe* II, 7 (November 1982), 26; James Will, "Reflections on the Role of the Catholic Church in Mediating the Present Crisis in Poland," in *Occasional Papers on Religion in Eastern Europe* II, 6 (September 1982), 20; Mary Lukens, "The Churches in the German Democratic Republic: Notes of an Interested Observer," Ibid. II, 1.

6. See *Christianity and Democracy*, issued by the Institute on Religion and Democracy, 1835 K St. N.W., Washington, D.C. 20006. For a critical discussion of this group see the March 21, 1983, *Christianity and Crisis* XLIII, 4, articles by Leon Howell, Wayne Cowan, and the editors. See also Cynthia Brown, "The Right's Religious Red Alert," *The Nation*, March 12, 1983, 301.

7. "Evangelicals for Social Action" (pamphlet). 25 Commerce St. S.W., Washington, D.C. 20005.

8. Sojourners, 1309 L St. S.W., Washington, D.C. 20005.

9. The principal voice of the most representative evangelical body is *Christianity Today* (465 Gunderson Drive, Carol Stream, Ill. 60187).

10. Vincent Yzermans, "The Catholic Revolution," *Christianity and Crisis* XLII, 3 (March 1, 1982), 39. For an interesting attempt to reclaim traditionally conservative symbols for a more progressive political purpose see: Joe Holland, *Flag, Faith and Family: Rooting the American Left in Everyday*

Symbols (Center for Concern, c. 1979, 3700 Thirteenth Street N.E., Washington, D.C. 20017).

11. Harvey Cox, *The Secular City—Urbanization and Secularization in Theological Perspective* (New York: Macmillan, 1965).

Chapter 1.

1. James E. Singleton, *The Fundamentalist Phenomenon or Fundamentalist Betrayal* (Tempe, Arizona: The Fundamentalist Press, n.d.).

2. The terms "conservative," "fundamentalist," and "evangelical" are somewhat slippery ones and have been used in different senses in different historical periods. For a more precise definition, see Chapter Two.

3. See Milton Yinger, "The Moral Majority Viewed Sociologically," in *Sociological Times* XV, 4 (October 1982), 289; Gabriel Fackre, *The Religious Right and Christian Faith* (Grand Rapids: Eerdmans, 1982); Gregory Baum and John Coleman, *Neo Conservatism: Social and Religious Phenomenon,* Concilium, January 1981 (Edinburgh: T. & T. Clark, 1981).

4. Jerry Falwell, "An Interview with the Lone Ranger of American Fundamentalism," *Christianity Today* XXV, 15 (September 4, 1981), 21.

Chapter 2.

1. Quoted from Anthony Wallace, *Religion, An Anthropological View* (New York: Random House, 1966).

2. Morton White and Lucia White, *The Intellectual Versus the City: From Thomas Jefferson to Frank Lloyd Wright* (New York: Oxford University Press, 1977).

3. *The Fundamentals* (Chicago: Testimony Publishing Company, 1910–1915), published in 12 parts.

4. Studies of fundamentalism and evangelicalism include James Barr, *Fundamentalism* (Philadelphia: Westminster, 1978); George Marsden, *Fundamentalism and American Culture: The Shaping of Twentieth-Century Evangelicalism 1870–1925* (New York: Oxford University Press, 1980); Ernest R. Sandeen, *Roots of Fundamentalism: British and American Millenarianism 1800–1930* (Chicago: University of Chicago Press, 1970); and Gary K. Claburgh, *Thunder on the Right: The Protestant Fundamentalists* (Chicago: Nelson Hall, 1974).

5. Jerry Falwell, *Listen, America* (New York: Doubleday, 1980).

6. Quoted in Carl F. H. Henry, "The Fundamentalist Phenomenon: The Ricochet of Silver Bullets," *Christianity Today* XXV, 15 (September 4, 1981), 30.

Chapter 3.

1. Quoted in George Marsden, *Fundamentalism and American Culture: The Shaping of Twentieth-Century Evangelicalism 1870–1925* (New York, Oxford University Press, 1980), p. 115.

2. Jean-François Lyotard, *La Condition Postmoderne: Rapport Sur le Savoir* (Paris: Les Editions de Minuit, 1979).

3. Rustum Roy, *Experimenting with Truth* (Oxford, England: The Pergamon Press, 1981).

4. Kenneth E. Stevenson and Gary R. Habermas, *Verdict on the Shroud* (Ann Arbor, Michigan: Servant Books, 1981).

5. Fritjof Schuon, *Stations of Wisdom* (London: Murray, 1961), p. 1.

Chapter 4.

1. Quoted in Carl F. H. Henry, "The Fundamentalist Phenomenon: The Ricochet of Silver Bullets," *Christianity Today* XXV, 15 (September 4, 1981), 30.

2. For recent descriptions of Jesus' relations to the political groupings of history, see *Jesus in His Time* (Philadelphia: Fortress Press, 1971), edited by Hans Jurgen Schultz, especially the essay by Paul Winter on "Sadducees and Pharisees."

3. A. G. Mojtabai, "Amarillo, the End of the Line," *Working Papers* IX, 4 (1982), 26ff.

4. Ibid., p. 28. For a best-selling statement of apocalyptic fundamentalist eschatology, see Hal Lindsey and C. C. Carlson, *The Late Great Planet Earth* (Grand Rapids: Bantam, 1970).

5. Tom Bisset, "Religious Broadcasting Coming of Age," *Christianity Today* XXV (September 4, 1981), 30.

6. Walter Benjamin, *Illuminations* (1955 Suhrkamp Verlag, Frankfurt and London; translation, New York: Harcourt, Brace and World, 1968). See also Eugene Lunn, *Marxism and Modernism: An Historical Study of Lukacs, Brecht, Benjamin and Adorno* (Berkeley: University of California Press, 1982).

7. Jurgen Habermas, "Modernity vs. Postmodernity," *New German Critique* XXII (Winter 1981), 18.

8. Ibid., p. 18.

Chapter 5.

1. Quoted in William R. Hutchinson, *The Modernist Impulse in American Protestantism* (Cambridge, Mass., and London, England: Harvard University Press, 1976), 266.

2. Quoted in George Marsden, *Fundamentalism and American Culture: The Shaping of Twentieth-Century Evangelicalism 1870–1925* (New York: Oxford University Press, 1980), p. 174.

3. John Carroll, "The Role of Guilt in the Formation of Modern Society: England 1550–1800," *Journal of Sociology* XXXII, 4 (December 1981).

4. Ibid. Quoted by Carroll from Lawrence Stone, *The Family, Sex and Marriage in England 1500–1800* (London: Weidenfeld and Nicholson, 1977), 93–98.

5. Mary Douglas, "The Effects of Modernization on Religious Change," *Daedalus* (Winter 1982), 18.

6. Owen Chadwick, *The Secularization of the European Mind in the Nineteenth Century* (New York: Cambridge University Press, 1975), 94.

Chapter 6.

1. Rudolf Siebert, "Ernesto Cardenal and the Nicaraguan Revolution–From Theological Theory to Revolutionary Practice," *Cross Currents* XXX, 3 (Fall 1980), 241.

2. Ernesto Cardenal, *Zero Hour and Other Documentary Poems* (New York: New Directions, 1980).

Chapter 7.

1. Pedro Trigo, "Espiritualidad y Cultura Ante la Modernización," *Christus* 529–530 (December 1979–January 1980), 73.

2. Pablo Richard, "El Evangelio Entre la Modernidad y la Liberación," *Servir* XIV, 76 (1978), 471.

3. Franz J. Hinkelammert, *Las Armas Ideológicas de la Muerte* (Ciudad Universitaria "Rodrigo Facio": Editorial Universitaria Centroamerica, 1977).

4. Gustavo Gutiérrez, "Two Theological Perspectives: Liberation Theology and Progressive Theology," in Sergio Torres and Virginia Fabella, *The Emergent Gospel* (Maryknoll, N.Y.: Orbis, 1976). See also Pablo Richard, op. cit., p. 472.

5. Ibid.

6. Jesus Antonio de la Torre Rangel, "La Modernidad, El Derecho y Tres Luchas Campesinas," *Christus*, 536–537 (July –August 1980), 22.

7. Juan Luis Segundo, *The Liberation of Theology* (Maryknoll, N.Y.: Orbis, 1976).

8. But for a highly critical conservative outlook on Roman Catholicism's

surrender to modernity, see James Hitchcock, *Catholicism and Modernity: Confrontation or Capitulation* (New York: Seabury, 1979).

Chapter 8.

1. I have changed the name of the village and of the priest to protect them.

2. Ignácio Ellacuria, *Freedom Made Flesh* (Maryknoll, N.Y.: Orbis, 1978).

3. Alvero Barreiro, S.J., *Basic Ecclesial Communities: The Evangelization of the Poor* (Maryknoll, N.Y.: Orbis, 1982).

4. Ibid., p. xii.

5. William Halsey, *The Survival of American Innocence: Catholicism in an Era of Disillusionment 1920–1940* (South Bend: University of Notre Dame Press, 1980).

Chapter 9.

1. Quoted in Alvero Barreiro, S.J., *Basic Ecclesial Communities: The Evangelization of the Poor* (Maryknoll, N.Y.: Orbis, 1982), p. 4.

2. Ibid., p. 71.

3. See M. D. Chenu, "Vatican II and the Church of the Poor," in *The Poor and The Church*, Norbert Greinacher and Alois Muller (eds.), Concilium 104 (New York: Seabury, 1977), 56–61.

4. Leonardo Boff, *Eclesiogenesis: Las Comunidades de Base Reinventan la Iglesia* (Santander, Spain: Sol Terrae, 1979).

5. *NTC News* (Rome: Italian Ecumenical News Agency) VI, 4 (February 1979), 3. Numbers 79, 81, and 82 of *Servir* (Third and Fourth Quarters of 1979) also contain extensive reports and evaluations of the Puebla meeting by Luiz Alberto Gómez de Souza; Luis Ramos, O.P.; Miguel Concha Malo, O.P.; Gustavo Gutiérrez; Enrique Dussel; Raul Vidales; and José Comblin.

6. Ibid., p. 4. The actual wording of the bishops' statement on the CEBs is: "As pastors we definitely seek to promote, orient and accompany the CEBs, according to the spirit of Medellín (and the criteria of *Evangelii Nuntiandi* 58), and to help to discover and gradually train animators for them. We must try especially to see how the small communities which are multiplying above all in the peripheral and rural zones can be adopted for pastoral work in the great cities of our continent." Quoted in "Documentos de Puebla," cited in Juan José Tamayo-Acosta, "Comunidades de Base y Lucha Contra la Pobreza," *Misión Abierta* (published in Madrid by the Claretian Fathers) LXXIV, 4–5 (November 1981), 595 (115), n. 1.

Chapter 10.

1. Giovanni Franzoni, "The CGC at the Crossroads Between Roman Catholicism, Protestantism, Working Class, Marginalized," *NTC News* (Rome: Italian Ecumenical News Agency) X, 1–2 (January–February 1983), 10.

2. "Grassroots Christian Communities," *NTC News* V, 22 (December 1978), 3.

3. "Sixth National Congress of Christian Grassroots Communities," *NTC News* X, 1–2 (January–February 1983), 9.

4. "The Netherlands—Manifesto of a Movement," *Christianity and Crisis* (September 21, 1981), 246.

5. Ibid., p. 246.

6. Ibid., p. 246.

7. Peadar Kirby, "The Threat of Peace; Church and State in East Germany," *Commonweal* CIX (June 6, 1982), 336–338. See also "Grassroots Communities Springing up in West Germany," *NTC News* VI, 6 (March 30, 1979), 7; "French Grassroots Communities," *NTC News* VI, 19–20 (October 15–30, 1978), 1.

8. Kate Pravera, "The United States: Realities and Responses," in *Christianity and Crisis* (September 21, 1981), 246. See also Reverend Frank Ponce, "Building Basic Christian Communities: *Comunidades Eclesiales de Base* in the U.S. Experience," in *Developing Basic Christian Communities—A Handbook* (Chicago: National Federation of Priests' Council, 1979).

9. Ibid., p. 248.

Chapter 11.

1. Foreword to Alvero Barreiro, *Basic Ecclesial Communities: The Evangelization of the Poor* (Maryknoll, N.Y.: Orbis, 1982), p. xii.

2. Johann B. Metz, *The Emergent Church: The Future of Christianity in a Post-Bourgeois World* (New York: Crossroads, 1981), 85.

3. Arnaldo Zenteno, "Las Comunidades Cristianas de Base ante el Proceso Popular," *Servir* XV (1979), 83–84.

4. Ibid., p. 577 (my translation).

5. Ibid., p. 578 (my translation).

6. Arnaldo Zenteno, "Las Comunidades de Base en el Marco de America Latina—Fortalecer la Hermandad Latinoamericana," *Servir* XVI, 90 (1980), 669.

7. Habermas himself, who often says insightful things in somewhat opaque language, puts it this way: ". . . we now observe . . . an overspill,

an encroachment by the system on areas no longer at all related to material reproduction. These areas of cultural tradition—social integration through values and norms, education, socialization of coming generations—are, however . . . held together by their very nature through the medium of communicative behavior. Once the steering media such as money and power penetrate these areas, for instance by redefining relations in terms of consumption, or by bureaucratizing the conditions of life, then it is more than an attack on traditions. The foundations of a life-world . . . are under assault. What is at stake is the symbolic reproduction of the life-world itself." From "The Dialectics of Rationalization: An Interview," *Telos* (St. Louis, Missouri: Sociology Department, Washington University) XLIX (1981), 20.

8. See Michael Bavarei, *New Communities, New Ministries: The Church Resurgent in Africa, Asia, and Latin America* (Maryknoll, N.Y.: Orbis, 1983); and Virgil Elizondo and Norbert Greinacher, *Tensions Between the Churches of the First and the Third World* (Edinburgh: T. & T. Clark, 1981).

Chapter 12.

1. Gustavo Gutiérrez, *A Theology of Liberation—History, Politics and Salvation* (Maryknoll, N.Y.: Orbis, 1973). See also Raul Vidales, "Perfil Teológico de Gustavo Gutiérrez," *Servir* XV, 82 (1979), 466.

2. Ibid., p. 243.

3. Gustavo Gutiérrez, "Two Theological Perspectives: Liberation Theology and Progressive Theology," in Sergio Torres and Virginia Fabella, *The Emergent Gospel* (Maryknoll, N.Y.: Orbis, 1976).

4. Ruben Dri, "Jesús y los Pobres," *Servir* XVI, 86 (1980), 211, and, by the same author, "La Conflictividad en la Vida de Jesús," *Servir* XVI, 85 (1980), 49.

5. Isabel Carter Heyward, *The Redemption of God* (Washington, D.C.: University Press of America, 1982).

Chapter 13.

1. David Tracy, *The Analogical Imagination—Christian Theology and the Culture of Pluralism* (New York: Crossroads, 1981), 1–43.

2. For a serious critique of liberation theology see Dennis McCann, *Christian Realism and Liberation Theology* (Maryknoll, N.Y.: Orbis, 1981).

3. See Ruben Dri, "Evangelización, Ideológia, Política," *Informativo Serie Puebla* LXXIX, 4 (Centro Nacional de Comunicaciones Sociales, A.C. Medellín 33, Mexico 7). See also Raul Vidales and Tokihiro Kudo,

276 *Notes*

Práctica Religiosa y Proyecto Histórico (Lima: Centro de Estudios y Publicaciones [EP], 1975).

4. See Jorge Pixley, "Pueblo de Dios y Mayorías Populares en la Biblia," *Servir* XIV, 77 (Quinto Bimestre de 1978), 603–622.

5. For a full-scale development of this view see Arend Th. van Leeuwen, *Christianity in World History* (New York: Scribner's, 1964).

6. Stephen Toulmin, *The Return to Cosmology: Postmodern Science and the Theology of Nature* (Berkeley: University of California Press, 1983).

7. Hector Diaz Valencia et al., "Dios y El Hombre," *Christus* XLV, 531 (February 1980), 18–53 (Centro de Reflexión Teológica, A.C. Rodin No. 355, Mexico 19, D.F.).

8. For an explication of this approach to the Bible, see Pablo Richard, "La Bible, Mémoire Historique des Pauvres," *Liaisons Internationales* 32 (September, 1982), 3 (published by Centre Oecuménique de Liaisons Internationales, Rue de Boulet 31, B-1000 Bruxelles, Belgium). See also *Romans Thirteen*, Working Papers from the Third Materialist Bible Reading Seminar (Geneva: World Student Christian Federation [Europe Region], December 1978) WSCF Quai Wilson, 1201 Geneva, 1979; and Sergio Rostagno, *Essays on the New Testament—A "Materialist" Approach* (Geneva: World Student Christian Federation, n.d.).

9. Ernesto Cardenal, *Gospel at Solentiname* (four vols., 1978–1982) (Maryknoll, N.Y.: Orbis).

10. There are some exceptions. See José Porfirio Miranda, *Being and the Messiah* (Maryknoll, N.Y.: Orbis, 1973) and the work of Juan Carlos Scannone, especially his essay "Transcendencia, praxis liberadora y lenguaje—Hacia una filosofía de la religión postmoderna y latinoamericamente situada," in *Hacia una Filosofía de la Liberación Latinoamericana* (Buenos Aires: Ed. Bonum, 1973).

11. Rosemary Ruether, "Basic Communities—Renewal at the Roots," *Christianity and Crisis* XLI, 14 (September 21, 1981), 236.

12. Gustavo Gutiérrez, "Comunidades Cristianas de Base—Perspectivas Eclesiologicas," *Servir* XVI, 90 (1980), 710.

13. García Ramirez, "Las Comunidades de Base Como Grupos Primarios," *Servir* XVI, 90 (1980), 583.

14. Katherine Auspitz, in *The Radical Bourgeoisie* (New York: Cambridge University Press, 1982), demonstrates that the change-oriented segments of the bourgeoisie have always advocated universal schooling as the most effective way of breaking the power of the corporate authorities such as church and state, which were seen as obstacles preventing the advance of the political goals the bourgeoisie supported, such as secularization, political democracy, meritocracy, and the equality of the sexes.

Chapter 14.

1. John Stuart Mill, *On Liberty* (London: 1859). Quoted in Owen Chadwick, *The Secularization of the European Mind in the Nineteenth Century* (New York: Cambridge University Press, 1975), p. 30.

2. For a radical critique of the political assumptions of the Enlightenment's anti-Christian bias see Lucien Goldmann, *The Philosophy of Enlightenment* (Cambridge, Mass.: MIT Press, 1973).

3. Ernest Renan, *The Life of Jesus* (New York: The Modern Library, 1927).

4. Ibid., p. 218.

5. Quoted in Chadwick, op. cit., p. 156.

6. See Edwin Sylvest, *Motifs of Franciscan Mission Theory in Sixteenth-Century New Spain Province of the Holy Gospel* (Washington, D.C.: Academy of American Franciscan History, 1975); and John Leedy Phelan, *The Millennial Kingdom of the Franciscans in the New World* (Berkeley: University of California Press, 1970 (first ed., 1956)).

7. Gustavo Gutiérrez, *A Theology of Liberation—History, Politics and Salvation* (Maryknoll, N.Y.: Orbis, 1973) p. 300.

8. Ibid., p. 302.

9. See Michael Walzer, *The Revolution of the Saints: A Study in the Origin of Radical Politics* (Cambridge, Mass.: Harvard University Press, 1982).

10. Renan, op. cit., p. 222.

Chapter 15.

1. Friedrich Schleiermacher, *On Religion—Speeches to Its Cultured Despisers* (New York: Ungar, 1955).

2. Joel Whitebrook, "Saving the Subject: Modernity and the Problem of the Autonomous Individual," *Telos* 50 (Winter 1981–82), 79.

Chapter 16.

1. Marshall Berman, *All That Is Solid Melts into Air: The Experience of Modernity* (New York: Simon and Schuster, 1982).

2. Ibid, p. 18.

3. Gabriel Daly in *Transcendence and Immanence: A Study in Catholic Modernism* (New York: Clarendon, 1980) makes a convincing case that Roman Catholic modernism had wholly different presuppositions from those of Protestant liberalism and that it ended not in exhaustion but because of

ecclesiastical censure. This is why Latin American theologians do not reject Blondel. See F. Guillén Preckler, SCH. P., "Tradición y Modernismo. El Pensamiento de Mauricio Blondel," *Christus* XLVI, 542 (February 1981), 30.

Chapter 17.

1. Quoted in Owen Chadwick, *The Secularization of the European Mind in the Nineteenth Century* (N.Y.: Cambridge University Press, 1975) p. 209.

2. Ibid., p. 209.

3. Daniel Bell, *The Coming of the Post-Industrial Society* (New York: Basic Books, 1973), 480.

4. Daniel Bell, *The Cultural Contradictions of Capitalism* (New York: Basic Books, 1976), 28.

5. Quoted in Hugh McLeod, *Religion and the People of Western Europe 1789–1970* (New York: Oxford University Press, 1981), 104.

6. Ibid., p. 105.

7. Peter Steinfels, *The Neo Conservatives—The Men Who Are Changing America's Politics* (New York: Simon and Schuster, 1979), 182.

8. James Fowler, *Stages of Faith* (San Francisco: Harper & Row, 1981).

9. Sharon Parks, "Faith Development and Imagination in the Context of Higher Education," Harvard University Dissertation, 1979, Microfilm.

Chapter 18.

1. Giovanni Franzoni, "The Earth Is God's," *NTC Summer Special 1978* V, 13 (July 1978) (Italian Ecumenical News Agency, 00184 Rome, via Firenze 38, Italy).

2. Auguste Comte, *Positive Philosophy* (New York: AMS Press, reprint of 1855 edition); *The Catechism of Positive Religion* (New York: Kelley, 1973).

3. Pablo Richard, "El Evangelio Entre la Modernidad y la Liberación," *Servir* XIV, 76 (1978), 471.

4. Marshall Berman, *All That Is Solid Melts into Air: The Experience of Modernity* (N.Y.: Simon and Schuster, 1982).

5. Katherine Maria Dyckman and L. Patrick Carroll, *Inviting the Mystic, Supporting the Prophet: An Introduction to Spiritual Direction* (Ramsey, N.J.: Paulist Press, 1981).

6. Quoted in Ernest Boyer, "Edges and Rhythms: The Spiritualities of Solitude and Community," *Sojourners* (June 1982), 14.

7. Jon Sobrino, *Christology at the Crossroads: A Latin American Approach* (Maryknoll, N.Y.: Orbis, 1978), 56.

8. See C.S. Song, "Many Peoples and Many Languages" (mimeograph), 1982; Tissa Balasuriya, *The Eucharist and Human Liberation* (Maryknoll, N.Y.: Orbis, 1979); Gerald H. Anderson, *Asian Voices in Christian Theology* (Maryknoll, N.Y.: Orbis, 1980); John C. England (ed.), *Living Theology in Asia* (Maryknoll, N.Y.: Orbis, 1982).

9. Michael Bavarei, *New Communities, New Ministries: The Church Resurgent in Africa, Asia and Latin America* (Maryknoll, N.Y.: Orbis, 1983).

Chapter 19.

1. Joel Whitebrook, "Saving the Subject: Modernity and the Problem of the Autonomous Individual," *Telos* 50 (Winter 1981–1982), 79.

2. Ibid., p. 75.

3. Fred Dallmayr, *The Twilight of Subjectivity: Contributions to a Post-Individualist Theory of Politics* (Amherst: University of Massachusetts Press, 1981).

4. Jurgen Habermas et al., "The Dialectics of Rationalization: An Interview," *Telos* 49 (1981).

5. Ibid.

6. Ibid.

Chapter 20.

1. Edward Schillebeeckx, *Jesus, an Experiment in Christology* (New York: Crossroads, 1981), 26.

2. See especially Ninian Smart, *Reasons and Faiths* (London: Routledge and Kegan Paul, 1958); John Hier (ed.), *Truth and Dialogue in World Religions* (Philadelphia: Westminster, 1974); George Rupp, *Christologies and Cultures—A Typology of Religious Worldviews* (The Hague and Paris: Motron, 1974); Stanley J. Samartha, *Course for Dialogue—Ecumenical Issues in Inter-Religious Relationships* (Maryknoll, N.Y.: Orbis, 1982); Peter Berger (ed.), *The Other Side of God—A Polarity in World Religions* (Garden City, N.Y.: Anchor Press, 1981), which includes the present author's "The Battle of the Gods? A Concluding Unsystematic Postscript."

3. Carl A. Raschke, "Religious Pluralism and Truth: From Theology to Hermeneutical Dialogy," *Journal of the American Academy of Religion* (March 1982), 35.

4. Wilfred Cantwell Smith, *Faith and Belief* (Princeton, N.J.: Princeton University Press, 1979); and *Towards a World Theology: Faith and Comparative History of Religion* (London: Macmillan, and Philadelphia: Westminster, 1981).

5. See especially Huston Smith, *Forgotten Truth* (New York: Harper & Row, 1976).

6. John Macquarrie, "The One and the Many: Complementarity of Religions," in Thomas A. Aykara (ed.), *Meeting of Religions, New Orientations and Perspectives* (Center for Indian and Inter-religious Studies, Rome. Bangalore, India: Dharmaram Publishers, 1978).

7. Raimundo Pannikkar, "The Myth of Pluralism: The Tower of Babel —A Meditation in Non-Violence," *Cross Currents* 29 (Summer 1979).

8. Eberhard Jungel, *The Doctrine of the Trinity: God's Being Is Becoming* (Grand Rapids: Eerdmans, 1976).

9. C.S. Song, "Many Peoples and Many Languages" (mimeograph), 1982.

10. Jon Sobrino, *Christology at the Crossroads: A Latin American Approach* (Maryknoll, N.Y.: Orbis, 1978).

11. Isabel Carter Heyward, *The Redemption of God* (Washington, D.C.: University Press of America, 1982).

12. Jerry Falwell, "An Interview with the Lone Ranger of American Fundamentalism," Christianity Today XXV, 15 (September 4, 1981), 24.

13. Tissa Balasuriya, "Latin American Theology of Liberation: An Asian View," in *The Church at the Crossroads*, IDOC Europe Dossier Six (Rome: IDOC International, 1978); see also Balasuriya's "The Asians," in Sergio Torres and John Eagleson (eds.), *The Challenge of the Basic Christian Communities* (Maryknoll, N.Y.: Orbis, 1981).

14. Ibid., p. 134.

15. See J. A. Lyons, *The Cosmic Christ in Origen and Teilhard de Chardin* (Oxford: Oxford University Press, 1982).

Chapter 21.

1. Roger Chartier, "Discipline and Invention: The Fête in France XV–XVIII," *Diogenes* 110 (Summer 1980).

2. Enrique Dussel, *The History of the Church in Latin America: Colonialism to Liberation*. Alan Neely, transl. (Grand Rapids: Eerdmans, 1981).

3. Jesús Antonio de la Torre Rangel in "La Modernidad, El Derecho y Tres Luchas Campesinas," *Christus* 536–537 (July–August 1980), shows how the efforts of peasant groups to preserve their lands and their rights often draw on a mixture of both traditional premodern and postmodern (socialist) views of law.

4. *Servir* XVII, 93–94 and XVII, 95–96.

5. Cardenal, *Gospel at Solentiname* (four vols., 1978–1982), (Maryknoll, N.Y.: Orbis).

6. See Robert Forster and Orest A. Ranum (eds.), *Ritual, Religion and the Sacred,* Selections from *Annales Economies, Sociétés, et Civilisations* 7 (Baltimore: Johns Hopkins University Press, 1982) for ten essays by scholars from the French *"annales"* school of historians on the role of popular religion in history.

7. Chartier, op. cit., pp. 46–47.

8. Ibid., p. 59.

9. Diego Irarrazával and Pablo Richard, *Religión y Política en America Central: Hacia una Nueva Interpretacion de la Religiosidad Popular* (Coleccion Centroamerica, Departmento Ecumenico de Investigaciones: n. d.). See also Diego Irarrazával, "Derechos del oprimido y su religiosidad," *Servir* XVI, 86 (1980), 257.

10. Ibid., p. 45.

11. See Rosemary Reuther, *Religion and Sexism* (New York: Simon and Schuster, 1974); Jean Chamberlain Engelsman, *The Feminine Dimension of the Divine* (Philadelphia: Westminster, 1979); Jean Bethke Elshtain, *Public Man, Private Woman: Women in Social and Political Thought* (Princeton, N.J.: Princeton University Press, 1981); Isabel Carter Heyward, op. cit.; Carol Ochs, *Women and Spirituality* (Totowa, N.J.: Rewman and Allanheld, 1983); Judith Plaskow, *Sex, Sin and Grace: Women's Experience and the Theologies of Reinhold Niebuhr and Paul Tillich* (Washington, D.C.: University Press of America, 1980).

12. Emily Culpepper, "Philosophia in a Feminist Key: Revolt of the Symbols" (unpublished dissertation: Harvard University, 1983; also available from University Microfilm International, Ann Arbor, Mich.).

13. Julia Kristeva, "Women's Time" (transl. by Alice Jardine and Harry Blake), *Signs* VII, 1 (August 1981), 16.

14. See Jean Bethke Elshtain, op. cit.

Chapter 22.

1. For a new approach to the interaction of religious and political strands see Otto Maduro, "Extraction de la Plus-Value, Repression de la Sexualité et Catholicisme en Amerique Latine," *Liaisons Internationales* 32 (September 1982) (OELI Brussels, Belgium).

2. James Obelkevich, *Religion of the People 800–1700* (Chapel Hill: University of North Carolina Press, 1979).

BIBLIOGRAPHY

Acquaviva, Sabino Samele. *The Decline of the Sacred in Industrial Society* (New York: Harper & Row, 1979).

Allen, Diogenes. "A Christian Theology of Other Faiths," *Theology Today* (October 1981), 305.

Ambler, Rex, and Haslern, David (eds.). *Agenda for Prophets* (London: The Bowerdean Press, 1980).

Anderson, Gerald H. *Asian Voices in Christian Theology* (Maryknoll, N.Y.: Orbis, 1980).

Auspitz, Katherine. *The Radical Bourgeoisie* (New York: Cambridge University Press, 1982).

Balasuriya, Tissa. "Latin American Theology of Liberation: An Asian View," in *The Church at the Crossroads*. IDOC Europe Dossier Six (Rome: IDOC International, 1978).

———. *The Eucharist and Human Liberation* (Maryknoll, N.Y.: Orbis, 1979).

———. "The Asians," in Sergio Torres and John Eagleson (eds.), *The Challenge of the Basic Christian Communities* (Maryknoll, N.Y.: Orbis, 1981).

Barr, James. *Fundamentalism* (Philadelphia: Westminster, 1978).

Barreiro, Alvero, S. J. *Basic Ecclesial Communities: The Evangelization of the Poor* (Maryknoll, N.Y.: Orbis, 1982).

Baum, Gregory, and Coleman, John. *Neo Conservatism: Social and Religious Phenomenon*, Concilium, January 1981 (Edinburgh: T. & T. Clark, 1981).

Bavarei, Michael. *New Communities, New Ministries: The Church Resurgent in Africa, Asia, and Latin America* (Maryknoll, N.Y.: Orbis, 1983).

Bell, Daniel. *The Coming of the Post-Industrial Society* (New York: Basic Books, 1973).

———. *The Cultural Contradictions of Capitalism* (New York: Basic Books, 1976).

———. "The Return of the Sacred: The Argument of the Future of Religion," *British Journal of Sociology* (December 1977).

Benjamin, Walter. *Illuminations* (1955 Suhrkamp Verlag Frankfurt and London. Translation, New York: Harcourt, Brace and World, 1968).

Berger, Peter. *Facing Up to Modernity* (New York: Doubleday, 1977).

———— (ed.). *The Other Side of God—A Polarity in World Religions* (Garden City, N.Y.: Anchor Press, 1981).

Berman, Marshall. *All That Is Solid Melts into Air: The Experience of Modernity* (New York: Simon and Schuster, 1982).

Bernamon, Michael, and Caramellow, Charles (eds.). *Performance in Postmodern Culture* (Madison: Coda Press, 1977).

Bisset, Tom. "Religious Broadcasting Comes of Age," in *Christianity Today* XXV (September 4, 1981), 30.

Bonhoeffer, Dietrich. *Letters and Papers from Prison* (rev. ed., New York: Macmillan, 1967).

Boyer, Ernest. "Edges and Rhythms: The Spiritualities of Solitude and Community," *Sojourners* (June 1982), 12–18.

Brown, Cynthia. "The Right's Religious Red Alert," in *The Nation*, March 12, 1983, 301.

Capra, Fritjof. *The Tao of Physics* (New York: Bantam, 1977).

————. *The Turning Point: Science, Society, and the Rising Culture* (New York: Simon and Schuster, 1982).

Cardenal, Ernesto. *Zero Hour and Other Documentary Poems* (New York: New Directions, 1980).

————. *Gospel at Solentiname* (four vols., 1978–1982) (Maryknoll, N.Y.: Orbis).

Carroll, John. "The Role of Guilt in the Formation of Modern Society: England 1550–1800," *Journal of Sociology* XXXII, 4 (December 1981).

Chadwick, Owen. *The Secularization of the European Mind in the Nineteenth Century* (New York: Cambridge University Press, 1975).

Chartier, Roger. "Discipline and Invention: The Fête in France XV–XVIII," *Diogenes* 110 (Summer 1980), 44.

Chenu, M. D. "Vatican II and the Church of the Poor," in *The Poor and the Church*, Norbert Greinacher and Alois Muller (eds.), Concilium 104 (New York: Seabury, 1977), 56–61.

Chodak, Szymon. "People and the Church Versus the State: The Case of the Roman Catholic Church in Poland," *Occasional Papers on Religion in Eastern Europe* II, 7 (November 1982). Published by Christians Associated for Relationships with Eastern Europe (Lafayette College, Easton, Pa. 18042).

Christianity and Democracy. Issued by the Institute on Religion and Democracy (1835 K Street N.W., Washington, D.C. 20006).

Christianity Today (465 Gunderson Drive, Carol Stream, Ill. 60187).

Claburgh, Gary K. *Thunder on the Right: The Protestant Fundamentalists* (Chicago: Nelson Hall, 1974).

Comte, Auguste. *Positive Philosophy* (New York: AMS Press, reprint of 1955 edition).

———. *The Catechism of Positive Religion* (New York: Kelley, 1973).

Cowan, Wayne et al. "Politics, Faith and Polemics," in *Christianity and Crisis* XLIII, 4 (March 1983).

Cox, Harvey. *The Secular City—Urbanization and Secularization in Theological Perspective* (New York: Macmillan, 1965).

———. "A Puebla Diary," *Commonweal* CVI, 5 (March 16, 1979), 141.

Culpepper, Emily. "Philosophia in a Feminist Key: Revolt of the Symbols (unpublished dissertation, Harvard University 1983; also available from University Microfilm International, Ann Arbor, Mich.).

Dallmayr, Fred. *Twilight of Subjectivity: Contributions to a Post-Individualist Theory of Politics* (Amherst: University of Massachusetts Press, 1981).

Daly, Gabriel. *Transcendence and Immanence: A Study in Catholic Modernism* (New York: Clarendon, 1980).

Dickinson, J. K. *The Later Middle Ages: From the Norman Conquest to the End of the Reformation* (New York: Barnes and Noble, 1980).

Douglas, Ann. *The Feminization of American Culture* (Avon: New York 1978).

Douglas, Mary. "The Effects of Modernization on Religious Change," *Daedalus* (Winter 1982), 1ff.

Dussel, Enrique. *The History of the Church in Latin America: Colonialism to Liberation.* Neely, Alan, transl. (Grand Rapids: Eerdmans, 1981).

Dyckman, Katherine Maria, and Carroll, L. Patrick. *Inviting the Mystic, Supporting the Prophet: An Introduction to Spiritual Direction* (Ramsey, N.J.: Paulist Press, 1981).

Elizondo, Virgil, and Greinacher, Norbert. *Tensions Between the Churches of the First World and the Third World* (Edinburgh: T. & T. Clark, 1981).

Ellacuria, Ignácio. *Freedom Made Flesh* (Maryknoll, N.Y.: Orbis, 1978).

Elshtain, Jean Bethke. *Public Man, Private Woman: Women in Social and Political Thought* (Princeton, N.J.: Princeton University Press, 1981).

Engelsman, Jean Chamberlain. *The Feminine Dimension of the Divine* (Philadelphia: Westminster, 1979).

England, John C. *Living Theology in Asia* (Maryknoll, N.Y.: Orbis, 1982).

Evangelicals for Social Action (pamphlet). 25 Commerce Street S.W., Grand Rapids, Mich. 49503.

Fackre, Gabriel. *The Religious Right and Christian Faith* (Grand Rapids: Eerdmans, 1982).

Falwell, Jerry. *Listen, America!* (New York: Doubleday, 1980).

———— (with Ed Hobson and Ed Hindson). *The Fundamentalist Phenomenon* Doubleday, 1981A).

————. "An Interview with the Lone Ranger of American Fundamentalism," *Christianity Today* XXV, 15 (September 4, 1981B), 22.

Fekete, John. "On Interpretation," *Telos* XLVIII (Summer 1981).

Fenn, Richard K. "A New Sociology of Religion," *Journal for the Scientific Study of Religion* II, 1 (March 1972), 17.

Forster, Robert, and Ranum, Orest A. *Ritual, Religion and the Sacred.* Selections from the *Annales Economies, Societies and Civilizations,* 7 (Baltimore: Johns Hopkins University Press, 1982).

Fowler, James. *Stages of Faith* (San Francisco: Harper & Row, 1981).

Franzoni, Giovanni. "The Earth Is God's," *NTC Summer Special 1978* V, 13 (July 1978) (Italian Ecumenical News Agency, 00184 Rome, via Firenze 38, Italy).

————. "The CGC at the Crossroad Between Roman Catholicism, Protestantism, Working Class, Marginalized," NTC News (Rome: Italian Ecumenical News Agency) X, 1–2 (January–February 1983), 10.

"French Grassroots Communities," *NTC News* VI, 19–20 (October 15–30, 1979), 1.

The Fundamentals (Chicago: Testimony Publishing Company 1910–1915), published in 12 parts.

Fung, Raymond. *Households of God on China's Soil* (Maryknoll, N.Y.: Orbis, 1983).

Goldmann, Lucien. *Christianity and Enlightenment* (Cambridge, Mass.: MIT Press, 1973).

"Grassroots Communities Springing up in West Germany," *NTC News* VI, 6 (March 30, 1979), 7.

Guardini, Romano. *The End of the Modern World: A Search for Orientation* (New York: Sheed and Ward, 1956).

Gutiérrez, Gustavo. A *Theology of Liberation—History, Politics and Salvation* (Maryknoll, N.Y.: Orbis, 1973).

————. "Two Theological Perspectives: Liberation Theology and Progressive Theology," in Sergio Torres and Virginia Fabella, *The Emergent Gospel* (Maryknoll, N.Y.: Orbis, 1976).

————. *The Power of the Poor in History* (Maryknoll, N.Y.: Orbis, 1983).

Habermas, Jurgen. "Modernity vs. Postmodernity," *New German Critique* 22 (Winter 1981).

————, Hanneth, Axel, Knodler-Bunte, Eberhard, and Widman, Arno. "The Dialectics of Rationalization: An Interview," *Telos* (St. Louis, Mo.: Sociology Department, Washington University) 49 (1981).

Halsey, William. *The Survival of American Innocence: Catholicism in an Era of Disillusionment, 1920–1940* (South Bend: University of Notre Dame Press, 1980).

Henry, Carl F. H. "The Fundamentalist Phenomenon: The Ricochet of Silver Bullets," in *Christianity Today* XXV, 15 (September 4, 1981), 30.

Heyward, Isabel Carter. *The Redemption of God* (Washington, D.C.: University Press of America, 1982).

Hier, John (ed.). *Truth and Dialogue in World Religions* (Philadelphia: Westminster, 1974).

Hinchcliff, Peter. *Holiness and Politics* (London: Derten, Longman and Todd, 1982).

Hitchcock, James. *Catholicism and Modernity: Confrontation or Capitulation* (New York: Seabury, 1979).

Holland, Joe. *Flag, Faith and Family: Rooting the American Left in Everyday Symbols* (Center for Concern, c. 1979, 3700 Thirteenth St. N.E., Washington, D.C. 20017).

Hunter, James Davidson. *American Evangelicalism: Conservative Religion and the Quandary of Modernity* (New Brunswick, N.J.: Rutgers University Press, 1983).

Hutchison, William R. *The Modernist Impulse in American Protestantism* (Cambridge, Mass., and London, England: Harvard University Press, 1976).

Joy, Donald (ed.). *Moral Development Foundations:* Judeo-Christian Alternatives to Piaget/Kohlberg (Nashville: Abingdon Press, 1983).

Jungel, Eberhard. *The Doctrine of the Trinity: God's Being Is Becoming* (Grand Rapids: Eerdmans, 1976).

Kirby, Peadar. "The Threat of Peace; Church and State in East Germany," *Commonweal* CIX, (June 6, 1982), 336–338.

Kristeva, Julia. "Women's Time" (transl. by Alice Jardine and Harry Blake), *Signs* VII, 1 (August 1981).

Lears, T. J. Jackson. *No Place for Grace: Antimodernism and the Transformation of American Culture, 1880–1920* (New York: Pantheon Books, 1981).

Lernoux, Penny. *Cry of the People* (New York: Doubleday, 1980).

Levinson, H. S. "Traditional Religion, Modernity and Unthinkable Thoughts," *Journal of Religion* LXI, 1 (January 1981), 37.

Lindsey, Hal, and Carlson, C. C. *The Late Great Planet Earth* (Grand Rapids: Bantam, 1970).

Lukens, Nancy. "The Churches in the German Democratic Republic: Notes of an Interested Observer," in *Occasional Papers on Religion in Eastern*

Europe II, 1 (November 1982). Published by Christians Associated for Relationships with Eastern Europe (Lafayette College, Easton, Pa. 18042).

Lynn, Eugene. *Marxism and Modernism: An Historical Study of Lukacs, Brecht, Benjamin and Adorno* (Berkeley: University of California Press, 1982).

Lyons, J. A. *The Cosmic Christ in Origen and Teilhard de Chardin* (Oxford: Oxford University Press, 1982).

Machen, J. Gresham. *Christianity and Liberalism* (New York: Macmillan, 1923).

Macquarrie, John. "The One and the Many: Complementarity of Religions," in Thomas A. Aykara (ed.), *Meeting of Religions, New Orientations and Perspectives* (Center for Indian and Inter-religious Studies, Rome. Bangalore, India: Dharmaram Publishers, 1978).

Marsden, George. *Fundamentalism and American Culture: The Shaping of Twentieth-Century Evangelicalism, 1870–1925* (New York: Oxford University Press, 1980).

Martin, David. *The Dilemmas of Contemporary Religion* (London: Basil Blackwell, 1978).

Massey, Marilyn Chapin. *Christ Unmasked: The Meaning of "The Life of Jesus" in German Politics* (Chapel Hill: University of North Carolina Press, 1982).

McCann, Dennis. *Christian Realism and Liberation Theology* (Maryknoll, N.Y.: Orbis, 1981).

McCoy, Charles S. *When Gods Change* (Nashville: Abingdon Press, 1982).

McLeod, Hugh. *Religion and the People of Western Europe 1789–1970* (New York: Oxford University Press, 1981).

Mendes-Flohr, Paul R. "Secular Religiosity: Reflections on Post-Traditional Jewish Spirituality," in *Bulletin of the Center for the Study of World Religions*, Harvard University (Spring 1982), 5.

Metz, Johann B. *The Emergent Church: The Future of Christianity in a Post-Bourgeois World* (New York: Crossroads, 1981).

———. "Toward the Second Reformation: The Future of Christianity in a Post-Bourgeois World," *Cross Currents* XXXI, 1.

Mill, John Stuart. *On Liberty* (reprint, New York: Norton, 1975).

Minnery, Tom. "The Man Behind the Mask: Bandit or Crusader?" *Christianity Today* XXV, 15 (September 4, 1981), 28.

Miranda, José Porfirio. *Being and the Messiah* (Maryknoll, N.Y.: Orbis, 1973).

Mojtabai, A. G. "Amarillo, the End of the Line," *Working Papers* IX, 4 (1982), 26ff.

"The Netherlands—Manifesto of a Movement," *Christianity and Crisis* (September 21, 1981), 246.

Northrup, F. S. C. *The Meeting of East and West: An Inquiry Concerning World Understanding* (New York: Macmillan, 1946).

"Grassroots Christian Communities," *NTC News* V, 22 (December 1978).

NTC News, 00184 Rome, via Firenze 38, Italy.

Obelkevich, James. *Religion of the People, 800–1700* (Chapel Hill: University of North Carolina Press, 1979).

Ochs, Carol. *Women and Spirituality* (Totowa, New Jersey: Rewman and Allanheld, 1983).

Palmer, Richard. "Toward a Postmodern Interpretive Self-Awareness," *Journal of Religion* 55 (1975).

Panikkar, Raimundo. "The Myth of Pluralism: The Tower of Babel—A Meditation on Non-Violence," *Cross Currents* 29 (Summer 1979).

Parks, Sharon Lea. "Faith Development and Imagination in the Context of Higher Education," Harvard University Dissertation, 1979, microfilm.

Pfeffer, Richard. *Working for Capitalism* (New York: Columbia University Press, 1982).

Phelan, John Leedy. *The Millennial Kingdom of the Franciscans in the New World* (Berkeley: University of California Press, 1970; first ed. 1956).

Plaskow, Judith. *Sex, Sin and Grace: Women's Experience and the Theologies of Reinhold Niebuhr and Paul Tillich* (Washington, D.C.: University Press of America, 1980).

Ponce, Reverend Frank. "Building Basic Christian Communities: *Comunidades Eclesiales de Base* in the U.S. Experience," in *Developing Basic Christian Communities—A Handbook* (Chicago: National Federation of Priests' Councils, 1979).

Pravera, Kate. "The United States: Realities and Responses," in *Christianity and Crisis* (September 21, 1981), 246.

"The Quest for Truly Human Communities," Pro Mundi Vita, Centrum Informationes, Brussels, *Pro Mundi Vita Bulletin* (September 1976) Rue de la limite 6, Brussels, Belgium (62).

Radhakrishnan, Sri. *Eastern Religions and Western Thought*, second ed. (New York: Oxford University Press, 1975).

Raschke, Carl A. "Religious Pluralism and Truth: From Theology to Hermeneutical Dialogy," *Journal of the American Academy of Religion* (March 1982), 35.

————. *The Alchemy of the Word: Language and the End of Theology* (New York: Scholars Press, 1983).

Renan, Ernest. *The Life of Jesus* (New York: The Modern Library, 1927).

Richard, Lucien J. U.M.I. *A Kenotic Christology* (Washington, D.C.: University Press of America, 1982).

Romans Thirteen Working Papers from the Third Materialist Bible Reading Seminar (Geneva, Switzerland: World Student Christian Federation [Europe Region] December 1978) WSCF 37 Quai Wilson, 1201 Geneva, 1979.

Rostagno, Sergio. *Essays on the New Testament—A "Materialist" Approach* (Geneva, Switzerland: World Student Christian Federation, n.d.).

Roy, Rustum. *Experimenting with Truth* (Oxford: The Pergamon Press, 1981).

Ruether, Rosemary. *Religion and Sexism* (New York: Simon and Schuster, 1974).

———. "Basic Communities—Renewal at the Roots," in *Christianity and Crisis* XLI, 14 (September 21, 1981), 236.

Runyon, Theo (ed.). *Santification and Liberation: Liberation Theologies in Light of the Wesleyan Tradition* (Nashville: Abingdon Press, 1981).

Rupp, George. *Christologies and Cultures—A Typology of Religious Worldviews* (The Hague and Paris: Motron, 1974).

Samartha, Stanley J. *Courage for Dialogue—Ecumenical Issues in Interreligious Relationships* (Maryknoll, N.Y.: Orbis, 1982).

Sandeen, Ernest R. *Roots of Fundamentalism: British and American Millenarianism 1800–1930* (Chicago: University of Chicago Press, 1970).

Schillebeeckx, Edward. *Jesus, An Experiment in Christology* (New York: Crossroads, 1981).

Schultz, Hans Jurgen (ed.). *Jesus in His Time* (Philadelphia: Fortress Press, 1971).

Schuon, Fritjof. *Stations of Wisdom* (London: Murray, 1961).

Schurmann, Reiner. "Anti-Humanism: Reflections on the Turn Toward the Post Modern Epoch," in *Man and World* XXI, 2 (1979).

Segundo, Juan Luis, S.J. *The Liberation of Theology* (Maryknoll, N.Y.: Orbis, 1976).

Schleiermacher, Friedrich. *On Religion—Speeches to Its Cultured Despisers* (New York: Ungar, 1955).

Siebert, Rudolf. "Ernesto Cardenal and the Nicaraguan Revolution—From Theological Theory to Revolutionary Practice," *Cross Currents* XXX, 3 (Fall 1980), 241.

———. "The Christianity of the Future—The Church from Below," Kung and Metz. *Cross Currents* XXXI, 1 (Spring 1981), 62.

———. *From Critical Theory to Theology of Communicative Praxis* (Washington, D.C.: University Press of America, 1979).

Singleton, Dr. James E. (ed.) *The Fundamentalist Phenomenon or Fundamentalist Betrayal* (Tempe, Arizona: The Fundamentalist Baptist Press, n.d.).

"Sixth National Congress of Christian Grassroots Communities." *NTC News* (Rome: Italian Ecumenical News Agency) X, 1–2 (January–February 1983), 9.

Smart, Ninian. *Reasons and Faiths* (London: Routledge and Kegan Paul, 1958).

Smith, Huston, *Forgotten Truth* (New York: Harper & Row, 1976).

———. *Beyond the Postmodern Mind* (New York: Crossroads, 1982).

Smith, Wilfred Cantwell. *Faith and Belief* (Princeton, N.J.: Princeton University Press, 1979).

———. *Towards a World Theology: Faith and Comparative History of Religion* (London: Macmillan, and Philadelphia: Westminster, 1981).

Sobrino, Jon. *Christology at the Crossroads: A Latin American Approach* (Maryknoll, N.Y.: Orbis, 1978).

Sojourners. 1309 L Street S.W., Washington, D.C. 20005.

Choan Seng Song, "Many Peoples and Many Languages" (mimeograph), 1982.

Spretnak, Charlene. *The Politics of Women's Spirituality: Essays on the Rise of Spiritual Power Within the Feminist Movement* (Garden City, N.Y.: Doubleday Anchor, 1982).

Steinfels, Peter. *The Neo-Conservatives—The Men Who Are Changing America's Politics* (New York: Simon and Schuster, 1979).

Stevenson, Kenneth E., and Habermas, Gary R. *Verdict on the Shroud* (Ann Arbor, Michigan: Servant Books, 1981).

Stokes, Henry Scott. "Korea's Church Militant," *New York Times Magazine*, November 28, 1982, p. 67.

Stone, Lawrence. *The Family, Sex and Marriage in England, 1500–1800* (London: Weidenfeld and Nicholson, 1977).

Sylvest, Edwin Edward, Jr. *Motifs of Franciscan Mission Theory in Sixteenth-Century New Spain Province of the Holy Gospel* (Washington, D.C.: Academy of American Franciscan History, 1975).

Torres, Sergio, and Fabella, Virginia. *The Emergent Gospel: Theology from the Underside of History* (Maryknoll, N.Y.: Orbis, 1978).

Toulmin, Stephen. *The Return to Cosmology: Postmodern Science and the Theology of Nature* (Berkeley: University of California Press, 1983).

Tracy, David. *The Analogical Imagination—Christian Theology and the Culture of Pluralism* (New York: Crossroads, 1981).

Van Leeuwen, Arend Th. *Christianity in World History* (New York: Charles Scribner's Sons, 1964).

Wallace, Anthony. *Religion, An Anthropological View* (New York: Random House, 1966).

Walzer, Michael. *The Revolution of the Saints: A Study in the Origin of Radical Politics* (Cambridge, Mass.: Harvard University Press, 1982).

Werblowsky, Zwi. *Beyond Tradition and Modernity* (London: Athlone Press, 1976).

White, Morton, and White, Lucia. *The Intellectual Versus the City: From Thomas Jefferson to Frank Lloyd Wright* (New York: Oxford University Press, 1977).

Whitebrook, Joel. "Saving the Subject: Modernity and the Problem of the Autonomous Individual," in *Telos* L (Winter 1981–1982), 79.

Will, James. "Reflections on the Role of the Catholic Church in Mediating the Present Crisis in Poland," *Occasional Papers on Religion in Eastern Europe* II, 6 (November 1982). Published by Christians Associated for Relationships with Eastern Europe (Lafayette College, Easton, Pa. 18042).

Winter, Paul. "Sadducees and Pharisees," in *Jesus in His Time* (Philadelphia: Fortress Press, 1971).

Yinger, Milton. "The Moral Majority Viewed Sociologically," in *Sociological Times* XV, 4 (October 1982), 289.

Yzermans, Vincent. "The Catholic Revolution," in *Christianity and Crisis* XLII, 3 (March 1, 1982), 39. (Reprinted from *New York Times*, November 14, 1981).

Foreign-Language Publications

Boff, Leonardo. *Eclesiogenesis: Las Comunidades de Base Reinventan la Iglesia* (Santander, Spain: Sol Terrae, 1979).

Comblin, José. "Comunidades Eclesias e Pastoral Urbana," *Revista Eclesiastica Brasiliera* XXX, 20 (1970).

De La Torre Rangel, Jesus Antonio. "La Modernidad, El Derecho y Tres Luchas Campesinas," *Christus* 536–537 (July–August 1980), 22.

Dri, Ruben. "Evangelizacion, Ideologia, Politica," *Informativo*. Serie Puebla 79, #4 (Centro Nacional de Comunicacion Social, A.C. Medellín 33, Mexico 7).

———. "Jesus y los Pobres," *Servir* XVI, 86 (1980), 211.

Dussel, Enrique. *Hipotesis Para Una Historia de la Iglesia en America Latina* (first ed. Barcelona: Editorial Estela, 1967).

——— and Espinosa, Felipe, S. J. "Puebla. Cronica e historia," *Christus* 520–521 (March–April 1979), 21–37. Published by Centro de Reflexion Teologica, A.C. Apartado Postel 19-213. Colonia Mixcoac, Del Juarez, Mexico, D.F. 03910.

Giminez, Gilberto. *Cultura Popular y Religion en el Anahuac* (Centro de Estudios Ecumenicas A.C. Mexico, D.F., 1978).

Gutiérrez, Gustavo. "La Fuerza Historica de los Pobres," in *Signos de Lucha y Esperanza* (Lima: Centro de Estudios y Publicaciones, 1978).

———. "Comunidades Christianas de Base—Perspectivas Eclesiologicas," *Servir* XVI, 90 (1980).

———. *El Dios de la Vida* (Lima: Pontificia Universidad Catolica, 1982).

Hinkelammert, Franz J. *Las Armas Ideologicas de la Muerte* (Ciudad Universitaria "Rodrigo Facio": Editorial Universitaria Centroamerica, 1977).

Instituto Superior de Ciencias Morales. *Modernidad y Etica Cristiana* (Madrid: P. S. Editorial, 1981).

Irarrazával, Diego. "Derechos del oprimido y su religiosidad," *Servir* XVI, 86 (1980), 257.

——— "Nicaragua: Una Sorprendente Religiosidad," in Pablo Richard and Diego Irarrazával. *Religión y Política en America Central: Hacia una Nueva Interpretación de la Religiosidad Popular* (Colección Centroamerica, Departmento Ecumenico de Investigaciones, n.d.).

——— and Richard, Pablo. *Religion y Politica en America Central: Hacia Una Nueva Interpretación de la Religiosidad Popular* (Coleccion Centroamerica, Departmento Ecumenico de Investigaciones, n.d.).

Kraft, Dieter. Die "Zweite Religiositat" theologische Anmerkungen zu einem geselschaflichen Thema. *Weissenseer Blatter* 4 (1982). 1157 Berlin, Ehrlichstr. 75.

Lyotard, Jean-François. *La Condition Postmoderne: Rapport Sur le Savoir* (Paris: Les Editions de Minuit, 1979).

Maduro, Otto. "Extraction de la Plus-Value, Repression de la Sexualité et Catholicisme en Amerique Latine," *Liaisons Internationales* 32 (September 1982) (OELI Brussels, Belgium).

Pixley, Jorge. *El Libro de Job: Comentario biblico latinoamericana* (San Jose, Costa Rica: Ediciones SEBILA, 1982).

———. "Puebla de Dios y Mayorias Populares en la Biblia," *Servir* XIV, 77 (Quinto Bimestre de 1978), 603–622.

Preckler, F. Guillen, SCH. P. "Tradición y Modernismo. El Pensamiento de Mauricio Blondel," *Christus* XLVI, 542 (February 1981), 30.

Ramirez, Garcia. "Las Comunidades de Base Como Grupos Primarios," *Servir* XVI, 90 (1980), 583.

Richard, Pablo. "La Bible, Memoire Historique des Pauvres," *Liaisons Internationales*. No. 32 (September 1982), 3. Centre Oecumenique de Liaisons Internationales, Rue de Boulet 31, B-1000, Bruxelles, Belgium.

————. "El Evangelio Entre La Modernidad y la Liberación," *Servir* XIV, 76 (1978), 471.

Rubert de Ventos, Xavier. *Ensayos Sobre el Desorden* (Barcelona: Editorial Kairos, 1976).

Scannone, Juan Carlos. "Transcendencia, praxis liberadora y lenguaje—Hacia una filosofia de la religion post-moderna y latinoamericanamente situada," in *Hacia una filosofía de la liberación latinoamericana* (Buenos Aires: Ed. Bonum, 1973).

Sobrino, Jon. *Resurrección de la Verdadera Iglesia—Los pobres, lugar teológico de la eclesiología* (Santander, Spain: Sal Terrae, 1982).

Tamayo-Acosta, Juan José. "Comunidades de Base y Lucha Contra la Pobreza," *Mision Abierta* XXIV, 4–5 (November 1981) (published by the Claretian Fathers, Madrid).

Trigo, Pedro, S. J. "Espiritualidad y Cultura Ante la Modernizacion," *Christus* 529–530 (December 1979–January 1980), 73.

Valencia, Hector Diaz, *et al.* "Dios y El Hombre. Una Historia," in *El Pueblo y Su Dios—Perspectivas desde el Antigua Testimento. Christus* XLV, 531 (February 1980), 18–53. Centro de Reflexión Teológica. A.C. Rodin No. 355, Mexico 19, D.F.

Vidales, Raul. "Perfil Teológico de Gustavo Gutiérrez," *Servir* XV, 82 (1979), 466.

———— and Kudo, Tokihiro. *Práctica Religiosa y Proyecto Historico* (Lima: Centro de Estudios y Publicaciones [EP], 1975).

Videla, Gabriela. *Un Senor Obispo—Sergio Mendez Arceo* (Cuernavaca, Mexico: Correo del Sur, 1982).

Zenteno, Arnaldo. "Las Comunidades Cristianas de Base en el Marco de America Latina—Fortalecer la Hermandad Latinoamericana," *Servir* XVI, 90 (1980).

————. "Las Comunidades Cristianas de Base ante el Proceso Popular," *Servir* XV, 83–84 (1979).

INDEX

"absolute other," 208
"affection," 206
African Methodist Episcopal
   churches, 110
aggiornamento concept, 111
ahimsa, 228
Allen, Jimmy, 33
All That Is Solid Melts into Air
   (M. Berman), 209
Amsterdam, Holland, base
   communities congress at
   (1978), 121
Anabaptists, 263
Analogical Imagination, The (Tracy),
   150
Ancien Régime, 197
Anthony, Saint, 195, 196, 210, 249
"antihumanists," 216
apologetics, in fundamentalism, 51,
   52, 61
Aquinas, Saint Thomas, 137, 216
"Are You Washed in the Blood of
   the Lamb?," 34
arribismo, 146
Asian religions, 208, 209, 212, 234,
   256
Assumption doctrine, 259–60
Augustine, Saint, 216
aura, decay of, 68
avant-gardeism, 151
Avvenire, 119

Baggio, Sebastiano, 116
Bahai religion, 207
Balasuriya, Tissa, 232, 233, 234, 237
Baptist Bible Fellowship, 44–45

Baptist churches, 110, 132, 182,
   267, 268
   fundamentalism in, 31, 32, 36,
      45, 48
Barnhouse, Donald Grey, 33
Barreiro, Alvero, 104
Barth, Karl, 57, 131, 177
base communities, Christian:
   Biblical teachings in, 99–101,
      108, 113, 114, 119, 120, 122,
      123, 124, 167, 168–69, 213
   at bishops' assembly in Puebla,
      Mexico (1979), 115–17, 119
   in Brazil, 108, 113, 114, 116,
      119, 129, 130, 131, 133, 144
   in Europe, 110, 118–24, 126,
      127, 132, 133, 134, 166, 167,
      214
   fundamentalism compared with,
      128–29, 140, 160
   growth of, 106, 107–15, 140,
      155–56, 260
   La Chispa as example of, 97, 98–
      103, 112, 136, 151, 214
   in Latin America, 59, 70, 97–
      103, 109–20, 123, 124, 126,
      132, 139, 140, 145, 151, 156,
      167–68, 214
   in Mexico, 115–17, 119, 129–31,
      133, 141
   middle-class members of, 119,
      121, 123
   political aspect of, 121, 122, 124,
      129–31, 140–44, 155–56, 157
   polyvalent character of, 132–34
   postmodern theology and, 126–
      127, 133, 134, 167–69

as reform movement, 262, 264, 266, 267
religious significance of, 139–40, 149, 158, 165, 230, 242
as secular communities, 130, 131, 133, 134
Sixth National Congress of (1982), 118–19
in U.S., 103, 124–25, 127, 133, 134, 166, 167
as viewed by Metz, 126–27, 128, 129
see also liberation theology
Basic Ecclesial Communities (Barreiro), 104
basismo, 130
Bayle, Pierre, 92
Beck, David, 52–53
Bell, Daniel, 198
Benedict, Saint, 195, 196
Benjamin, Walter, 68
Berlin Appeal, 123
Berman, Harold, 62–63
Berman, Marshall, 181, 209
Berrigan, Daniel, 87, 88
Bible:
authority of, 40, 42, 43, 53, 56, 65, 181
in fundamentalism, 30–31, 32, 35, 61, 65, 69, 152–53, 154, 168, 169
historical criticism of, 42, 44, 92, 154, 168, 169, 177, 224
interpretation of, 168–69
in liberation theology, 137, 139, 140, 144, 148, 152–53, 166, 167, 168–69
as taught in base communities, 99–101, 108, 113, 114, 119, 120, 122, 123, 124
see also individual books
Bible Baptist churches, 31
Big Gap theory, 160
Bisset, Tom, 67
black religious experience, 202, 209, 214, 232, 237, 257
Blavatsky, Elena, 202

Bloch, Ernst, 217
Boff, Clodovis, 130
Boff, Leonardo, 114, 161
Bonhoeffer, Dietrich, 147, 175, 202, 204, 205
born-again Christians, 35, 42, 66
Brazil, base communities in, 108, 113, 114, 116, 119, 129, 130, 131, 133, 144
Brunner, Emil, 57
Bryan, William Jennings, 34, 64
Buber, Martin, 217
Bultmann, Rudolf, 177
Buñuel, Luis, 165n
Butler, Bishop Joseph, 92–93

Calvin, John, 42, 263
Calvinism, 163, 164, 165
Campus Crusade, 47
capitalism, as basis of modern world, 82, 90, 133, 183, 185, 189–90, 218, 220, 221
Capra, Fritjof, 53, 55
Cardenal, Ernesto, 36, 37, 154n
as radical Christian, 85–90, 92n, 247
Carroll, John, 77
Catholic Church:
as church of poor people, 108, 110, 114, 125, 126, 139–40, 143
liberal agenda for, 111–12, 113
Protestantism compared to, 42, 43, 92–97, 106, 109, 110, 113, 114, 120–21, 122, 127, 132, 137, 139, 148, 168–69, 265
Reformation and, 92, 262, 264
Second Vatican Council in, 108, 110, 111–13, 117, 118, 139, 145
secularization and, 93, 94, 97, 112
in U.S., 97, 103–6, 108, 109
see also base communities, Christian
Chadwick, Owen, 80
Chartier, Roger, 250

Chavez, César, 246
Christian academies, 47
Christianity:
  clergy in, 131, 132, 157, 164,
    198, 257, 264
  hierarchy in, 132, 156, 168, 175,
    214
  in Middle Ages, 76, 77, 79, 143–
    144, 195–96
  monastic movement in, 193–94,
    195–96
  as official religion of Roman
    Empire, 192–93, 194
  in Reformation period, 77–78, 92,
    127, 163, 164, 194, 210, 262–
    267
  see also base communities,
    Christian
Christianity and Liberalism (Machen),
  73
Christianity Today, 67
Christology, 141, 234, 235, 236
church and state, separation of, 93,
  94–95, 96, 97, 128, 183–84
cities, religion in, 80–81, 170, 171,
  268
*Coming of the Post-Industrial Society,
  The* (Bell), 198
Common Prayer, Book of, 39
Commonweal, 123
communications, alternative
  channels of, 119, 132
communicative praxis theory, 218–
  219, 238
communism, 185, 190, 208
Comte, Auguste, 206, 207, 267
comunidades eclesiales de base (CEBs),
  see base communities, Christian
Condition Postmoderne, La (Lyotard),
  53
Constantine I, conversion of, 192–
  193, 194
"contemplative intelligence," 58,
  220
convergence of faith, 226, 227
"Courses for a Better World," 113
creo quia absurdum est concept, 55

Daedalus, 79
Dallmayr, Fred, 217
Daniel, Book of, 65, 140
Darrow, Clarence, 34
Darwin, Charles, 161
Day, Dorothy, 211
Deck, Allan Figueroa, 104, 106, 126
Descartes, René, 183
"detoxification" process, 243, 268
dialogy, 228, 229
"Dios y El Hombre: Una Historia,"
  153
Doctrine of the Trinity, The (Jüngel),
  229
Dominguito, Fiesta of, 253–54
Dormition doctrine, 259–60
Douglas, Mary, 79
Durkheim, Emile, 204
Dussel, Enrique, 242

ecclesial viewpoint, 92n
ecclesiogenesis concept, 114
Eddy, Mary Baker, 202
Edwards, Jonathan, 46, 78
Eliot, T. S., 203
Ellacuria, Ignácio, 102, 161
Elms, Royce, 65–66
Enlightenment period, 92, 201, 217,
  219, 266
Episcopal churches, 39
Epplemann, Rainer, 123
Equal Rights Amendment, 48
Erasmus, Desiderius, 191
Erikson, Erik, 194
"estate," definition of, 143–44
Evangelicals for Social Action, 46
evangelism, 45–47, 57, 61, 62
evolution theory, fundamentalist
  opposition to, 34–35, 40, 56,
  71
existentialism, 177, 216
Experimenting with Truth (Roy), 54
Ezekiel, Book of, 65

faith:
  in fundamentalism, 55, 56–59,
    61, 153

nature of, 93–94, 95, 175, 203, 204
in world religions, 224, 226, 227
Falwell, Jerry:
  as fundamentalist, 31, 34–37, 44, 45, 46, 47, 48, 51, 60, 63, 64, 65, 230, 231
  personality of, 29, 33–34
  as preacher, 32–33, 34, 68, 69, 70
fêtes, French, 250, 252
Finney, Charles Grandison, 46, 78
Fire Company Fair (Malvern, Pa.), 250
Ford, J. Alan, 65
Fowler, James, 204
Francis de Sales, Saint, 143
Francis of Assisi, Saint, 143
Francis Xavier, Saint, 103
Franzoni, Giovanni, 118, 120
freedom, religious vs. secular view of, 127, 217, 160, 170–71, 218
Freedom Made Flesh (Ellacuria), 102
Freiraum concept, 123
French revolution (1830), 163–64
French theologians, 111
Freud, Sigmund, 49, 194, 203
FSLN movement, 87
Fuller, Charles, 33
fundamentalism:
  academic rejection of, 49–53
  antimodernism of, 34, 60–62, 68, 69, 71, 72–75, 79, 81–82
  apologetics in, 51, 52, 61
  in Baptist churches, 31, 32, 36, 45, 48
  base communities compared with, 128–29, 140, 160
  as basis of postmodern theology, 57, 59, 63–71, 72–82, 267–68
  Biblical teachings in, 30–31, 32, 35, 61, 65, 69, 152–53, 154, 168, 169
  eschatology of, 45, 65–67
  evangelicalism compared with, 45–47, 57, 61, 62
  evolution theory opposed by, 34–35, 40, 56, 71

faith as important to, 55, 56–59, 61, 153
  as ideology, 36, 48, 60–71
  liberalism opposed by, 31, 46, 48, 53, 62, 71, 73
  liberation theology compared with, 57, 60, 62, 64, 85, 91, 155, 160
  mass media's effect on, 32–33, 34, 43–44, 67–71, 128, 132, 140, 169
  modern theology vs., 49–50, 51, 53–54, 56, 72, 73, 74, 81, 82
  origins of, 44, 60, 74
  poor rural basis of, 63–64, 74
  popular religion and, 249–50, 252
  premodern theological attitudes in, 54, 57, 59
  rational discourse in, 49, 50–53
  as "redneck religion," 35, 42–43, 55, 60, 63, 64
  religious pluralism and, 46, 47, 59, 63, 222, 223, 224, 230–31
  revival of, 36, 44–48, 74
  scientific method and, 40, 49, 53–56, 61
  as subculture, 50, 51, 56, 57, 60, 62, 63
  as theology, 49–59, 60, 63
  see also Falwell, Jerry
Fundamentals, The, 44

García Ramírez, Roberto, 157
Garden of Eden, 42
Genesis, Book of, 56
Germany, East, base communities in, 123
Gethsemane, Ky., Trappist monastery at, 85, 86
God:
  as deity of religion, 39, 57, 200–201
  as *el dios pobre,* 147, 151, 166, 260, 263
  existence of, 92, 201, 210–11, 229
  grace of, 66, 127, 144, 263

God (*cont.*)
  justice of, 91, 146, 152, 157
  religion as visible sign of, 101,
    102, 131, 132, 257–58
  as universal concept, 178–79,
    213, 238
"God's Microphone," 113
"gospel glut," 68
Gospel of Solentiname, The
  (Cardenal), 154n
Graham, Billy, 33, 46
grassroots communities movement,
  see base communities, Christian
Great Awakening, 46
Great Commission, 233
Green, Thomas Hill, 92
guadalupismo, see Our Lady of
  Guadalupe, folk worship of
"Guidelines for Christian Living"
  (Falwell), 33
Gutiérrez, Gustavo, as liberation
  theologian, 95, 135–36, 139,
  141, 144, 146, 156, 157, 158,
  165, 252

Habermas, Gary, 54
Habermas, Jürgen, 69, 133
  critical modernist position of,
    218–21
Haitian Baptists, 167
Halloween celebrations, 250–52
Halsey, William, 105
Harrison, Beverly, 255
Hegel, Georg Wilhelm Friedrich,
  204
Heidegger, Martin, 217, 219
Helms, Jesse, 70
Herodians, 30, 64, 65
heteronomous societies, 62
Heyward, Isabel Carter, 229
Hidalgo, Miguel, 246, 257
Hindson, Ed, 30–31, 35, 60
Hinduism, 50, 227
"Hindu solution," 227
*History of the Church in Latin
  America, The* (Dussel), 242
Holiness churches, 110

Holland, base communities in, 121–
  123
"Homage to the Indians"
  (Cardenal), 89
Humbard, Rex, 67
Hutchinson, Anne, 202
"hypers," 31

Idea of the Holy, The (Otto), 40
independent churches, 31
infallibility doctrine, 93
instrumental reason, 218, 220
Intellectual Versus the City, The
  (White and White), 41
interfaith dialogue, 238, 239
internal proletariat, 192, 267
Intervarsity, 47
"invisible hand" concept, 95
*Inviting the Mystic, Supporting the
  Prophet,* 210
Iranian revolution, 169
Irarrazával, Diego, 252, 253, 254
Islam, 50
Italy, base communities in, 119–21,
  166

James, Saint (Santiago), 147
James, William, 154
Jerome, Saint, 195, 196
"Jesus and His Critics" (Hindson),
  30–31
Jesus Christ:
  divine vs. human nature of, 31,
    44, 181
  Great Commission of, 233
  kenosis of, 141–43, 144
  Last Supper of, 99–100
  in liberation theology, 235–36,
    263
  as personal savior vs. Cosmic
    Christ, 236–39
  politics of, 64, 102, 193, 234,
    235, 237, 262
  Renan's biography of, 161–62,
    170
  Resurrection of, 54, 55, 209, 214–
    215, 263

Joan of Arc, 143
John of the Cross, Saint, 79
John XXIII, Pope, 105, 110, 111, 113, 126, 265
John Paul II, Pope, 115
jouissance, 258, 260
Juan Diego, 244, 247, 257
Judas, Christ betrayed by, 99–100
Julião, Francisco, 114–15, 160
Jung, Carl, 49
Jüngel, Eberhard, 229
justification doctrine, 57

Kant, Immanuel, 92–93
Kennedy, John F., 105
kerygma, 205
Kierkegaard, Sören, 55, 236
King, Martin Luther, Jr., 35, 202, 211
Kirby, Peadar, 123
Kristeva, Julia, 258, 259
Kung, Hans, 57, 127, 241

La Chispa base community, 97, 98–103, 112, 136, 151, 214
Latin America:
    base communities in, 59, 70, 97–103, 109–20, 123, 124, 126, 132, 139, 140, 145, 151, 156, 167–68, 214
    theological developments in, 153–155, 162, 164, 165, 166, 212–213, 223, 232, 263, 267
    see also Brazil; Mexico
"leap of faith" concept, 55
legal principles, religious foundation of, 62–63, 199–200
Lercaro, Cardinal, 111, 114, 125, 145
"liberating core, 207–8
liberation theology:
    and academic theology, 150, 151–155
    antimodernism of, 85, 89, 91
    applied theology vs., 136, 144
    as basis of postmodern theology, 157, 158, 160, 167–69, 213, 267–68
    Bible as used in, 137, 139, 140, 144, 148, 152–53, 166, 167, 168–69
    Christ's significance to, 235–36, 263
    as church theology, 92n, 150–51, 211
    conflict as strategy of, 138, 140–141, 143, 144–46, 148–49, 151–52
    "consulting the faithful" in, 136, 137
    ecclesiology of, 137–38, 141, 142, 148
    fundamentalism compared with, 57, 60, 62, 64, 85, 91, 155, 160
    God or "theos" component in, 137–38, 146–49, 151, 152–54
    Gutiérrez as proponent of, 95, 135–36, 139, 141, 144, 146, 156, 157, 158, 165, 252
    modern theology vs., 82, 91–97, 150, 157–58, 159–71
    poor people in, 139–40, 143, 145, 151, 154, 156, 164, 165–67, 176, 208, 214, 230
    popular religion and, 240–43, 246, 248, 252, 255, 257, 258, 260
    as public theology, 150, 151, 155–158
    as reform movement, 262, 264, 266, 267
    religious pluralism and, 222, 223, 224, 230, 231–34
    as theology of praxis, 136–37, 154
    world or "logos" component in, 137–46, 148, 151–52
    see also base communities, Christian
Liberty Baptist College, 32, 33, 36, 51–53, 54, 65
Liberty Baptist Seminary, 36, 51

Life of Jesus, The (Renan), 161–62,
170
life-worlds, communicative, 69, 70,
221
liminality, 250, 251
Lippmann, Walter, 73
literal verbal inspiration theory, 168
Lombardi, Father, 113
Louis IX, king of France, 143
Luke, Gospel of, 99
Luther, Martin, 42, 94, 137, 262,
263
Lyotard, Jean-François, 53

Machen, J. Gresham, 60, 72–73
Macquarrie, John, 226–27
Maillard, Abbé, 199, 201
Maritain, Jacques, 177
Marx, Karl, 62, 164, 203
Marxism, 102, 243
Mary, mother of Christ, 188, 256,
259–60
masses, vernacular, 108, 111, 112
Mater et Magistra encyclical, 113
Matthew, Gospel of, 30–31
Matthiesen, Leroy, 65
Medellín, Colombia, bishops'
assembly at (1968), 143
Merton, Thomas, 85, 86, 87
metanoia, 140, 144
metatheology, 155
Metz, Johannes B., 89, 90
base communities as viewed by,
126–27, 128, 129
Mexico, base communities in, 115–
117, 119, 129–31, 133, 141
Christianity in, 76, 77, 79, 143–
144, 195–96
Mill, John Stuart, 160, 162, 200,
208
Miskito Indians, 88, 89, 90
modern theology, *see* theology,
modern
modern world:
airline terminal as symbol of, 184–
188

bourgeois society in, 81–82, 90,
92, 93, 128, 162–64, 179, 197,
198, 200, 201, 202–3, 220
bureaucracy in, 40, 79–80, 134,
183, 188, 189, 218, 221
capitalism in, 82, 90, 133, 183,
185, 189–90, 218, 220, 221
communism in, 185, 190, 208
corporate-conflict vs. homeostatic
model of, 148, 151–52
science and technology in, 39–40,
41, 44, 49, 67–68, 94, 183,
184, 186, 188, 189
secularization of religion in, 39,
41–42, 75, 80, 81, 170–71,
183, 185–86, 188, 189, 190,
196–204, 210, 217, 236, 268
separation of church and state in,
93, 94–95, 96, 97, 128, 183–
184
socialism in, 109, 114, 185, 221
sovereign national states in, 183,
184, 186, 188–89
see also religion
Mojtabai, A. G., 65, 66
Moltmann, Jürgen, 147
morality, nonreligious basis for, 93,
95, 206, 218, 219, 220
Moral Majority, 36, 65, 230, 231
Muñoz, Padre, 98, 99, 100, 101–2
Murray, John Courtney, 111

Nation, 73
National Association of
Evangelicals, 46
National Congress of Christian
Grassroots Communities
(1980), 120
National Council of Churches, 40,
46
National Council of Churches of
Holland, 122
nature mysticism, 80, 81
New Eloise, The (Rousseau), 182
New Evangelicalism, 46
New Guinea, religious rituals in, 75–
77

New Republic, 73
Newton, Isaac, 54
Nicaragua:
    popular religion in, 252–54
    revolutionary movement in, 86,
        87, 88, 89–90
"Nicaraguan Canto" (Cardenal), 87
Nietzsche, Friedrich Wilhelm, 201
Noble Savage myth, 76, 129
nuclear arms, as religious issue, 65–
    66, 78, 123, 189

Old Time Gospel Hour, 33, 36, 68,
    70, 230
On Liberty (Mill), 160
Origin of Species, The (Darwin), 161
Osservatore Romano, 119
Otto, Rudolf, 40, 176
Our Lady of Guadalupe, folk worship
    of, 243–48, 249, 256, 257,
    259, 260, 261
Our Lady of Solentiname monastery,
    86–88, 89, 90
Our Lady of the Airways, 185, 188

Pacem in Terris encyclical, 113
pacifism, 87, 88
paideia concept, 233
Panikkar, Raimundo, 227, 228, 238
"panthers," 223
Papal States, 93
Paris Commune (1870), 197
Parsons, Talcott, 204
Pastoral Plan, First, 113
Pauck, Wilhelm, 177
Paul, Saint, teachings of, 46, 141,
    142, 145, 219, 263
Paul VI, Pope, 195
Pentecostal churches, 110
Peter, Saint, 54
Peter, Second Epistle of, 65
Pharisees, 30, 31
Philippians, Epistle to the, 141, 142
pilgrimages, 252, 253, 254
Pius XII, Pope, 113
"political apocalyptic" belief, 65

poor people:
    conflict as strategy of, 140–41,
        143, 144, 146, 148–49, 157,
        187–88
    in liberation theology, 139–40,
        143, 145, 151, 154, 156, 164,
        165–67, 176, 208, 214, 230
populism, religious, 151
positivism, 206
postmodern theology, *see* theology,
    postmodern
practical reason, 218, 220
Pravera, Kate, 124
prayer in public schools, 36, 70
"privatization," 128
projection, psychological, 79, 81
Protestantism:
    Catholic Church compared to, 42,
        43, 92–97, 106, 109, 110, 113,
        114, 120–21, 122, 127, 132,
        137, 139, 148, 168–69, 265
    see also fundamentalism
Proverbs, Book of, 23, 33
Puebla, Mexico, bishops' assembly at
    (1979), 115–17, 119, 141
Puritan piety, 78

Quinet, Edgar, 162

radio communities, 113
Rapture, definition of, 45, 66
Raschke, Carl, "truth question"
    examined by, 225, 226, 227,
    228, 229, 237
Rawls, John, 219
Reagan, Ronald, 36, 70
reason, types of, 218, 219–20
"redneck religion," fundamentalism
    as, 35, 42–43, 55, 60, 63, 64
Reformation period, 77–78, 92, 127,
    163, 164, 194, 210, 262–67
religion:
    in Asian cultures, 208, 209, 212,
        234, 256
    autonomy of, 94, 128, 185, 188,
        200–201

religion (*cont.*)
    base communities as important to, 139–40, 149, 158, 165, 230, 242
    as based on reason, 50–51, 204, 205–7
    black experience of, 202, 209, 214, 232, 237, 257
    in cities, 80–81, 170, 171, 268
    communication in, 218–21, 238
    corporate structures in, 148, 151–152, 196, 210, 213–15, 231, 262–68
    feeling of awe as basis of, 40, 79, 228
    form vs. substance in, 68–70, 74, 198
    fundamentalism and pluralism of, 46, 47, 59, 63, 222, 223, 224, 230–31
    God as deity of, 39, 57, 200–201
    human need for, 197–98, 203–4, 206
    as interpreted by modern theology, 175–77, 183, 208, 209
    legal principles founded on, 62–63, 199–200
    liberation theology and pluralism of, 222, 223, 224, 230, 231–234
    in modern vs. premodern times, 74, 75, 76, 77–82, 143–44, 195–96
    mystical tradition in, 85, 86, 90, 91, 128, 129, 131, 145
    political tradition in, 90, 92n, 93, 94, 128, 129, 131
    science and, 92, 93, 94, 153n
    secularization of, 39, 41–42, 75, 80, 81, 170–71, 183, 185–86, 188, 189, 190, 196–204, 210, 217, 236, 268
    Taine's views on, 197–98, 200, 203–4, 206, 208
    truth question in, 224, 225–29, 230, 237
    as visible sign of God, 101, 102, 131, 132, 257–58
    women's experience of, 124, 131, 167–68, 202, 207, 208, 209, 214
    see also liberation theology; modern world; theology, modern; theology, postmodern
religion, popular:
    festivals in, 248–54, 256
    fundamentalism and, 249–50, 252
    guadalupismo as example of, 243–248, 249, 256, 257, 259, 260, 261
    liberation theology and, 240–43, 246, 248, 252, 255, 257, 258, 260
    piety in, 176, 180, 191, 221, 241, 248, 252, 255, 257
    women's role in, 254–61
Renaissance period, 188, 194
Renan, Ernest, 161–62, 170
reproduction, mechanical, 68, 71
Return to Cosmology, The (Toulmin), 153n
Revelation, Book of, 65, 140
Ricca, Paolo, 120
Rich, Adrienne, 209
Richard, Pablo, 204, 207, 208, 209
Roberts, Oral, 67
Robertson, Pat, 67, 69
Romero, Oscar Arnulfo, 211
Rosenzweig, Franz, 217
Rossi, Father, 113–14
Rousseau, Jean-Jacques, 181–82, 184
Roy, Rustum, 54
Ruether, Rosemary, 156, 168, 255
Rule (Saint Benedict), 195

Sadducees, 30, 64, 65
St. Francis Xavier parish (Hyannis, Mass.), 103–6, 108, 126, 166
St. Paul's Outside the Walls, 119–120, 166

saints, 79, 81, 147
  festivals of, 248–49, 253–54
  see also individual saints
Sandino, César Augusto, 88
Santiago (Saint James), 147
Schleiermacher, Friedrich, 176–77
Schuon, Fritjof, 58–59, 153, 220
science:
  distrust of, 39–40, 41, 44, 49, 67–
    . 68, 94, 183, 184, 186, 188, 189
  fundamentalism and, 40, 49, 53–
    56, 61
  religious belief vs., 92, 93, 94,
    153n
  Shroud of Turin and, 54–55, 61
scientific creationism, 40, 53, 54
Scopes, William, 71
Scopes "monkey trial," 34–35, 53,
  55–56, 71
"secular city" concept, 170, 171,
  267, 268
*Secularization of the European Mind in
  the Nineteenth Century*
  (Chadwick), 80
secular world, *see* modern world
security checks in airports, 187–88,
  190
Segundo, Juan Luis, 243, 245
"Septuagint" group, 121
Servir, 245
Shroud of Turin, scientific
  investigation of, 54–55, 61
sin, nature of, 100–101, 138, 232
Sixth National Congress of base
  communities (1982), 118–19
Smith, Wilfred Cantwell, 225–26,
  227, 233
Sobrino, Jon, 57, 211, 229
social contract theory, 93
Social Encyclicals, 96
Social Gospel, 96
socialism, as basis of modern world,
  109, 114, 185, 221
Sojourners, 46
sola fide concept, 137, 263, 267
Solentiname monastery, 86–88, 89,
  90, 247

Somoza family, 86, 88, 253, 254
Song, C. S., 229
Southern Baptist Convention, 47,
  48
Southwest Baptist Church
  (Amarillo, Tex.,), 65, 166
space/time sensibility, 258
*Speeches on Religion to Her Cultured
  Despisers* (Schleiermacher),
  176–77
Stations of Wisdom (Schuon), 58
Steinfels, Peter, 203
subject, decentering of, 217
Survival of American Innocence, The
  (Halsey), 105

Taine, Hippolyte, religion as viewed
  by, 197–98, 200, 203–4, 206,
  208
Tao of Physics, The (Capra), 53, 55
technology, distrust of, 39–40, 41,
  44, 49, 67–68, 94, 183, 184,
  186, 188, 189
televised religious services, 32–33,
  34, 43–44, 67, 68–69, 70–71
teología de la liberación, La
  (Gutiérrez), 135–36
"testimony," 131
theology, modern:
  as academic discipline, 223–24,
    242
  development of, 92–97, 159–64,
    181–204
  ecclesiocentric vs. history-
    centered approach to, 138–39,
    157, 158, 160, 178, 231, 234,
    236
  fundamentalism vs., 41–43, 49–
    50, 51, 53–54, 56, 72, 73, 74,
    81, 82
  inversion of influences in, 175–
    180, 188, 192, 194, 195, 196,
    208, 210, 221, 229, 261, 262,
    265
  liberalism in, 31, 46, 48, 53, 62,
    71, 73, 138, 157–58, 266, 267,
    268

theology, modern (*cont.*)
"logos" and "theos" elements in, 176, 177–80
philosophical traditions in, 53, 153, 213, 216, 221
praxis-oriented theology vs., 136–137, 154, 224, 238
religion as interpreted by, 175–77, 183, 208, 209
see also individual theologians
theology, postmodern:
base communities and, 126–27, 133, 134, 167–69
Christ's significance to, 234–39, 263
corporate structures in, 210, 213–215, 231, 262–68
fundamentalism and, 57, 59, 63–71, 72–82, 267–68
liberation theology and, 157, 158, 160, 167–69, 213, 267–68
modernist positions on, 216–21, 267–68
personal identity in, 210–11, 214
as reform movement, 210, 262–68
theological vision of, 210, 211–13
see also liberation theology
theonomous societies, 62
Third World, 91, 106
base communities in, 128, 134, 213
religious worship in, 127, 164, 242
Thomas Road Baptist Church (Lynchburg, Va.). 29–34, 35, 36, 45, 63, 69, 230
Tillich, Paul, 62, 177
Toulmin, Stephen, 153n
tourbillon social, 181–82
Toynbee, Arnold, 192, 267
Tracy, David, 150, 151, 157, 158
Trappist order, 86
Trent, Council of, 264

Turner, Victor, 250
Twilight of Subjectivity, The (Dallmayr), 217

usury laws, 93

Varieties of Religious Experience, The (James), 154
Vatican Council, Second, 108, 110, 111–13, 117, 118, 139, 145
vía activa, vía contemplativa vs., 86
Viridiana (film), 165n
Vitória, Brazil, base communities meeting at (1975), 114, 121
Voltaire, François, 162

Waldensian Theology Faculty of Rome, 120
Waldo, Peter, 120
Wallace, Anthony, 39
Wall Street Journal, 33, 64
Warfield, Benjamin B., 51
White, Morton and Lucia, 41
Whitebrook, Joel, 216
White League, 115
"Wild Man of Borneo" figure, 251–252, 256
women:
in popular religion, 254–61
religious experience of, 124, 131, 167–68, 202, 207, 208, 209, 214
word processors, 70–71
"Work of Art in the Age of Mechanical Reproduction" (Benjamin), 68
World Council of Churches, 40

Zapata, Emiliano, 245, 246, 257
Zenteno, Arnaldo, 129, 130, 131, 132, 247
"Zero Hour" (Cardenal), 87
Zumárraga, Bishop, 244, 247, 257